P9-APU-179

St. Olaf College Libraries

Gift of Robert Entenmann

The Archaeology
of the Indian Subcon
and Sri Lanka

The Archaeology
of the Indian Subcontinent
and Sri Lanka

A Selected Bibliography

Robert B. Marks Ridinger

Bibliographies and Indexes in Anthropology, Number 10

GREENWOOD PRESS
Westport, Connecticut • London

DS
418
R53
2001

Library of Congress Cataloging-in-Publication Data

Ridinger, Robert B. Marks, 1951–
    The archaeology of the Indian subcontinent and Sri Lanka : a selected bibliography /
Robert B. Marks Ridinger.
        p.   cm.—(Bibliographies and indexes in anthropology, ISSN 0742–6844 ; no. 10)
    Includes bibliographical references and index.
    ISBN 0–313–30001–1 (alk. paper)
    1. India—Antiquities—Bibliography.   2. Excavations
(Archaeology)—India—Bibliography.   3. Sri Lanka—Antiquities—Bibliography.   4.
Excavations (Archaeology)—Sri Lanka—Bibliography.   5. South
Asia—Antiquities—Bibliography.   6. Excavations (Archaeology)—South
Asia—Bibliography.   I. Title.   II. Series.
    Z3208.A8R53   2001
    [DS418]
    016.934—dc21   00–042673

British Library Cataloguing in Publication Data is available.

Copyright © 2001 by Robert B. Marks Ridinger

All rights reserved. No portion of this book may be
reproduced, by any process or technique, without the
express written consent of the publisher.

Library of Congress Catalog Card Number: 00–042673
ISBN: 0–313–30001–1
ISSN: 0742–6844

First published in 2001

Greenwood Press, 88 Post Road West, Westport, CT 06881
An imprint of Greenwood Publishing Group, Inc.
www.greenwood.com

Printed in the United States of America

The paper used in this book complies with the
Permanent Paper Standard issued by the National
Information Standards Organization (Z39.48–1984).

10 9 8 7 6 5 4 3 2 1

44133137

Contents

Preface

"The world is a bridge: pass over it, but build no house upon it." *Inscription carved at Fatehpur Sikri on the orders of the Emperor Akbar, 1601.*

India — the very name conjures up a series of powerful images in the western mind- tall snowpeaks bearing temples with wind bells "lost behind the ranges," the bathing ghats at Varanasi where the faithful come to purify themselves in the sacred waters of Mother Ganga, newsreels of Mahatma Gandhi, sacred cows wandering through crowded streets, and the entire vanished world of the Raj. Less familiar to students of the subcontinent's past is the story of the inception and development of the science of archaeology in South Asia. This is due to several factors: the unfamiliarity of the majority of European scholars with the ancient languages and scripts of the subcontinent, chief among them Sanskrit, Prakrit and Kharoshthi; the interwoven strands of numismatics, linguistics, epigraphy, field excavation and laboratory analysis whose histories may be traced through over two hundred years of publications by both government agencies and scientific societies; and the sheer volume of monographs and articles available to be scanned. The present bibliography has been assembled with a view to providing the researcher who is unfamiliar with this massive body of literature a framework for both introduction and more detailed independent investigation. Given the local orientation of many of the publications in this genre, organization of this bibliography has been done by contemporary political unit of the subcontinent rather than physiographic region, with the exception of the Ganges Valley. Older provincial and regional terms widely used during the colonial era have been included under the more modern form of name. Entries within each category have been arranged in chronological order by either the date of publication or, in the cases of volumes reporting the proceedings of a specific conference, the year the conference was held. This feature permits the reader to follow the gradual growth of regional archaeological knowledge and its varied interpretations. Coverage extends from the writings of James Prinsep in 1788 to the 1990s.

This work is dedicated to my great-aunt, Florence Jones, who walked the land of India as a medical missionary decades ago, and left a heritage of carved teakwood and slippers with curled toes to inspire further dreams of far-off lands.

India

1. Jones, William. "A Discourse on the Institution of a Society, for inquiring into the History, civil and natural, the antiquities, arts, sciences, and literature, of Asia," in *A Sourcebook of Indian Archaeology* edited by F. Raymond Allchin and Dilip K. Chakrabarti. New Delhi: Munshiram Manoharlal, 1979: 5-8.

Originally published in the first volume of *Asiatic Researches* in Calcutta in 1788, this ambitious essay lays out Sir William Jones' ideas for the progress of the then newly-created Asiatic Society of Bengal. Archaeology and epigraphy lie within the focus of the "antiquities" mentioned in the title, although Jones himself states that he considers "languages as the mere instruments of real learning," (p. 7) an interesting observation given the important role the collection and translation of inscriptions was to play in the development of Indian archaeology in the following century.

2. Prinsep, James. "On the Ancient Roman Coins in the Cabinet of the Asiatic Society," *Journal of the Asiatic Society of Bengal*, 1, n. 9 (September, 1832): 392-405.

Noting that "it was not until the year 1814, that the Society opened a museum, and publicly invited contributions to it of the natural productions, antiquities, coins and other curious monuments of the country," (p. 392) the author (at that time Director of the Calcutta Mint) presents an illustrated *catalog raisonne* of the fifty to sixty Roman coins possessed by the Society in 1832. They represent almost one thousand years, from the era of Augustus Caesar to 290 A.D. Sharp criticism is leveled at those collectors who, following their tours of duty in the East, subsequently carried off their finds to London, rather than presenting them to the Society "where, from their rarity, they would have been prized and, from their presence, have promoted the acquisition of further stores for antiquarian research from the whole continent of India." (p. 393) A valuable window into the beginnings of scientific antiquarian research in India, in the words of one of its most influential founders. All illustrations included were drawn by Prinsep himself.

3. Prinsep, James. *Essays On Indian Antiquities, Historic, Numismatic and Palaeographic*. London: J. Murray, 1858.

A posthumous collection and publication of twenty-one of the articles authored by the Indian scholar and numismatist James Prinsep (1799-1840) which originally appeared in the *Journal of the Asiatic Society of Bengal* between September, 1832 and July, 1838. Selected entries from this collection been entered separately in the present bibliography.

4. Prinsep, Henry. "Memoir on the Author," in *Essays On Indian Antiquities, Historic, Numismatic and Paleographic* by James Prinsep. Varanasi: Indological Book House, 1971. 2 volumes: I-xvi.

The only extant biographical essay on one of the earliest serious investigators of India's past, this invaluable work summarizes both the tragically brief life and scientific contributions of James Prinsep (1799-1840). Assay Master of the mint established in Calcutta by the East India Company. Following training at the Royal Mint and appointment by the Company, he arrived in India in 1819, working first in the newly created mint facility at Benares, where his architectural knowledge was applied in 1823 to the stabilization of the minarets of the Masjid of Aurangzeb. With the abolishment of the Benares mint in 1830, Prinsep was recalled to Calcutta, where he contributed articles to a newly-founded periodical, *Gleanings In Science*, issued by the Bengal Asiatic Society. In 1831, he took over the management of this periodical, and in 1832 changed its named to the *Journal of the Asiatic Society of Bengal*. His brother notes that "through this close connection with the Asiatic Society, James Prinsep now felt the necessity of devoting himself...to the study of the antiquities of India, and especially applied himself to the deciphering of ancient inscriptions." (p. x) His translation of the edict pillars of Ashoka at Delhi and Allahabad provided the first documented bridge between Indian archaeology and Western history. The collecting of ancient coins with Greek or bilingual inscriptions had become a popular way of investigating antiquities, and many of these were sent to Calcutta, where Prinsep translated and published them. In 1838, he began to suffer from headaches and sickness, eventually being forced to return to England, where his condition continued to deteriorate. His death on April 22, 1840 robbed the study of the Indian past of one of its foremost scholars. Researchers on the beginnings of Indian archaeology will find this excellent background to the articles by Prinsep which appeared in the *Journal* between 1832 and 1838.

5. Prinsep, James "On The Ancient Roman Coins In the Cabinet of the Asiatic Society," in *Essays On Indian Antiquities, Historic, Numismatic and Palaeographic,* London: J. Murray, 1858: 1-6.

The first article on Indian numismatics written by Prinsep, this text (even in the amended version reprinted here) provides a clear picture of the approach to the collection and analysis of antiquities popular in the early nineteenth century. Between fifty and sixty coins are reviewed, with the observation that "the pieces found in India are chiefly of the lower denominations, the common currency of the eastern part of the empire." (p. 4) Similar essays on Greek, Bactrian and ancient Hindu coinage and their possible relationships with then-known mints in the classical world are also presented in this collection.

6. Cunningham, Alexander. *Four Reports Made During the Years 1862-63-64-65.* Volume II. Varanasi: Indological Book House, 1972.

This second volume of the Archaeological Survey of India's *Report* continues the accounts of the four initial survey reports filed with the Government of India by Alexander Cunningham in his capacity as "Archaeological Surveyor" on the results of his travels across the subcontinent in the mid-nineteenth century for the years 1863 through 1865. The first page of the 1863-64 report states his purpose as "the identification of those famous peoples and cities whose names have become familiar to the...world through the expedition of Alexander the Great...To find the...sites of those cities amongst the...ruined mounds of the present day, I propose...to follow the track of Alexander himself." (p. 60) This strategy resulted in a presentation of data from the banks of the Indus eastward, a point readers should bear in mind when interpreting the text. The report is divided into two sections on "Ethnology and Antiquities," the latter comprising the majority of the publication and centering on such ruins as were still extant in the Punjab and the northern extremity of the Northwest Province at that time. The descriptions left by Chinese pilgrims and the companions of Alexander the Great were also used as sources for the identification of sites. Thirty-two sites were visited and described, including Taxila, Peshawar, Badarpur and Thanesar. The 1864-65 report covers the continuation of the survey into Rajputana, Central India and the Bundelkhund region of Uttar Pradesh.Twenty-three sites were investigated in this period, many well known such as Jaipur, Ajmer, Gwalior and Khajuraho. Researchers wishing to have a comprehensive picture of the initial explorations at many of the sites which would be worked by later generations of Indian archaeologists will find Cunningham's detailed descriptions invaluable. A section of maps, sections and site plans for some of the sites named in the two reports is appended, and an index to the entire volume is provided.

7. Watson, John Forbes. *Report on the Illustration of the Archaic Architecture of India.*London, India Museum, 1869.

The content of this text addresses the means by which India's ancient monuments and structures may be depicted and "the utilization of the materials and of the information obtained." (p. 1) What follows this sweeping statement is virtually a technical manual of archaeological techniques related to architectural copying and documentation as they existed in the mid-nineteenth century and their potential applications in the Indian context. Specific subjects covered in addition to photography are drawings, plans and sections, models, moulds and casts. Attached to this preliminary paper are seven appendixes written by field investigators familiar with India such as James Fergusson, Meadows Taylor, and Alexander Cunningham. While Fergusson's document addresses the conservation and representation of ancient monuments, it is the latter two which are more important to the history of Indian archaeology. Cunningham's memorandum discusses "the Archaeological Remains of India," which he classifies into architecture, sculpture, coins and inscriptions (accompanied by full lists of the more important items), a division revealing of the mindset of the day regarding antiquities. Colonel Meadows Taylor focuses on "the subject of the Pre-historic Archaeology of India," which he sees as having "a high rank for consideration." (p. 35) The perspective used to buttress his argument for the separate study of this aspect of India's past (chiefly rock constructions ranging from dolmens and rock temples to cairns) is drawn from prior work in Europe. He notes that "until...a general investigation of the whole of India has been made, the subject must...remain incomplete for scientific, ethnological or archaeological purposes." (p. 35)

8. Cunningham, Alexander. *The Ancient Geography of India.I. The Buddhist Period, Including The Campaigns of Alexander and the Travels of Hwen-Thsang.* London: Trubner, 1871.

In the preface to this massive volume, Sir Alexander Cunningham notes that "my researches were signally successful in fixing the sites of many of the most famous cities of ancient India." (p. xiv) Published ten years after his appointment by the Viceroy, Lord Canning, as "Archaeological Surveyor," *Ancient Geography* is rooted in his initial charge in this post, to conduct a survey of the monuments and ancient remains of northern India. At the time, the travel accounts left by two Chinese Buddhist pilgrims of the fifth and seventh centuries A.D. had been newly translated, the longer and more detailed being that of Hsuan Tsang, who spent fifteen years studying in India from 629 to 645 A.D. Much of Cunningham's methodology in this work is based upon corroborating the voluminous references given by both classical Greek and Muslim geographers through his own contemporary journeys, using their measurements and physiographic descriptions in an effort to establish the locations and boundaries of individual cities and political units, of which Hsuan Tsang's account notes no fewer than eighty. *Ancient Geography* lists one hundred and thirty-one specific places and regions, including Afghanistan, Kashmir, the Punjab and Sind, as well as the central, eastern and southern portions of India, with Ceylon covered in a separate chapter. Having previously written *The Bhilsa Topes, or Buddhist Monuments of Central India*, published in 1854, Cunningham's interest in Buddhist India came to full flower in this compilation. Many of his site identifications were later confirmed by archaeological excavation. Researchers will find this work most valuable for descriptions of individual sites as they existed in the middle decades of the nineteenth century and as a convenient source for published references. The maps tracing both the campaigns of Alexander the Great in Sind and the intricate route of Hsuan Tsang are particularly valuable.

9. Cunningham, Alexander. *Report of the Year 1871-72.* Varanasi: Indological Book House, 1966.

Originally issued by the Office of Government Printing in Calcutta in 1873 as the third public record of the Archaeological Survey, this text and the fourth volume summarize the field activities of Cunningham and his assistants in 1871-72. The third volume covers only Cunningham's own work in the northern regions of the North-West Frontier Provinces. Of particular interest is his *Memorandum of Instructions* to his field workers, whose main attention was focused on architectural features. He visited and explored thirty-three sites during this season, providing detailed descriptions of their condition at this time and his activities, with the exceptions of "the ancient Muhammadan cities of Gaur, Sunargaon and Delhi, the account of which I reserve for future illustration." (p. xii) Among the major sites subsequently worked covered in this volume are Nalanda and Rajagriha. Plans, maps, copies of inscriptions and drawings of architectural elements from Mathura, Bodh Gaya, Rajagriha and Kiyul are appended.

10. Cunningham, Alexander. "Memorandum Of Instructions," in *A Source-book of Indian Archaeology* edited by F.Raymond Allchin and Dilip Chakrabarti. New Delhi: Munshiram Manoharlal, 1979: 25-27.

Originally published in the *Report* of the Archaeological Survey of India for the year 1871-72, this document states clearly the types of materials considered by Cunningham to be of primary value, which he defines as "all ancient remains whatever that will help to illustrate the manners and customs of former times." (p. 25) Particular emphasis is placed on architectural remains and fragments of sculptures (together with any associated inscriptions). Existing standards of weights and measures, agricultural implements and cart construction are cited as examples of areas where recording of contemporary practices may help to clarify both literary references and scenes carved on public buildings. The casual approach taken by Cunningham to excavation is also reflected in his comment on the smaller mound groups, which "may be opened at once,as the work would not occupy more than a few days." (p. 25)

11. *Archaeological Survey of India Report Volume IV. Report for the Year 1871-72. Delhi* by J.D. Beglar: *Agra* by A.C.L.Carlleyle. Varanasi: Indological Publishing House, 1966.

Due to delays, the archaeological campaign of 1871-72 planned by Sir Alexander Cunningham was unable to begin until February, 1871. To spare his assistants overexposure to the hot season, he assigned them the exploration of the major architectural monuments and sites of the cities of Delhi and Agra, said reports to be included as supplementing his own work in the North-West Frontier Provinces. This fourth volume of the *Report* presents the results of these surveys. Beglar's text is given first and notes one hundred and thirteen significant buildings extant in

Delhi at that time, including the two pillars raised by Ashoka, the Qutb Masjid and Minar, Adilabad, and Tughlaqabad. A listing of all structures and the publications where they are discussed provides useful access to this body of early scientific writing on Indian archaeology. Carlleyle's review of Muslim Agra is the longer of the two, and provides data on numerous small sites in the vicinity of the city as well. In contrast to Beglar's work, Carlleyle includes many of the inscriptions found scattered about Agra through the reuse of building elements from former mosques and other public structures, and is the only one of the reports to provide plans of specific buildings. While valuable sources of popular folklore and notation of the condition of many sites which were subsequently destroyed or radically altered, these reports also stand as the first work done in Indian archaeology by Cunningham's proteges.

12. Cunningham, Alexander. *Report for the Year 1872-73*. Varanasi: Indological Book House, 1966.

First issued in 1875 by the government printer in Calcutta as the fifth *Report* of the Archaeological Survey of India, "the present volume contains the results of a tour through the Punjab during the cold season of 1872-73." (p. v) Cunningham was accompanied by a company of workmen and made soundings at or visited over thirty sites and mounds, including Taxila, Shorkot, the Buddhist stupa at Mainikyala and the Ashokan pillars at Delhi. The known local history and folklore associated with each place are summarized in each entry. During this tour, much of his attention was focused on the retrieval of sculptural elements and the copying of inscriptions. Of particular significance for later Indian archaeology is the section of the *Report* dealing with his visit to the "ruins of Harapa," (p. 105) where he notes the discovery of "a seal...a smooth black stone without polish. On it is engraved very deeply a bull, without hump...above the bull there is an inscription in six characters, which are quite unknown to me. They are certainly not Indian letters: and as the bull which accompanies them is without a hump, I conclude that the seal is foreign to India." (p. 108) This is the first recorded description of a specimen of what would later be recognized as the writing system of the Indus civilization and its distinctive square seals. Fifty plates are appended, covering cross sections and plans of major monuments visited and features of the several types of Indian architecture discussed in the text.

13. Carlleyle, A.C.L. *Report of A Tour in Eastern Rajputana in 1871-72 and 1872-73*. Calcutta: Office of the Superintendent of Government Printing, 1878.

Issued as the sixth *Report* from the Archaeological Survey of India, this is the record of two seasons field work and survey at twenty-three locations and sites scattered across Rajputana (the area of eastern Rajasthan and westernmost Uttar Pradesh.) His first area of investigation was in the Fatehpur Sikri hills west of Agra and in several smaller villages close to the city, followed by an examination of notable remains (ranging from stone circles and cairns to fortresses and an inscription of Ashoka) over a wide area of eastern and southeastern Rajasthan, including the Bayana Hills. A preface by Sir Alexander Cunningham notes the more significant of his finds. Readers should bear in mind that most if not all of the place names referred to by Carlleyle have changed their forms in the intervening 125 years and have a modern map of the region available for reference. Twenty-four plates (chiefly views of monuments, plans of structures and general maps of the larger sites) are appended. For the archaeologist working in this region of India, this text provides invaluable historical background.

14. Beglar, J.D. *Report of a Tour in Bundelkhand and Malwa, 1871-72 and in the Central Provinces, 1873-74.* Calcutta: Superintendent of Government Printing, 1878.

This volume (the seventh *Report* in the series issued by the Archaeological Survey of India) presents two detailed accounts of field surveys of ruins extant across the Bundelkhand Uplands of Uttar Pradesh and the Malwa Plateau (1871/72) and a second journey from Jabalpur to Bharhut two years later. Although the first trip yielded numerous inscriptions dating to between 600 and 1400 A.D.(as well as descriptions of many sites which have since vanished), a primary goal was the photographic recording of the temple complexes of Khajuraho, Udaipur and Pathari. The later survey noted fifty-nine individual sites, although the major sites examined as a team with Sir Alexander Cunningham are not included in the text. Researchers should examine the body of survey data compiled by Beglar as historical background to later archaeological work in these regions.

15. Beglar, J.D. *Report of a Tour Through the Bengal Provinces*.Calcutta: Superintendent of Government Printing, 1878.

Beglar's "tour" was carried out in 1872/73 in Bihar, Chota Nagpur and West Bengal, and covered a total of 4,500 miles by both rail and foot. During this survey, he visited fifteen districts and no fewer than one hundred and three localities (among them Bodh Gaya, Rajgir, and Bihar), beginning in Bihar at Patna on the Ganges and ending at Hugli in modern West Bengal. This eighth *Report* of the Archaeological Survey of India provides extremely valuable background for the archaeologist dealing with the history of fieldwork in the northeastern part of the subcontinent. Notable in this report is his tracing of the ancient course of the Son river and his use under Cunningham's influence of the recently translated accounts of the Buddhist pilgrim Hsuan Tsang and other Buddhist annals as a guide for the identification of possible sites of monasteries and cave retreats. The reader will note the frequent description of mounds and temples as having been damaged through looting for reusable bricks. Twenty-one plates (chiefly maps of individual sites, sections and architectural elements) are appended as illustration.

16. Carlleyle, A.C.L. *Report of Tours in the Central Doab and Gorakhpur in 1874-75 and 1875-76.* Calcutta: Superintendent of Government Printing, 1879.

The bulk of this twelfth *Report* of the Archaeological Survey of India is devoted to Carlleyle's identification of the location of the city of Kapilavastu, birthplace of the Buddha, and major sites within it. The "Central Doab" region of the title corresponds to the southern two-thirds of the modern state of Uttar Pradesh. Other sites covered at length are the mound of Indor Khera southwest of Anupshahr, Sambhal, and Sankara. Fourteen black and white plates provide a map of the region of Indor Khera, plans and elevations of several of the structures mentioned in the text, as well as a plan of the area identified as Kapilavastu.

17. Cunningham, Alexander. *Report of A Tour in the Central Provinces, 1873-74 and 1874-75.* Calcutta: Superintendent of Government Printing, 1879.

At the beginning of the 1873 leg of this research, Cunningham noted the ruins of the major Buddhist stupa at Bharhut, which he subsequently published as a separate study. The "Central Provinces" of the title correspond to portions of modern Maharashtra and Madhya Pradesh. A portion of this text is devoted to Cunningham's review of known inscriptions from the region and their significance in fixing the precise beginning of the Gupta era. Twenty-eight communities and their associated ruins or surviving temples and other public buildings are described, creating valuable documentation for later archaeological studies in central India. Thirty line drawings, plans, sections and reproductions of copper plate inscriptions are appended. This publication appeared as the ninth *Report* from the Archaeological Survey of India.

18. Cunningham, Alexander. *Report of Tours in Bundelkhand and Malwa 1874-75 and 1876-77.* Calcutta: Superintendent of Government Printing, 1880.

The author notes that the high points of these two field seasons in the Malwa Plateau and Bundelkhand Uplands were "the discovery of several monolith capitals and other remains of the time of Asoka and his successors, and of numerous undoubted specimens of the architecture of the Gupta period." (p. v) Major sites included in Cunningham's journey are Kausambi, Khajuraho, Sanchi and Udaipur. Much of the clearance work and excavation done at the twenty-three places visited in these explorations was done with the objective of ascertaining the presence of inscribed materials, and where such were present their translations are included. An appendix covers Cunningham's continuing efforts at elucidating the beginnings of the era of Gupta rule. References are made from this tenth *Report* of the Archaeological Survey to earlier observations published in previous volumes of the series.

19. Cunningham, Alexander. *Report of Tours in the Gangetic Provinces from Badaon to Bihar, 1875-76 and 1877-78.* Calcutta: Superintendent of Government Printing, 1880.

"Many curious and interesting remains of Hindu architecture and sculpture of all ages" (p. 1) ranging from Buddhist times to the Muslim eras are the subject of this report covering two field seasons spent examining ancient sites in the network of rivers comprising the Ganges drainage in eastern Uttar Pradesh and Bihar. Thirty-six sites are noted, beginning with the city of Badaon in northwestern Uttar

Pradesh. Each section reviews the state of the site at the time of survey (including inscriptions and their translations when done), together with recording local legends and citing extant historical textual references. The first of the forty-four illustrations is a map of the Ganges Valley with all locations mentioned in the *Report* precisely noted. Major sections of text are devoted to Sravasti, Bodh Gaya, Patna, Bhitargaon, and Jaunpur. This *Report* is the eleventh issued by the Archaeological Survey of India.

20. Fergusson, James and James Burgess. *The Cave Temples of India*. Delhi: Oriental Books Reprint Corporation, 1969.

First published in 1880, this work began with a paper presented by James Fergusson in 1843 to the Royal Asiatic Society, summarizing the results of several field journeys made between 1836 and 1842. His objective was to build upon the recent translation work done by James Prinsep and others elucidating and clarifying the early history of both Buddhism and Hinduism. Prior to this paper, studies of individual temples had been published, as had studies in the *Journal of the Asiatic Society of Bengal*.

The present volume is the result of Fergusson's decision to travel to the major cave sites of both eastern and western India and to apply the new knowledge to their classification. Researchers unfamiliar with the precise sequence of investigation of the caves and their publication in the scientific literature produced between 1843 and 1880 will find Fergusson's preface invaluable. High quality illustration is provided by ninety-eight plates and seventy-three woodcuts. Sites included are divided into Buddhist, "Brahmanical" (Hindu) and Jain. Among the groups visited are temples at or near at Barabar, Rajgir, Katak, Hathi Gumpha, Mahavallipur, Ajanta, Bagh, Elura, Kathiawar, Gwalior, and Elephanta. Readers studying any cave temple should consult this work to obtain essential background on the history of this particular aspect of Indian archaeology.

21. Anderson, John. *Catalogue and Hand-Book of the Archaeological Collections in the Indian Museum*. Calcutta: The Museum, 1882-3. Reprinted New Delhi: Gayatri Offset Press, 1977.

Prepared by an author whose training lay in zoology rather than archaeology or any other antiquarian field, this two-volume work was intended to revise and amplify an earlier guide issued in 1879. The *Catalogue*'s goal was to "give some explanation, however imperfect, of the various Archaeological objects exhibited in the Museum." (p. vi) The Indian Museum's collections as represented here were divided into four distinct galleries-Asoka, Indo-Scythian, Gupta and Mahomedan-each centering upon a clearly defined epoch of history. Anderson notes the augmentation of Museum holdings since its inception in 1866 with sculptures and bas-reliefs from Bharhut, Gandhara, Bodh Gaya and Orissa. Each gallery's contents are profiled individually. The first volume covers the Asokan and Indo-Scythian galleries, while the second is principally concerned with Buddhist, Jain,

"Brahmanical" (Hindu) and Islamic sculptures. A forty-five-page section on "General Archaeology" reviews artifacts whose provenience is unknown. Researchers will find this set a useful window into the manner in which archaeology was viewed at its inception in India and the intellectual approaches taken to the preservation and analysis of artifacts.

22. Beglar, J.D. *Report of Tours in the South-Eastern Provinces in 1874-75 and 1875-76.* Calcutta: Superintendent of Government Printing, 1882.

Sixty individual sites were visited in the course of this highly descriptive account of two survey seasons. Their focus was to expand available data on the existence and status of ancient sites and structures in "the little known and unexplored places...lying between Chhatisgarh and Katak." (p. 1) The "South-Eastern Provinces" of the title correspond roughly to modern central and eastern Orissa, southern Bihar and southwestern West Bengal. Sites noted as being newly recorded are the temple of Chandrehi in the Rewa district of northeastern Madhya Pradesh, and the ruins at Ranipur-Jural in north central Bihar. This text was issued as the thirteenth *Report* of the Archaeological Survey of India.

23. Cunningham, Alexander. *Report of a Tour in the Punjab in 1878-79.* Calcutta: Superintendent of Government Printing, 1882.

The fourteenth *Report* to appear in the first series of scientific documents published by the Archaeological Survey of India, this document describes the results of Cunningham's lengthy re-survey of the Punjab (in its old geographic sense, which includes a large section of modern Pakistan) and sections of northern Haryana. His goal was "to complete as far as possible a general exploration of the province." (p. 1) Beginning at the stupa of Manikyala sixteen miles south of Rawalpindi, his travels included the sites of Taxila, Kurukshetra, the Salt Range, and Thanesar, as well as numerous small temples, inscribed monuments, and mound groupings. The preface serves to place the results of this tour in the context of previous explorations. Fourteen plates (some lithographed copies of photographs) illustrate selected monuments in both plan and cross-section.

24. Cunningham, Alexander. *Report of a Tour in Bihar and Bengal in 1879-1880 From Patna to Sunargaon.* Calcutta: Superintendent of Government Printing, 1882.

This season of exploration took place in the cold season of 1879-1880, and began in central Bihar near Patna. Thirty-five localities, the majority in Bengal, were visited, including a return trip to Bodh Gaya. Of particular note are the lengthy descriptions of the ancient capital of Bengal lying between the Mahanadi and Ganges Rivers, Gaur, covering its citadel, city and suburban areas, and the later cities of Mahasthan and Sunargaon. As in other accounts by Cunningham, frequent reference is made to accounts of the Buddhist pilgrim Hsuan Tsang. Illustrations depict views of the Jahngira hermitage as well as major inscriptions from Gaur and plans of Sunargaon and Mahasthan. This was the fifteenth *Report* in the *Old Series* published by the Archaeological Survey.

25. Burgess, James. *Report on the Buddhist Cave Temples and Their Inscriptions.* London: Trubner and Company, 1883.

The lengthy subtitle of this volume designates it as being based upon the third, fourth and fifth seasons of fieldwork carried out by the Archaeological Survey of Western India between 1876 and 1879. Burgess intended this work to supplement Fergusson's 1880 publication *The Cave Temples of India* by providing highly detailed descriptions of some of the more striking groups of Buddhist cave shrines than the previous encyclopedic work was able to give. Twelve cave complexes are reviewed here, beginning with the vihara at Bhaja in western India and including a lengthy treatment of the Pitalkhora, Junnar, Nasik, and Ajanta cave shrines as well as other less familiar localities. Approximately half the work is devoted to the presentation and translation of inscriptions from each site. Illustration is provided by sixty engraved plates and twenty woodcuts. The volume was reissued in 1964 by the Indological Book House in Varanasi. Researchers may wish to consult the companion work, *Report on the Elura Cave Temples and the Brahmanical and Jain Caves in western India*, also published in 1883.

26. Cunningham, Alexander and H.B.W.Garrick. *Report of Tours in North and South Bihar in 1880-81.* Calcutta: Superintendent of Government Printing, 1883.

The first section of this sixteenth *Report* of the Survey, while covering the recording and excavation done at twenty-seven major and minor sites across Bihar (including a lengthy section on the ruins of Vaisali), omits a detailed consideration of Cunningham's further work at Bodh Gaya. The latter consisted of clearing debris out of the temple, attempting to identify specific sites of pilgrimage and reviewing materials uncovered by his assistant Beglar. The second portion reports on the work of Garrick, much of which was the creation of photographic documentation for known structures. In contrast to some of the earlier reports in this series, separate data obtained by each investigator at the same site are not blended into one account.

27. Cunningham, Alexander. *Report of a Tour in the Central Provinces and Lower Gangetic Doab in 1881-82.* Calcutta: Superintendent of Government Printing, 1884.

The objective of this field work was the exploration of the old cities of Rajim, Arang and Sirpur in the valley of the Mahanadi River. Cunningham observed that "the remains at these three ancient sites are extremely interesting, as they differ from all the other temples that I have examined in Northern India, not only in their plans but in their decorations." (p. iii) The cities of Mathura and Maha-Kosala (the modern Chattisgarh) were investigated as well among the thirty-three sites visited. Two essays on demon worship and the Savara tribal people complete this seventeenth *Report* of the Archaeological Survey.

28. Carlleyle, A.C.L. *Report of A Tour in the Gorakhpur District in 1875-76 and 1876-77.* Calcutta: Superintendent of Government Printing, 1883.

The district under consideration in this volume lies in the easternmost region of Uttar Pradesh. A central feature of this eighteenth *Report* of the Archaeological Survey is Carlleyle's account of his re-investigation of the site of Kusinagara, and its identification with the city where the Buddha died. Readers will find this report an extension in part of Carlleyle's earlier work (covered by the twelfth *Report* in 1879) in which he identified the location of Kapilavastu, birthplace of the Buddha. Much of the methodology of this campaign is based upon identifying places mentioned in the pilgrim accounts of Hsuan Tsang and Fa Hsien. Seven plates (chiefly maps of locales visited by Carlleyle) are appended.

29. Garrick, H.B.W. *Report of A Tour Through Behar, Central India, Peshawar and Yusufzai, 1881-82.* Calcutta: Superintendent of Government Printing, 1885

The author opens this account of his survey and recording trip through northeastern and central India and a portion of Afghanistan with the observation that "during the cold season of 1881-82 I traveled 3,450 miles…forty-one places of archaeological interest have been visited." (p. 1) Garrick began at Simla on August 1, 1881 and journeyed eastward across Bihar, south to Baghelkhand then west to Peshawar. Major sections of this report are devoted to the sites of Charsada and Shabazgarhi. The full text of the memo of instructions received by Garrick from Alexander Cunningham detailing the seven most prominent sites and ruins to be investigated as part of a British mission to explore the mineral resources of the Yusufzai country of Afghanistan is included. Most of the illustrations are lithographs of standing temples or plans of individual sites. The *Report* is the nineteenth of the series of monographs issued for a general audience by the Archaeological Survey of India.Garrick's expedition was concluded on May 20, 1882.

30. Cunningham, Alexander. *Report of A Tour in Eastern Rajputana in 1882-83.* Calcutta: Superintendent of Government Printing, 1885.

In this twentieth *Report* of the Survey, director Cunningham recounts his researches and travels across eastern Rajputana, which at the time included portions of five native states and the British-administered districts of Mathura, Delhi and Gurgaon. The region examined corresponds to modern Haryana,western Uttar Pradesh and eastern Rajasthan. Among the results of the trip (which are arranged by district) were eighteen new inscriptions from the Muslim era. Readers will find the preface a useful summary of all major sites visited and the activity at each, while the thirty-eight plates alternate between plans of structures and copies of inscriptions. Readers of the 1966 reprint should be aware that a binding error gives volume 20 the same title as volume 21.

31. Cunningham, Alexander. *Reports of A Tour in Bundelkhand and Rewa in 1883-84, and A Tour in Rewa, Bundelkhand, Malwa and Gwalior, in 1884-85.* Calcutta: Superintendent of Government Printing, 1885.

The region examined in these *Reports* (the twenty-first volume issued to inform the public of the work of the Archaeological Survey) corresponds to portions of contemporary Madhya Pradesh, West Bengal, and Uttar Pradesh. Seventy-five locations were visited, with selection emphasizing "places which had not been reported upon by officers of …the Survey." (p. iii) Among the major structures covered in the text are the fortresses of Kalanjara and Ajaygarh, Kausambi, and the temple complex of Khajuraho. Forty-two plates provide maps of the regions investigated, reproductions of early photographs, copies of inscriptions from Khajuraho, Kalanjara and Ajaygarh, architectural elements and plans of selected buildings.

32. Carlleyle, H.C.L. *Report of Tours in Gorakhpur, Saran and Ghazipur in 1877-78-79 and 80.* Calcutta: Superintendent of Government Printing, 1885.

In this text, the twenty-second publication of the Archaeological Survey's first series of scientific monographs, Carlleyle continued his research into "the identification of several other important sites in the early history of Buddhism." (p. iii) Over four field seasons, his travels centered on the area of easternmost Uttar Pradesh, the adjoining districts of Bhojpur and Siwan, and the Saran Plain of northwestern Bihar. Like his mentor Cunningham, he used the account of Hsuan Tsang as a guide to pinpoint further significant places of pilgrimage southeast of the Buddha's birthplace of Kapilavastu, whose location Carlleyle had established in the mid-1870's. Contents are arranged chronologically by individual years.

33. Garrick, H.B. W. *Report of A Tour in the Panjab and Rajputana in 1883-84.* Calcutta: Superintendent of Government Printing, 1887.

This volume (the twenty-third and final monograph covering ongoing archaeological survey and recording done under the government of the Raj) describes in detail data obtained during a lengthy exploration of northern and central Rajasthan, northwest Haryana, and the adjoining region of the Punjab. Among the twenty-seven places visited during this field season were Jaipur, Ajmer, and the forts of Hansi, Sirsa, Bathinda and Chitor. The tour began at Simla on October 1, 1883 and ended at Agra on March 31, 1884. Twenty-eight plates (some reproducing photographs, others reprints of lithographs depicting specific buildings and inscriptions) are appended.

34. Archaeological Survey of India. *Annual Report 1902-03.* Varanasi: Indological Book House, 1970.

Written by John Marshall, then Director of the Survey, this is the inaugural issue of what was intended to be a more regular means of informing the public of the agency's accomplishments in the fields of archaeology, epigraphy, and conservation.The model for the envisioned series was the annual reports issued by the Egypt Exploration Fund, whose impact on the public had been substantial in raising awareness of the antiquities of that country. The introduction covers in some detail the past history of the Survey and its functions as they existed in 1903. The text itself is divided into three major sections, the first, on conservation, dealing only with projects of special importance, mainly in Bengal, at Agra and

Ajmer. Actual field excavation is reported under the heading "Exploration and Research," although Marshall notes that "considering the vast and promising field which India offers for exploration, the record of what has been done in it during the past year may appear to be a somewhat meagre one…it must be remembered that it is the preservation of the known monuments rather than the exploration of the unknown which has the first claim upon the time of the Survey officers." (p. 104) Continuing work at the cemetery of Adittanallur near Madras and at Charsada in the North West Frontier province are the main campaigns reported upon. The final section covers recent work in the field of epigraphy, ranging from newly found copper plate inscriptions to salvage work done at temples threatened with demolition.

35. Lord Curzon. "On Archaeology In India," in *A Source-book of Indian Archaeology* edited by F. Raymond Allchin and Diulip K. Chakrabarti. New Delhi: Munshiram Manoharlal, 1979: 27-28.

An extract from an article originally published in the *Annual Report* of the Archaeological Survey of India for the year 1902-1903, issued in 1904. Lord Curzon, then recently apppointed as the British Viceroy, was principally responsible for the revival of the Survey as an active and regularly funded agency of the imperial bureaucracy. In this text, he states that he "regarded the conservation of ancient monuments as one of the primary obligations of Government….of an even more binding character in India than in many European countries" (p. 27) due both to the absence of private institutions which can take up some of the necessary work and "the combined ravages of a tropical climate, an exuberant flora and…a local and ignorant population who see only in an ancient building the means of inexpensively raising a modern one for their own convenience." (p. 27) Conservation, epigraphic collection and study of inscriptions and excavation are noted as being equally vital portions of the Survey's work.

36. "Ancient Monuments Preservation Act of 1904," in *India Code, Being A Compilation of unrepealed Central Acts arranged chronologically.Volume 4*. New Delhi: Ministry of Law, Justice and Company Affairs, 1994: 260-271.

Also known as Act. No.7 of 1904, this is the full text (with English and Hindi versions on facing pages) of the document. It begins with a sweeping definition of an ancient monument, which it takes to be "any structure, erection or monument or any tumulus or place of interment, or any cave, rock-sculpture, inscription or monolith, which is of historical, archaeological or artistic intent, or any remains thereof." (p. 263) The body of the Act is divided into five sections, covering ancient monuments, the traffic in antiquities, protections of carved objects and sculptures of all kinds, archaeological excavation and general related issues. Authority touching directly upon field excavation covers designating an area as protected, issuing licenses for digging, and the power to acquire an area to save it from being despoiled.

37. "The Temples of India," *National Geographic* 20 (2) (November, 1909): 922-971.

A lengthy portfolio of fifty-four photographs with accompanying text illustrating some of the major temple complexes of India as they existed in 1909. Sites of archaeological interest included are Sarnath, Bodh (Buddha) Gaya, Sanchi, Ujjain, Bhubaneshwar and the cave temples of Ellora. Much of the focus of this presentation is on details of carving.

38. *The Periplus of the Erythraean Sea ; Travel and Trade In The Indian Ocean By A Merchant of the First Century.* Translated from the Greek and annotated by Wilfred H.Schoff. London: Longmans, Green and Company, 1912.

Perhaps the most frequently referenced of the surviving ancient documents dealing with India, the *Periplus* (a combination of sailing directions and market information handbook, written sometime in the first century A.D.) deals with the system of trade routes established between the Roman empire and the subcontinent. A wide range of products is listed as being exported from the various centers of trade on both the east and west coasts of India, including indigo, pearls, pepper and linen. It was this document which provided a context for the numerous finds of Roman coins made in southern India in the late nineteenth and early twentieth centuries. Readers dealing with data from such identified trading sites as Arikamedu should read the *Periplus* for historical background on the archaeology of southern India. The bulk of this edition is devoted to notes on the places, products and individuals mentioned in the document.

39. Foote, Robert Bruce. *The Foote Collection of Indian Prehistoric and Protohistoric Antiquities: Catalog Raisonne.* Madras: Government Press, 1914, 1916. 2 volumes.

This set represents the culmination of thirty-three years of collecting by Robert Bruce Foote, member (and later Superintendent) of the Geological Survey of India from 1858 to 1891. His discovery of a chipped stone implement at Pallavaram near Madras on May 30th,1863 established the presence of an Indian stone age and began a career-long interest in gathering specimens of this type of artifact during his extensive travels for the Survey across a considerable part of southern India. Many of the items which Foote assembled into his large collection came from the Madras Presidency, Mysore and Hyderabad. The collection was purchased by the Madras government in 1904, and a special room built to house it in the Art and Ethnological Section of the Madras Museum. Prior to his death on December 29, 1912, Foote had overseen several proofs of the catalogue.

The first of the two volumes provides a descriptive list of the objects in the collection according to the twenty-eight districts of India where they were found (as well as including items from Ceylon presented to Foote). The second (not published until 1916) is subtitled "Notes On Their Ages and Distribution" and presents the researcher with Foote's classification of the artifacts into Palaeolithic,

Neolithic, Early and Later Iron Ages and a discussion by district of the items found. The section entitled *General Notes* is valuable for the history of Indian archaeology through its preservation of Foote's views on the proper approach to research. He notes that "prehistoric artifacts should be treated historically, and be assigned respectively to one or other of the several stages of man's progress in civilization," (p. 1) while stating that he had deliberately left untouched such graves and barrows as he found, preferring to leave them for excavation by the Archaeological Survey. A list of sites represented in the collection, twenty-five pages of appendixes, and sixty-four monochrome plates illustrating both stone tools and pottery complete the work. A sheet map of all sites is provided in a pocket at the end of the volume.

40. *Indian Archaeological Policy, 1915*. Calcutta: Superintendent of Government Printing, 1916.

Subtitled "a resolution issued by the Governor General in Council on the 22nd October 1915", this description actually applies only to the first two pages. The remaining thirty-seven pages, entitled *Note On Archaeology*, consist of an assessment of the history and current status of archaeology as practiced in India in 1915, written by Sir John Marshall, then director of the Archaeological Survey. Beginning with Sir Alexander Cunningham's initial survey of the monuments of northern India in 1862 (and a similar survey done in the Bombay and Madras Presidencies in 1874), he notes the creation of a "Curatorship of Ancient Monuments" in 1881 and attempts during the 1880's to unify site surveying throughout the country. With the beginning of financial retrenchment in 1889, the post of Director General was allowed to go unfilled. In 1899, India was divided into five circles, each in the charge of a surveyor, whose duties "were to be limited almost exclusively to conservation." (p. 2) It was this system which Lord Curzon overhauled in 1902, reviving the position of Director General, increasing the number of local circles and staff, appointing two Imperial Epigraphists to cope with the flood of inscription material and instituting scholarships for the training of Indian personnel in archaeology. The emphasis in Marshall's report lies with setting forth the full structure and functioning of the Archaeological Department. This includes the various categories of staff members and their assigned duties (superintendents being advisors to local governments, and charged with inspecting the monuments in their area and making recommendations for preservation). Epigraphists at the local level receive help from two government specialists, who divide Persian/Arabic and Sanskrit between them and edit the two official journals *Epigraphia Indica* and *Epigraphia Indo-Moslemica*. Other topics included are the need for recruitment of Indian staff, the role of archaeology in what were then termed "the Native States" (based upon an invitation issued by the Government of India in 1901), conservation progress and monuments preserved between 1910 and 1915. This last is divided into Muslim, Hindu and Buddhist structures and fortresses.

The longest section of the entire report, *Exploration*, traces the work done by the Survey since 1902, beginning with an initial period of work between 1902 and

1910 devoted to a re-examination of Buddhist sites already identified to recheck the sometimes conflicting conclusions of prior excavators. Upon the completion of this phase, fresh field work was begun. Sites noted as having been investigated between 1910 and 1915 include Bhita (near Allahabad), Taxila, Pataliputra (capital of the Mauryan empire), Besnagar, Sanchi, and Avantipur in the valley of Kashmir. Exploratory travels beyond the frontiers of India proper resulting in new knowledge and artifact collections cited are the 1909 journey of Dr. A.H. Francke to Ladakh and the three prolonged trips into Central Asia and western China carried out by Sir Aurel Stein since 1901, all of which have been copiously published. Researchers beginning literature searches in any aspect of Indian archaeology, linguistics and history will find the *Publications* section an invaluable history of scientific work issued by the Survey up to the time of writing.

41. Coggin Brown, J. *Catalogue Raisonne of the Prehistoric Antiquities in the Indian Museum at Calcutta*. Simla: Government Central Press, 1917.

Compiled by the curator of the Geological Survey of India (and the anthropological secretary of the Asiatic Society of Bengal) on the orders of Sir John Marshall (who served as editor) this catalogue lists "antiquities...collected by officers of the Geological Survey of India between 30 and 40 years ago," (p. 1) placing the finds in the period 1877-1887. The collection is arranged into four groups on the basis of chronology (palaeoliths, neoliths, copper antiquities and early Iron Age) with each subdivided by geographic area of origin. Palaeolithic tools are noted as being primarily made of quartzite, although Coggin Brown rejects Robert Bruce Foote's contention that ten distinct forms could be recognized. Areas of India represented in the collection are heavily weighted towards the southern portion of the subcontinent for palaeoliths, although finds are noted from the Narbada and Godavari valleys, the Central Provinces, Bihar, Bengal, Orissa and Rajputana. Neolithic specimens are listed from northern and southern India equally, with the Indus Valley, Baluchistan and Assam noted as well. Copper artifacts were less numerous, coming from Bengal, the United Provinces and the Central Provinces. Researchers will find this volume of great value in delineating those portions of India which had been subjected to intensive study up to this point and the approach taken in the application of European categories of prehistory to the subcontinent. The *catalogue raisonne* of the lithic collections amassed by Robert Bruce Foote in the Government Museum at Madras (used as the master index of such artifacts) published in 1914 should also be consulted. Ten black and white photographic plates illustrate celts, hammerstones, choppers and flakes. There is no bibliography.

42. Chanda, Ramaprasad. *The Indus Valley in the Vedic Period*. Calcutta: Government of India, Central Publications Branch, 1926.

Issued as the thirty-first *Memoir* of the Archaeological Survey of India, this short monograph by the superintendent of the Archaeological Section of Calcutta's Indian Museum was written at a time when Harappa and Mohenjo-daro were only recently found, and the long-accepted picture of civilization's history in the subcontinent under massive revision. "It may now be hoped that archaeology will one day enable students to fix the chronology of the Vedic literature with a greater degree of certainty ...I propose to discuss in this paper some of the passages in the Vedic literature that throw light on the early history of the Indus Valley." (p. 1) Topics addressed through quotation and translation of lines from specific hymns and other texts contained in various Vedic scriptures include the drying up of the Sarasvati River, the coming of the Aryans and a detailed presentation on styles of burial and other customs for the disposal of the dead. Aspects of Mohenjo-daro and Harappa as then known are cited as proving the accuracy of the Vedas, although no attempt is made to give a precise date to either.

43. Chanda, Ramaprasad. *Survival of the Prehistoric Civilization of the Indus Valley*. Calcutta: Government of India, Central Publication Branch, 1929.

"The relics of the prehistoric period discovered at Mohenjo-daro and Harappa leave no room for doubt that the Chalcolithic civilization of the Indus Valley was something quite different from the Vedic civilization." (p. 1) Beginning with this sweeping statement, the author (curator of the Archaeological Section of the Indian Museum in Calcutta) examines the ten books of the *Rigveda*, noting "how cautious one should be in attaching ethnological significance to the language." (p. 31) Succeeding sections of this detailed essay discuss the roles of king and priest (relating them to the ongoing debate over the origin of the caste system), human sacrifice, the original meaning of the practice of yoga, with stone statuettes from Mohenjo-daro cited as evidence (as are numerous lines from the *Upanishads* and Buddhist scriptures) and the cult of tree-worship. Perhaps most relevant to the archaeologist considering the Vedic literature as a reflection of vanished cultural practices is Chanda's rejection of the classic Aryan conquest myth in favor of a different model. "The hypothesis that seems to fit in best with the evidence...may be stated thus...on the eve of the Aryan immigration the Indus Valley was in possession of a civilized and warlike people. The Aryans...came to seek their fortune in small numbers more or less as missionaries of the cults of Indra, Varuna, Agni and other gods of nature and settled in peace under the protection of the native rulers who...employed them to secure the assistance of the Aryan gods against their...enemies by offering sacrifices with the recitation of hymns." (p. 25) A valuable window into a time when traditional Indian scholarship was attempting to absorb the results of archaeological investigations. This is the forty-first *Memoir* of the Archaeological Survey of India.

44. Richards, F.J. "Geographical Factors In Indian Archaeology," *Indian Antiquary* 62 (December 1933): 235-243.

A detailed examination of the geography of India and the cultural divisions which parallel it. Areas delineated are the Indus basin, the Ganges basin, the central belt of hills and desert, and the southern peninsula. While heavily oriented towards historic relics, this essay provides a useful topographic framework for the researcher attempting to sort out numerous sites and their relation to the subcontinent's physical features.

45. Gordon, D.H. "The Microlithic Industries of India," *Man* 38 (February, 1938): 21-23.

A review of the then-known distribution of flake and core tools across India. Areas represented are Western India (specifically Sind, Kathiawar and Gujarat), Bihar, Orissa, the Bombay Presidency, Hyderabad, the Mahadeo Hills and Narbada River regions, and Madras. The author notes that "it is unsafe to go far as yet in the matter of equation with similar cultures in the West." (p. 23) There is no bibliography.

46. *Revealing India's Past. A Co-Operative Record of Archaeological Conservation and Exploration in India and Beyond* edited by Sir John Cumming. London: The India Society, 1939.

Originating as an idea of the Council of the India Society in London, this volume of contributed articles is perhaps the most comprehensive attempt made to assess the status of archaeology in India prior to World War II. The twenty-five essays focus specifically on work done by the Archaeological Survey of India in the peninsula itself, India, Indian Tibet and Burma as well as ten of what were at the time referred to as "Native States." Sir John Marshall, director of the Survey from 1902 to 1931, opens the collection with a lengthy review of the history of his organization, covering both the forty years prior to its restructuring under Lord Curzon's administration and the subsequent era of controlled scientific excavation. Topics addressed in other sections of the volume are conservation (including methodologies as well as Buddhist, Hindu and Muslim structures), the status of excavations at prehistoric, Buddhist and Hellenic period sites (this last referring to Taxila and Mathura), the role played by epigraphy in the foundation and development of Indian archaeology, publications, and the condition of extant archaeological museums in the region. A series of thirty-three black and white photographs is appended, offering portraits of Alexander Cunningham, James Burgess, Lord Curzon, Sir Aurel Stein and K.N.Dikshit as well as illustrations of sites as diverse as the Great Bath at Mohenjo-Daro, the cave temples of Ajanta and the stupa at Sanchi. Researchers will find the chapter on *Publications* essential for tracing the vast literary output of the Survey but should also review the relevant chapters for specific bibliographical references. Several of the essays from this volume have been entered separately in the present bibliography.

47. Bhandarkar, D.R. "Epigraphy: Prakrit and Sanskrit Inscriptions," in *Revealing India's Past: A Co-Operative Record of Archaeological Conservation and Exploration in India and Beyond* edited by Sir John Cumming. London, The India Society, 1939: 200-211.

Beginning with a review of the major substances (principally stone and metal) used to record inscriptions at various times in Indian history, this essay both explores the history of script decipherment and illustrates the vital role Hindu epigraphy has played in the evolution of archaeology in the subcontinent. The role of the Brahmi alphabet as ancestral to all modern hands in use in the region and the contributions of Charles Masson and James Prinsep in deciphering the Kharoshthi script through the use of bilingual coins from the Indo-Bactrian Greek kingdoms are noted. Fields as diverse as geography, history, trade, political history, religion, the role of women and immigration are linked to information contained in sources as varied as the edict columns of Ashoka and sheet copper deeds. Researchers unfamiliar with the history of Indian archaeology will find this a useful summary but should also read the companion piece by Zafar Hasan on Muslim inscriptions, entered separately in the present bibliography.

48. Dikshit, Kashinath Narayan. "Conservation," in *Revealing India's Past: A Co-Operative Record of Archaeological Conservation and Exploration in India and Beyond*. London: The India Society, 1939: 34-42.

A review of the special problems faced by archaeological conservators in the Indian subcontinent, written by the Director General of the Archaeological Survey. Specific natural factors noted as complicating preservation work are the annual heavy rainfall of the monsoon seasons, the rapid growth of vegetation which demands a regular program of clearance, high levels of salt in the groundwater in northern and northwest India which can cause the disintegration of ancient brickwork (the site of Harappa being offered as an example), erosion due to the shifting of rivers, and earthquakes, particularly in northern India, Baluchistan and Assam. Human impact on ruins is also noted, having taken the form of destruction through warfare and domestic practices such as expanding agriculture and mining ancient structures for building materials. At the time this piece was written, 2,662 monuments were under the protection of the Government of India.

49. Dikshit, Kashinath Narayan. "Buddhist and Hindu Monuments," in *Revealing India's Past: A Co-Operative Record of Archaeological Conservation and Exploration in India and Beyond* edited by Sir John Cumming. London: The India Society, 1939: 43-55.

A status report on the major structures associated with Buddhism and Hinduism being conserved as of 1939. The author observes that "one of the main difficulties which face the conservator…is the fact that the use of mud mortar in masonry and the corbelled or pillar-and-lintel mode of construction render these buildings peculiarly liable to destruction." (p. 48) The listing of major sites ranges from the edict pillars of Ashoka to the temple complexes of Konarak and Khajuraho and the caves of Elephanta. The text presupposes familiarity with a substantial portion of India's geography, and readers unfamiliar with the region may wish to have an atlas for reference.

50. Hargreaves,Harold. "Archaeological Museums," in *Revealing India's Past: A Co-Operative Record of Archaeological Conservation and Exploration In India and Beyond*, London, The India Society, 1939: 222-236.

A highly detailed account of the creation and evolution of the approximately one hundred museums of India and Burma as they existed in 1939. Beginning with a reminder that "the first museum collection in India was founded as long ago as 1796" (p. 222) by employees of the East India Company involved with the Asiatic Society of Bengal in Calcutta, the essay notes that, while archaeological curiosities were frequently part of locally assembled holdings, their firm place as a focus of museum activity was only solidified in 1860. That year saw the constitution of the Archaeological Survey of India by the Viceroy, Lord Canning, who appointed General (later Sir) Alexander Cunningham as Archaeological Surveyor. Under the administration of Lord Curzon, the philosophy of keeping retrieved artifacts at their place of provenience was adopted, and the Survey founded ten museums. These are reviewed in the final section of the essay, beginning with the oldest museum of all, the Indian Museum (based on the Asiatic Society collection). They are the Taj Museum in Agra, the Delhi Fort and Lahore Fort Museums, the Archaeological Museum of Nalanda, the site museums at Mohenjo-Daro, Harappa and Taxila, and the Central Asian Antiquities Museum (based on the expeditions of Sir Aurel Stein in 1906-08 and 1913-16).

51. Hasan, Zafar. "Epigraphy: Muslim Inscriptions," In *Revealing India's Past: A Co-Operative Record of Archaeological Conservation and Exploration in India and Beyond* edited by Sir John Cumming. London; The India Society, 1939: 211-221.

Noting that "the activities of the Archaeological Department, constituted in 1862, were originally restricted to the survey of ancient monuments," (p. 218) the author, Superintendent of the Northern Circle of the Archaeological Survey of India, presents a history both of the scripts used to record Muslim inscriptions since the twelfth century A.D. and the publications devoted to scholarship related to them. The founding of the biennial journal *Epigraphia Indo-Moslemica* in 1907 is seen as a necessary outgrowth from the *Epigraphia Indica*. At the time this piece was written, fourteen issues had appeared, the majority published in Hyderabad. An expansion of government staffing resources in this area is called for.

52. Konow, Sten. "Publications," in *Revealing India's Past: A Co-Operative Record of Archaeological Conservation and Exploration in India and Beyond* edited by Sir John Cumming. London: The India Society, 1939: 237-253.

One of the chief problems facing the researcher unfamiliar with Indian research in any field is the bewildering mass of local and national scientific publications and series which appeared at various times under the government of the Raj. This chapter gives a clear and concise overview of the scope and and contents of all major official series, beginning with Sir Alexander Cunningham's initial *Archaeological Survey of India* in 1871.Types of materials included are museum catalogs, items issued by the archaeological departments of individual states, works on prehistory, art, architecture and inscriptions. Researchers intending to start work on any subject related to ancient India will find this chapter indispensable, particularly for tracing specific works which appeared as several volumes of more general titles such as the *New Imperial Series*.

53. Marshall, Sir John H. "The Story of the Archaeological Department in India," in *Revealing India's Past: A Co-Operative Record of Archaeological Conservation and Exploration in India and Beyond* edited by Sir John Cumming. London: The India Society, 1939: 1-33.

This essay is without question the best history of Imperial British government involvement with archaeological work in the Indian subcontinent. Written by the man who had been appointed the first Director General as part of the reforms of the Curzon administration in 1902, it is divided into two sections. The first covers the period from the appointment of Alexander Cunningham as "Director of Archaeology" in 1862 to the early twentieth century and is especially valuable for clarifying the political and fiscal factors and policies of the era which so sharply hampered the evolution of the Archaeological Department. The primary (and continuing) focus on site survey, assessment of the structural status of monuments of all eras, and the necessity of conservation in the highly damaging tropical climate are explored. The many changes in the internal administration of the Department are also traced. The second portion is Marshall's review of the primary accomplishments, strategies, and problems of the Department under his administration between 1902 and 1938. Investigators who have read the document *Indian Archaeological Policy 1915* will find much of this information familiar. Of particular interest are his quotations from several speeches of Lord Curzon in which the priorities of the Department – epigraphy, preservation and excavation – are explicitly stated. Marshall notes that "one of the principal reasons for my appointment as Director-General was that I might introduce into India the scientific methods of digging which had yielded such brilliant results in Greece and Crete," (p. 23) an intention quickly carried out at Charsada, Rajagriha, Kasia, Basar and Adittanallur. The choice was made to center initial campaigns of excavation on major Buddhist sites due to both the substantial body of information available about them and the possibility of significant finds to attract desirable publicity in support of badly needed financial assistance. Areas in which the Department was active are noted as the foundation of archaeological museums and the creation of a large reference library with a photographic collection of more than 40,000 items.

54. Mohammed Sana Ullah. "Science and Conservation," in *Revealing India's Past: A Co-Operative Record of Archaeological Conservation and Exploration in India and Beyond* edited by Sir John Cumming. London: The India Society, 1939: 86-90.

This essay assesses frankly the chemical problems of preservation in the Indian environment. The author, the country's first Archaeological Chemist, recounts his training at the British Museum and initial assignment to the Indian Museum in Calcutta in 1917. Contexts of preservation work are discussed, ranging from working with copper and bronze artifacts from Harappa and Mohenjo-daro to assisting in cleaning and saving the frescoes of Ajanta. Factors traced as affecting preservation are extreme temperature fluctuations, salt extrusion, and rainfall.

55. De Terra, Helmut and T.T. Paterson. *Studies On The Ice Age in India and Associated Human Cultures.* Washington, D.C.: Carnegie Institution of Washington, 1939.

This substantial volume contains the record of what may be considered the most concentrated effort to integrate the human prehistoric record with the geologic processes of the Indian subcontinent carried out prior to World War II. A joint international project of field research was carried out between March and December of 1935. Five areas were selected for study: the Valley of Kashmir, the Potwar-Indus area in the northwestern Punjab, the Narmada Valley in Madhya Pradesh at Hoshangabad and Narsinghpur, Madras, and the lower Indus region at Sukkur and Rohri. The first and most lengthy chapter outlines the data obtained on the glacial sequence in the Himalayas and its correlation with the Pleistocene of both Kashmir and the Upper Indus Valley. Little attention is given to the prehistory of Kashmir from an archaeological perspective, beyond noting the megalithic site at Burzahom and extensive collections of flaked stone tools made at various locations on the Jhelum River. Chapter two contains a section by Patterson on the prehistory of the Potwar and Indus regions, including a typology of stone tools from the area as then known. The Narmada valley Pleistocene study notes two culture-bearing localities at Hoshangabad and Narsinghpur, yielding a range of forms from handaxes to flake tools. For Madras, site of the discovery of the first Pleistocene-era stone tools by R.B. Foote in the nineteenth century, a general typological and stratigraphic framework for the palaeolithic is presented. The final chapter reports on a survey done to see how far the Old Stone Age cultures identified in the Himalayan foothills could be traced towards the Indus delta using two groups of sites near Sukkur and Rohri. A bibliography of relevant literatures is provided.

56. Piggott, Stuart. *Some Ancient Cities of India.* London: Oxford University Press, 1945.

A brief guide "for those who, with an interest in Indian history and its monuments or art and architecture, have no specialized knowledge and want a reliable background to give their visits to ancient sites some significance." (p. iii) Following an introductory chapter on Indian prehistory, Piggott covers Mohenjo-Daro, Taxila, the Great Stupa at Sanchi, Muttra, the caves of Ajanta, the rock-cut temple complex at Ellora, the sacred Hindu and Jain shrines of Mount Abu, various monuments of Delhi, the Deccan citadel of Daulatabad, the imperial Mogul city of Fatehpur Sikri (built in 1575) and Agra (specifically, the Agra Fort and the Taj Mahal). Readers unfamiliar with any of these sites may wish to read the relevant essay prior to beginning work with more technical archaeological literature and will find the plans included useful.

57. Wheeler, Robert Eric Mortimer. "Notes," *Ancient India* 1 (January 1946): 1-3.

The introductory essay marking the appearance of a new post-war journal from the Archaeological Survey of India, *Ancient India*, whose intent was "to put archaeology regularly on the bookstalls" (p. 1) and create a greater awareness of it among the Indian public. Papers comprising this initial issue review repair work done to the Taj Mahal, a comparative study of the known cultures of northwest India with established sequences from Iran by noted European prehistorian Stuart Piggott, a hoard of bar coinage from Taxila found in 1945, the local pottery industry from the site of Ahichchattra (Uttar Pradesh), and the first season's work at Adilabad, part of the "fourth" city of Delhi. The closing technical section is intended to present regular coverage of such topics as field methods and new applications of technology. Individual articles from this volume have been entered separately in the present bibliography.

58. Piggott, Stuart. "The Chronology of Prehistoric Northwest India," *Ancient India* 1 (January 1946): 8-26.

A detailed analytic exploration of the relationship of the Harappan culture and nine other artifact assemblages from northwestern India, both to each other and the more solidly established archaeology of Iran and Iraq. Piggott begins by defining the Zhob, Harappan, Quetta, Amri, Nal, Kulli, Shah-i-tump, Jhukar and Jhangar ceramics and associated material culture as then known, moving next to comparisons of available stratigraphic sequences and stylistic features. Excellent line drawings illustrate type artifacts from each culture. Much of the accompanying text lays out the possible correlations with known sites from Sumeria. A clear example of the traditional approach to the complex picture presented by the interlocking array of archaeological sites found in this region. Researchers may wish to check Piggott's conclusions against later work done with such dating techniques as radiocarbon to assess the accuracy of his reconstruction and correlations.

59. Mohammed Sana Ullah. "Notes On The Preservation Of Antiquities In The Field," *Ancient India* 1 (January 1946): 77-82.

Written by the retired archaeological chemist of the Archaeological Survey of India, this essay reviews the chief classes of materials found in the subcontinent and their proper treatment for preservation. Types of artifacts covered include bone and ivory, pottery, textiles and paper, metals (at this time limited to gold, silver, iron, copper and lead), silk, horn and leather. A listing of equipment "required for an archaeological field laboratory at a major excavation" (p. 81) is appended. A unique perspective on the level of technical expertise available for Indian archaeologists in the early 1940's.

60. Wheeler, R.E.M. "Archaeological Planning For India:Some of the Factors," *Ancient India* 2 (July 1946): 125-133.

The full text of the address given by the author, then Director General of Archaeology in India, to the Anthropology and Archaeology section of the Indian Science Congress at its January 1946 meeting in Bangalore. His principal question for the assembled was "how are we in India to harness the natural sciences in the service of the study of man?" (p. 127) The potential roles to be played in Indian archaeology by geography, geology, botany, soil science, the then-new technique of tree-ring dating, biology, chemistry and physics are assessed. Among the projects envisioned is a correlation of the glacial sequences of Europe with those of the subcontinent. The present constellation of lectureships in archaeology scattered among several universities is criticized and the creation of a central school of archaeology called for, a development which had already begun to be realized in 1944 at the northern Indian site of Taxila.

61. Krishnaswami, V.D. "Stone Age India," *Ancient India* 3 (January 1947): 11-57.

The question of the presence of stone tool industries in the Indian subcontinent, their distinctive features, and the various methods of obtaining relative dating for each are set in context in this paper. The author was an associate of the Yale-Cambridge Expedition of 1935, which focused attention on "the relationship of Quaternary glaciations...to Early Man and his cultures" (p. 14) with specific reference to Kashmir and the adjoining regions of the Punjab. After reviewing the history of awareness of stone tool manufacture in India (beginning with the finds made near Madras in 1863 by Robert Bruce Foote of the Indian Geological Survey), recent collections from southern India are noted. The principal work of this paper is to explore strategies of correlating the Himalayan glacial cycles as represented in Kashmir (and their associated stone tool assemblages such as the Sohan) with similar finds from central and southern India. While the goal of setting artifactual complexes within a datable geological framework is achieved for northern India, Krishnaswami notes ruefully that "in South India the vast and valuable collections of Foote in the Madras Museum remain as yet wholly uncorrelated to the Quaternary sequence." (p. 42) Researchers will find the lengthy bibliography covering field work on this aspect of Indian archaeology from 1863 to date of special value, as many of the items cited come from local Indian journals.

62. Wheeler, R.E.M. "The Recording of Archaeological Strata," *Ancient India* 3 (January 1947): 143-150.

A technical note on the application of the principles of controlled stratigraphy to archaeological excavation and an assessment of past practice in Indian fieldwork. Noting that "the rising generation of Indian archaeologists is rapidly becoming familiar with them," (p. 143) Wheeler then severely criticizes the history of site excavation in India, taking work done at Mohenjo-daro, Harappa and Chanhu-daro as examples, where the outdated technique of measuring the distance of found objects from a predetermined bench level and their consequent assignment into arbitrary strata (a technique used in early field work in mass excavations in Egypt and Mesopotamia) resulted in distortion of the site occupation record.

63. Wheeler, R.E.M. "Notes," *Ancient India* 4 (July, 1947-January, 1948): 1-3.

The final editorial written by Sir Mortimer Wheeler for *Ancient India*, this essay reflects upon the impact of the political partition of India and Pakistan on the future of archaeology in the subcontinent. The historical focus of Indian archaeology in the northwestern region on such sites as Mohenjo-daro, Harappa, and Taxila is recognized, and a shift in priorities to equally intensive investigation of the Ganges Valley and southern India called for.

64. "Notes," *Ancient India* 5 (January 1949): 1-3.

This editorial addresses the fate of the archaeological remains lying in the approximately five hundred and fifty former political divisons of India known as "Native States" as a consequence of the widespread political changes following Partition on August 15, 1947. While a few of these areas had possessed archaeological departments of their own, the majority had made no efforts toward the preservation of historical sites. Under the new independent Indian administration, the Archaeological Survey of India was to assume primary responsibility for both initiating new explorations and tackling long-needed stabilization work. Archaeology was also retained as a subject in the draft of the new Constitution of India as a matter falling within the authority of the central government.

65. Wheeler, R.E.M. "Archaeological Fieldwork In India: Planning Ahead," *Ancient India* 5 (January 1949): 4-11.

This article is the publication for general circulation of an internal memorandum to the Archaeological Survey of India, written by its former director, which outlines a logical plan for addressing "our present main need:...systematizing the protohistoric and early historic cultures of India." (p. 10) Fieldwork carried out between 1944 and 1947 is summarized, with emphasis on the extension of the dated first century culture known from the site of Arikamedu in Madras across much of southern India through excavations at Brahmagiri and Chandravalli in Mysore. The problems of Indian archaeology are best addressed through following the natural division of the subcontinent into the North Indian Plain and the region south of the Vindhyas. Future work is called for to extend the southern sequence to link up with established information from the north, and excavation at two specific sites, Amaravati and Shishupalgarh, recommended as profitable. In the north, the long-deferred comprehensive surface survey of the Ganges Valley is seen as vital. Researchers will find the specific articles referred to by Wheeler entered in the present bibliography under the appropriate Indian state.

66. Krishnaswami, V.D. "Megalithic Types Of South India," *Ancient India* 5 (January 1949): 35-45.

This article assesses the state of investigation of megalithic structures within India, noting the confusing use of multiple and ill-defined terminology derived from

European study of similar monuments since 1848. Agreement on a common language of scientific description is necessary, as are regional studies of megaliths and their accurate planning. Surveys from three areas of southern India carried out since 1944 (in Madras, Pudukkottai, and Cochin on the Kerala coast) are presented and the types of constructions defined by actual features found. Two appendixes note the continuing tradition of erecting megaliths among tribal peoples of northeastern India and list the glossary of terms being employed by the Department of Archaeology for their description.

67. Chhabra, B.Ch. N. Lakshminarayan Rao and M. Ashraf Hussain. "Ten Years of Indian Epigraphy (1937-1946)," *Ancient India* 5 (January 1949): 46-61.

During World War II, the practical work of village surveying for inscriptions continued in India, albeit at a much reduced level. This lengthy review of the resulting four thousand inscriptions found in that decade is divided chronologically into sections covering copper-plate inscriptions, stone inscriptions, miscellaneous finds (such as the fragments of Dravidian writing on pottery sherds from Arikamedu) and two hundred Muslim inscriptions which clarify the dates of construction of several public buildings. Samples of the materials recovered are illustrated in monochromatic plates.

68. Gordon, D.H. "The Stone Industries of the Holocene in India and Pakistan," *Ancient India* 6 (January 1950): 64-89.

A general article presenting a synthesis of available information on the microlithic stone tool assemblages from sites in both India and Pakistan. Beginning with a discussion of various stratigraphic sequences in which such implements have been found(principally the established succession from cores to microliths at Khandivli north of Bombay and data from the Lower Godavari region), the author considers the typology of Indian microliths, their distribution, and evidence indicating the contemporary use of such products with very early pottery. The most important sites for the latter are Hirpura and Langhnaj in Gujarat. The then-recent excavations at Brahmagiri in Mysore are also cited. A provisional date of ca. 8000 B.C. is assigned to the first appearance of this culture. The field collections and excavations upon which this summary is based were carried out between 1889 and 1948. Readers unfamiliar with the terminology used in European prehistory may find the text confusing. The bibliography usefully gathers a widely scattered literature for convenient reference.

69. Piggott, Stuart. *Prehistoric India*. Harmondsworth: Penguin Books, 1950.

A work intended as "an account of our knowledge of Indian prehistory from the earliest times to the settlement of the Aryans... a stock-taking of our incomplete evidence and interpretation...as...incentive to further work in the field." (p. 9) Piggott quite frankly states that much of the material in this work is either newly synthesized from existing data or draws upon information previously completely unpublished, with the "argument addressed to the specialist in oriental archaeology." (p. 9) The resulting volume is therefore highly detailed and may be somewhat difficult reading for researchers lacking background in South Asian geography and prehistory. Chapters dealing with the Bronze Age communities of western India, the cities of the Punjab and Sind, and the ending of the Harappan civilization are based upon fieldwork done in Indian museums between 1942 and 1945. Useful as a summary of knowledge and the state of archaeological theory regarding India at the beginning of the postwar era. Bibliographies are brief and appended to each section of text. A reprint of this volume appeared in 1962.

70. Lal, B.B. "Examination of Some Ancient Indian Glass Specimens," *Ancient India* 8 (1952): 17-27.

Tracing the origin of glassmaking in the ancient world has long been problematic due to the fragile nature of the compound. This article addresses the question of the beginning and persistence of glass crafting in India through analysis of specimens ranging in age from classical to medieval times. Available data indicate that the chemistry of Indian glass is unique in its virtual lack of barium and low use of lead. Sites providing samples are Arikamedu, Ahichchhatra, Nalanda, Kurukshetra, Assam, Udaigiri and Taxila.

71. Roy, Sourindranath. "Indian Archaeology From Jones To Marshall," *Ancient India* 9 (1953): 4-28.

This highly detailed readable article concisely summarizes the history of archaeological investigation in the Indian subcontinent, providing an essential framework for any beginning researcher to the complex scientific publication record created under the Raj. Beginning with the formation of the Asiatic Society under the direction of Sir William Jones in 1788, all major events, acts of legislation, field surveys (both architectural and epigraphic) and excavations are noted and their place in the evolving knowledge of India's past clarified. Copious footnotes provide full bibliographic information on all cited literature. Among the investigators whose work is reviewed are James Prinsep, Sir Alexander Cunningham, James Burgess and James Fergusson. The coverage ends with the arrival of Lord Curzon as Viceroy in 1898 and the appointment of John Marshall as Director General of the Archaeological Survey in 1901. The subsequent history and activities of the Survey are traced in the article by A. Ghosh, "Fifty Years of the Archaeological Survey of India," in the same issue of *Ancient India*.

72. Ghosh, A. "Fifty Years of the Archaeological Survey of India," *Ancient India* 9 (1953): 29-52.

Taking up where Sourindranath Roy's excellent summary article "Indian Archaeology from Jones to Marshall" in the same issue of *Ancient India* leaves off, this essay provides a clear picture of the programs and priorities of archaeology in the subcontinent up to and after Partition in 1948. Issues addressed include the reorganization of the Survey in 1902, the administration of Sir John Marshall and his emphasis upon consistent rules for the conservation of buildings and monuments, the evolution of both protective legislation and central government responsibility for archaeological work, the shifting of areas of coverage among the existing "Circles" coordinating field research, and the move away from literary to practical fieldwork. A report solicited from eminent prehistorian Sir Leonard Woolley in 1939 on the state of Indian archaeology is noted. Special emphasis is placed upon the political and budgetary factors which affected the limits placed on field investigations. Researchers will find the map of the archaeological Circles as they existed in 1953 of particular use as a reference when seeking for regional reports. Publications of the Survey, the creation of archaeological departments by governments of individual states, and the involvement of Survey personnel on the international scientific scene conclude the review.

73. Lal, B.B. "Archaeological Chemistry and Scientific Studies," *Ancient India* 9 (1953): 199-206.

The position of Archaeological Chemist was first added to the staff of the Archaeological Survey of India in 1917, with responsibility for "the scientific examination and chemical treatment and preservation of museum-objects and other antiquities recovered in the course of excavations and explorations." (p. 199) This essay discusses the methods and techniques developed since that time to treat and preserve ceramics, metal objects, mural paintings, stone monuments (such as the caves of Elephanta, where large-scale preservation was first tried in 1937) and the limited work done to that date in the fields of soil analysis as an aid to environmental reconstruction.

74. Krishnaswami, V.D. "Progress In Prehistory," *Ancient India* 9 (1953): 53-79.

The identification of the presence of stone tools in ancient India occurred in the same year that geological evidence for the antiquity of man was first published by Lyell. On May 13, 1863, Robert Bruce Foote of the Geological Survey of India made the first discovery of a palaeolithic era tool in a gravel bed near Madras. This ignited an interest which he would pursue for the next forty-three years, eventually identifying varieties of stone tools across a wide area of southern India below a line from the Kathiawar peninsula to Bengal. This lengthy article presents the gradual evolution of knowledge about the Palaeolithic, Mesolithic and Neolithic eras amassed over the first ninety years of research. The opening historical section notes that "till 1930, the Old Stone Age in India was very loosely interpreted on the basis of the prevailing European nomenclature, which should not have been applied freely without understanding their geological connotations." (p. 55) The correlation of glacial sequences in Kashmir and handaxes from the Punjab with datable river gravel deposits by Helmut De Terra in 1935 is discussed and his two stone tool complexes, the Sohan (identified as a flake and pebble tool assemblage) and the Madras (characterized by handaxes similar to Foote's original find) outlined. Recent palaeolithic discoveries from Gujarat, Maharashtra, Karnataka, Orissa and the Singrauli basin in Uttar Pradesh are summarized and the issue of placing the pebble tools within the Lower Palaeolithic sequence noted. The largest section of text is devoted to the Upper Palaeolithic, Mesolithic and Neolithic, with attention centering on the widespread microlithic industries, the appearance of pottery (from the sites of Nasik, Jorwe and Maheshwar), the rise of copper-using technologies in western snd southwestern India, and the place of proto-Neolithic flint industries and their long thin blades in Pakistan and India. Correlations are drawn with contemporary data on these eras from the Middle East and Indo-China.

75. Srinivasan, K.R. and N.R. Banerjee. "Survey of South Indian Megaliths," *Ancient India* 9 (1953): 103-115.

First noted in scientific literature in 1872, a comprehensive survey of the megaliths of southern India was recommended by R.Sewell in 1882, but not initiated until 1944. The present article summarizes the results of recent work, in particular the delineation of two distinct typological groups (replacing the former confusing tangle of names borrowed from European prehistory) their distribution and results of excavation at Brahmagiri, Porkalam and Sanur. Associated pottery and other grave goods are reviewed as well.

76. Sharma, Y.D. "Exploration of Historic Sites," *Ancient India* 9 (1953): 116-169.

This lengthy essay presents a highly detailed summary of the information available on fifty-four specific sites from the historical period where survey and excavation had been carried out up to 1953. In this context, the term "historical" is defined as beginning with the second half of the first millennium B.C. Contents cover the northwestern plains and highlands, the Ganges-Yamuna drainage, the Central Ganges Basin, Rajputana, eastern, western and central India, the Deccan and the southern peninsula, and the southeast. Readers unfamiliar with most of the major site work in India will find this background invaluable for interpreting individual research reports and data analysis.

77. Ramachandran, T.N. "Preservation of Monuments," *Ancient India* 9 (1953): 170-198.

"The ancient monuments of India constitute her cultural heritage...a variety of causes, not to speak of age and age-long neglect, has combined to produce a decay and devastation unparalleled in the history of any country." (p. 170) Beginning with this unfortunately accurate statement, this review notes both natural and human agencies as contributing to the problem, the latter ranging from using sites as sources for building materials (a threat posed to even, at one point, the Taj Mahal) to quartering troops in them. The history of formal conservation is followed from the systematic survey of ancient monuments by Alexander Cunningham in 1861 to the appointment of H.H. Cole in 1881 with preservation as his specific mandate. Topics addressed include vegetation and its effects, the role of excavation in restoration work, repair and consolidation of masonry (with methods used given in some detail), archaeological gardens, and the issues raised by contemporary irrigation schemes. Approaches taken to the special needs of prehistoric and protohistoric sites are considered separately. The final sixteen pages present notable sites from the jurisdiction of each of the nine Circles (administrative units) of the Archaeological Survey where major consolidation and conservation projects had been completed up to the time of publication.

78. Chhabra, B.Ch. "Epigraphy and the Archaeological Survey," *Ancient India* 9 (1953): 207-211.

A concise overview of the longstanding relationship of the disciplines of epigraphy and archaeology in India. The importance of the collection, translation and publication of inscriptions, begun in the early nineteenth century by James Prinsep, Charles Masson and others' work on the Brahmi and Kharoshthi scripts, was recognized by the appointment of a Government Epigraphist as part of the reorganization of the Archaeological Survey in 1902. Useful to the nonspecialist are the sections dealing with the types of publications available at this time which presented both regional and nationwide inscription researches, such as the *Corpus Inscriptionum Indicarum* series. Some thirty thousand inscriptions had been uncovered by both excavation and a village to village survey by the time this article was written.

79. Sircar, D.C. "Inscriptions In Sanskritic and Dravidian Languages," *Ancient India* 9 (1953): 212-224.

Focusing on the past of two of the subcontinent's major language families, this article opens with a review of the particular importance of inscriptions to the reconstruction of Indian history, which lacks the types of chronicles present in Western classical civilizations. As early as 1837, James Prinsep and his colleagues in the Asiatic Society of Bengal had begun to collect and publish inscriptions, a tradition carried on by the *Indian Antiquary* and *Epigraphia Indica* later in the century. The decipherment of the Brahmi and Kharoshthi alphabets by European scholars and the problems of the Indus script are noted. The remainder of the paper is devoted to an explication of the types of epigraphs known, both those engraved by an authority or governmental official, and those memorializing private individuals. Separate sections discuss copper-plate grants, eulogies, techniques of engraving, types of seals used, and the dating of inscriptions.

80. Desai, Z.A. "Arabic and Persian Inscriptions," *Ancient India* 9 (1953): 224-232.

The voluminous literature created by over a century of study of inscriptions dating to the time of Muslim rule in India is briefly reviewed in the opening section of this article. Researchers unfamiliar with the development of major journals such as the *Epigraphia Indo-Moslemica* will find this a useful reference. Arabic and Persian were used as inscriptions on a wide range of public structures ranging from bridges and forts to gateways and mosques, as well as many types of personal possessions. The types of records available, the shifts in languages used (including bilingual inscriptions using one of the Indian languages such as Telugu), styles of calligraphy and the various historical uses of this class of inscription are reviewed.

81. Sivaramamurti, C. "The Museums In India: A Survey," *Ancient India* 9 (1953): 233-240.

Stating that "the genesis of the museum-movement is to be traced to the Asiatic Society of Bengal" (p. 233) and its cabinet of antiquities, this detailed outline sets forth the sometimes complicated history of the idea of a museum in India. The role played by the Archaeological Survey as a source of materials for collections and in the administration of provincial museums is emphasized. Researchers should also review the companion article by J.K.Roy on the museums operated directly by the Department of Archaeology.

82. Roy, J.K. "Museums of the Department of Archaeology," *Ancient India* 9 (1953): 241-249.

By the time the report *Museums of India* was issued by the Museums Association in London in 1936, its authors were able to state that "the discoveries of the Archaeological Survey...have stimulated in no small measure feelings of nationalism and directed the attention of Indians to the need for preserving their archaeological treasures." (p. 241) This had been achieved both through excavation and a program of active conservation, part of which was the creation of several museums at major sites to retain a local context for artifact studies. While Sir Leonard Woolley's 1939 recommendations to the Government of India on archaeological matters advised closing the site museums, his suggestion was disregarded. This article presents the history to date of the Museums branch of the Department of Archaeology since its formation in 1946 and the major features of the twelve collections maintained by it before and after Partition. Sites represented are Mohenjo-daro and Harappa, Taxila, Sarnath, Sanchi, Amaravati, Nagarjunakonda, Kondapur, Nalanda, Khajuraho, Hampi (Vijayanagara), the Red Fort at Delhi and Fort St. George at Madras.

83. Basham, Arthur Llewellyn. *The Wonder That Was India*. London: Sidgwick and Jackson, 1954.

Subtitled "a survey of the culture of the Indian sub-continent before the coming of the Muslims," this is principally a general work of history. Its connection to the archaeology of the region lies in the second chapter "The Harappa Culture and the Aryans," which illustrates one interpretation of the then-available data on the Indus Valley civilization. The introduction is also of value, as it summarizes concisely the birth of the field of Indology and the early history of the Archaeological Survey of India. This source was reprinted in two American editions in 1959 and 1962.

84. Gordon, D.H. *The Pre-Historic Background of Indian Culture*. Bombay: N.M. Tripathi, 1958.

An early work for a mass audience reflecting the state of knowledge of the Indian Stone Age, Mesolithic and Chalcolithic cultures prior to much of the significant post-Partition archaeological work. An unusual feature is a separate chapter on the pottery of the Makran Coast, Baluchistan and Sind. A bibliography and thirty-two black and white photographs are appended.

85. Soundara Rajan, K.V. "Quaternary Pebble, Core and Flake Cultures of India-An Appraisal of the Data," *Ancient India* 17 (1961): 68-85.

In this useful survey of then-recent work done on the stone tool assemblages of the Indian subcontinent since the time of Partition, the author begins by remarking on the variety of specializations evident, a variety he views as limited only by ecology, raw materials and choice of function. His stated intention is "to trace the broad technological criteria involved in the tool… industries of…Stone Age India…with a view toward comparing their interrelated tendencies with those in the other Asian-African areas." (p. 68) Following a discussion of production techniques, the Sohan industry of the Punjab is compared with sites in central India (notably in the Narmada Valley of Madhya Pradesh) and a greater affiliation is found with known tool industries from Africa. A six-page appendix illustrates tool types from the site of Bariarpur in Madhya Pradesh. Researchers should be aware that the text presupposes familiarity with the terminology used to describe the European Palaeolithic.

86. Sankalia, H.D. *Indian Archaeology Today*. New York: Asia Publshing House, 1962.

This volume is a collection of the full texts of the three addresses delivered by the author as the first Heras Memorial Lectures in 1960, a series inaugurated to honor the memory of the Bombay archaeologist and historian Rev. Henry Heras. Sankalia's first text deals with the changing objectives of Indian archaeology, standard field methods and then-new technical methods ranging from thermoluminescent dating to magnetic surveying. The second and longest speech covers recent investigations into prehistory (including all stone tool industries then known) and protohistory, the latter defined as 5000-2500 B.C. and ending with the rise of the Indus Valley civilization. The third lecture treats the megalithic monuments of India, the site of Ranghmahal on the now-dry Ghaggar river, epigraphic analysis, numismatics and sculpture, ending with a call for archaeological planning, centering on the study of regional problems. At the time he delivered these speeches, Sankalia was the Joint Director of the Deccan College Postgraduate and Research Institute in Poona.

87. Wheeler, Robert Eric Mortimer. "Ancient India: The Civilization of A Sub-Continent," in *The Dawn of Civilization: The First World Survey of Human Cultures in Early Times*. New York: McGraw-Hill, 1962: 229-252.

A general summary of Indian prehistory as known in the early 1960's written for an audience unfamiliar with the region. Topics covered include the Indus civilization and its possible precursors, the Ganges Valley, and central and southern India. Readers should be aware that the majority of this chapter is photographs of representative sites and artifacts with accompanying text, useful as an introduction to the subject.

88. Allchin, F.R. "Upon the Antiquity and Methods of Gold Mining in Ancient India," *Journal of the Economic and Social History of the Orient* 5 (1962): 195-211.

This unusual paper begins by examining the evidence for gold mining in India, defining both alluvial washing and direct excavation of shafts tracing gold-bearing reefs and veins as the primary extractive techniques of numerous fields whose "potentials had been largely exhausted before the opening of the 19th century," (p. 195) The two most important regions worked for alluvial gold were the Chhota Nagpur Plateau and the Himalayas, while direct mining is best known from the Dharwar band of southern India in the Mysore district of Karnataka. A concentration of mines between Hutti and Maski in Karnataka is used to illustrate construction technologies employed and the difficulties of dating mine remains to a particular period. An analysis of both historical records (including the *Arthasastra*) and the limited number of artifacts from Hutti examined by the author indicate the period of active extraction to have been between the fourth century B.C. and the first two centuries A.D., although the clustering of known Neolithic settlements around the gold fields (such as Maski and Piklihal) indicate activity at an earlier time.

89. Singh, S.D. "Iron in Ancient India," *Journal of the Economic and Social History of the Orient* 5 (1962): 211-216.

A review of both archaeological and literary evidence associated with the introduction of iron technology to the Indian subcontinent, challenging the suggestion by Mortimer Wheeler that this event occurred in the sixth century B.C. Finds of iron fragments and finished objects from early levels at Kausambi, Sravasti, Purana Qila (Delhi) and Hastinapura indicate a date of introduction ca. 1000 B.C., which fits well with the textual reference to *syama ayas*, "black metal" in the Vedas. Researchers may also wish to consult the 1963 article by D.D.Kosambi on "The Beginning of the Iron Age in India."

90. Goetz, Hermann. "Building and Sculpture Techniques In India, Part I: The Pre-Classical Phase," *Archaeology* 15 (4) (December, 1962): 252-261.

Written by a noted archaeologist and art historian with thirty years experience in India, this is the first of two essays presenting a detailed discussion of the evolution of construction techniques in both stone and wood throughout the country. After reviewing the varied regional geologies and their relationship to local options in architectural materials, building styles are traced, beginning with the brick house platforms from the Indus civilization site of Lothal, the first Buddhist stupas and the timber architecture of the fifth through seventh centuries, and the history of stonework as it was then known. Special note is made by the author of the role of cave temples as models of contemporary wooden construction and the methods of rock cutting used to create such massive edifices as the Kailasa temple at Ellora.

Attention is also given to military building, the reuse of statuary and portions of older public works in fortress walls, and the religious significance of the design and execution of irrigation systems. A sequel to this article, covering the Classical and Islamic eras, appears in the March 1963 issue of *Archaeology*.

91. Kosambi, D.D. "The Beginning of the Iron Age in India," *Journal of the Economic and Social History of the Orient* 6 (1963): 309-318.

This essay takes as its focus the question "when was iron first produced from natural ores in India, in quantity sufficient to be important in the means of production?" (p. 309) The argument is developed for the start of Indian iron use ca.800-700 B.C. through a combination of both literary references (notably the *Yajurveda* and the Pali *Sutta-nipata*) and placement of the main iron ore fields in northern Bihar, thus refuting the proposition that Persian rule brought this technology to the region.

92. Goetz, Hermann. "Building and Sculpture Techniques in India, Part II: Classical and Later Times," *Archaeology* 16 (1) (March, 1963): 47-53.

A sequel to the article of December, 1962 covering the architectures of the Indus Valley civilization and Buddhist India, this essay presents a detailed discussion of stone construction in both the classical Hindu temples and Muslim buildings erected after the twelfth century. Particular attention is given to the varieties of vaulting, wall construction, and the transportation of materials. Researchers unfamiliar with Indian architecture will find the two Goetz entries useful background.

93. Lal, B.B. "A Decade of Prehistoric and Protohistoric Archaeology in India, 1951-1960," *Asian Perspectives*, v.7, nos. 1-2 (Summer-Winter 1963): 144-159.

A clear and readable overview of the major developments and state of knowledge of the regional archaeologies of India amassed between 1951 and 1960, this essay opens with a brief discussion of the structure of organized investigation at both the national and state levels. This is of particular value for the reader unfamiliar with the agencies involved, ranging from the Archaeological Survey itself to private research institutes. Three sections assess then-current data on the Stone Age, the protohistoric period and historic site excavation. A map showing "Principal Sites Explored and Excavated Since Independence" is provided. The attached bibliography is stated to cover "the more noteworthy publications during the decade." (p. 156)

94. Khatri, A.P. "Recent Exploration for the Remains of Early Man in India," *Asian Perspectives* v.7, nos. 1-2 (Summer-Winter 1963): 160-182.

A report on the results of the 1959-1960 season of test excavations carried out in three areas of India previously identified as possessing substantial deposits of stone tools and fossils. These regions are the Siwalik Hills in Himachal Pradesh (specifically, the site of Hari Talyangar), the upper portion of the Narmada Valley, and the Kurnool region of Andhra Pradesh. While no fossil hominid remains were located, excavations did clarify questions of cultural and climatic succession. A major feature of this text is the page-length drawings of the hand-axes and cleavers recovered from the Narmada Valley.

95. Goetz, Hermann. "An Indian Bronze From South Arabia," *Archaeology* 16 (3) (9 September, 1963): 187-189.

An analysis of a bronze figurine excavated in 1953 in Oman at the site of Khor Rori. Stylistic features identify it as a tree goddess, dating to the beginning of the third century A.D. Commentary on the cultural attitudes towards sea trade and travel among different population groups in India is included.

96. Lal, B.B. "India," *Asian Perspectives* v.8, n.1 (Summer 1964): 84.

A summary report on archaeological activity and exploration in India carried out between April 1962 and March 1963, consisting of several river valley surveys and the excavating of thirty sites with dates ranging from the Stone Age to historic times. A lengthy bibliography of publications describing the results of these seasons is appended. Area covered include the Narmada and Suvarnarekha valleys, Madras, Gujarat's Kathiawar region, Kalibangan, the site of Eran in Madhya Pradesh, Atranjikhera, Rajghat, and the states of Bihar, Uttar Pradesh, West Bengal and Andhra Pradesh.

97. *Archaeological Remains, Monuments and Museums, Parts I and II*. New Delhi: Archaeological Survey of India, 1964.

Originally published in a limited edition for the twenty-sixth International Congress of Orientalists, held in New Delhi from January 4-10, 1964, this two-volume set was subsequently reworked from a handbook format to a more general treatment of the past of the subcontinent. The nine chapters were all written by staff members of the Archaeological Survey and edited by the director A. Ghosh. Topics covered are protohistoric remains, early historical sites, northern and southern Buddhist monuments, rock-cut monuments, northern and southern temples and Islamic monuments and museums. Within each chapter, contents are divided by geographic region and political units, with major sites treated individually. Ninety-six black and white photographs provide illustration of many striking examples of public architecture and excavations as well as sample artifacts from museum collections. An index to the set is included at the end of the second volume.

98. Lal, B.B. *Indian Archaeology Since Independence*. Delhi: Motilal Banarsidass, 1964.

In May,1962, the author gave a series of lectures in the United Kingdom, one of which, for the Society of Antiquaries in London, was on "Recent Archaeological Discoveries in India." The present book is an expansion of that lecture, concisely covering sixteen years and updated with then-current information on conservation, the organization of archaeological science in India, museums, and Indian archaeology's role in such international efforts as the rescue work in Nubia. Among the projects reviewed is the massive salvage effort at Nagarjunakonda in Andhra Pradesh. A limited bibliography is also provided, with readers referred to the *Annual Bibliography of Indian Archaeology*. Forty-two black and white photographs illustrate the range of subjects investigated by India's archaeologists, from coinage and inscriptions to architectural history.

99. Prakash, Satya and N.S. Rawat. *Chemical Study of Some Indian Archaeological Antiquities*. Bombay: Asia Publishing House, 1965.

The "antiquities" of the title whose analyses are presented in this monograph are ancient mortars and plasters, pigments and pottery glazes, glass, copper and bronze objects, and coins. Samples are drawn from a variety of sites including Mohenjo-daro, Kausambi, Harappa, Arikamedu, Ajanta, Taxila, Nalanda, and Ahichchhatra. The original work was sponsored by the State Council of Scientific and Industrial Research of Uttar Pradesh. A bibliography of related literature in print as of the early 1960's is appended.

100. Sahney, Vimala. *The Iron Age of South India*. Ph.D dissertation, University of Pennsylvania, 1965.

In the preface to this dissertation, the author notes that "There are thousands of grave sites covering nearly the whole of peninsular India and part of the Deccan which contain iron objects and also a ceramic which is apparently technologically homogeneous. Nothing is known about the relationship of one site to another." (pp. 2-3) At the time this research was carried out, only a few stratified Iron Age sites were known, including Brahmagiri and Piklihal. Sahney's objective in his research was to attempt to establish a chronology for the undated sites by creating a chronology of grave types at the stratified sequences and tying undated localities yielding datable materials to the resulting sequence by means of typological similarities of eleven grave forms. The dating terminology used in this research (Lower and Upper Neolithic, Iron Age, and Early Historical) is carefully redefined from the local Indian context and does not simply represent a transfer of European chronology. Areas represented in the study are Upper Mysore, the Deccan, Andhra Pradesh, the coastal plain of Tamil Nadu, southern Mysore and the Ghats, Kerala and the Nilgiri Hills. Major Iron Age sites reviewed include Brahmagiri, Maski and Piklihal in Mysore, Nagarjunakonda, Yeleswaram and Amaravati in Andhra Pradesh, Sanur in Tamil Nadu, and Porkalam in Kerala. The origins of the Iron Age cultures in adjoining regions are also considered. Results indicate a time span for the so-called "Megalithic" graves from ca. 500 B.C. to the sixth and seventh centuries A.D. Researchers will find the extensive bibliography useful.

101. Abu Imam. *Sir Alexander Cunningham and the Beginnings of Indian Archaeology*. Dacca: Asiatic Society of Pakistan, 1966.

The only extant biography of one of the founding fathers of Indian archaeology, this work "is an attempt at giving an outline of the history of Indian archaeology from the end of the eighteenth century to the end of the nineteenth." (p. vii) Cunningham's career in the British Army is followed from his initial appointment in May, 1828 as a member of the Bengal Engineers to his retirement from active service in 1861, by which time he had already contributed antiquarian studies on the ancient temples of Kashmir and the geography of Ladakh to the scientific literature. The text then explores the seminal contributions to Indian archaeology made by James Prinsep (1790-1840), chief of the Calcutta mint, who infected Cunningham with his enthusiasm for investigating ancient India, the Asiatic Society of Bengal and its journal *Asiatick Researches*, founded in 1788. Discussion of the early emphasis on the reconstruction of Indian history through numismatics and the problems of site identification provide background to the extensive series of surveys and limited excavations done by Cunningham. Following his appointment by the Viceroy, Lord Canning, in November, 1861 as "Archaeological Surveyor", his duties were specified as carrying out "a detailed and accurate account of the archaeological remains of Upper India." (p. 55) This task was to occupy him for the next twenty-four years, often using the then-newly translated accounts of two Buddhist travelers of the fifth and seventh centuries A.D., Hsuan Tsang and Fa Hsien, as guides. Beginning with a visit to Bodh Gaya in December, 1861, his inspections and work at such major sites as Nalanda (Bihar), Pataliputra, Sravasti, Kausambi, Mathura, Kapilavastu and his survey work in the Punjab, Central India and Bengal are next reviewed. The third chapter, "Interpretation of the Remains," offers a valuable picture of the history of the usage of coins and inscriptions as the first focus of archaeology in India, along with the preservation of architectural remains and the retrieval of sculpture. The final section evaluates Cunningham's work as to the dangers of exploration in his time, methods of dating and excavation (the latter not up to date even by the standards of the day), his comprehensive definition of archaeology, management of the Survey and the reactions of his critics. The dates of publication of all of his reports, a lengthy bibliography (including both original unpublished sources, published works and secondary sources) and his role in ascertaining the function of the Buddhist *stupa* complete the work. Essential background for all students of the Indian past.

102. Wheeler, Sir Mortimer. *Civilizations of the Indus Valley and Beyond*. New York: McGraw-Hill, 1966.

Originally written in 1961, this volume presents a comprehensive review of the state of knowledge of Indian prehistory and ongoing research as they existed in 1965. While the central focus is the ancient culture of the Indus Valley as represented by its type-sites of Harappa and Mohenjo-daro, coverage is included of the archaeology of the northwestern border region, Central India and the Ganges Basin up to the beginning of the Mauryan Empire. Numerous color and black and white illustrations make this a good introductory volume on the periods indicated. Specific sites noted as significant include Charsada, Lothal, Kalibangan, Chanhu-daro, Amri, Kot-Diji, Sutkagen-Dor, Navdatoli, Hastinapura, Ahichchhatra, Kausambi, Taxila, Pataliputra, Shishupalgarh, Ujjain, Brahmagiri and Arikamedu.

103. Maloney, Clarence Thomas. *The Effect of Early Coastal Sea Traffic on the Development of Civilization in South India.* Ph.D dissertation, University of Pennsylvania, 1968.

This dissertation interweaves a variety of textual resources which collectively comprise the historical records of south India (here defined as the south and southwestern parts of the peninsula) from earliest times through the third century A.D. with then-available archaeological information from both Tamil Nadu and Kerala as well as Sri Lanka in an examination of the cultural roles played by local and long distance maritime connections. Sources used are the Tamil literature of the Sangam period (the first three centuries A.D.) and the Sri Lankan chronicles the *Dipavamsa* and *Mahavamsa,* as well as accounts by Greek historians (from Herodotus, Ptolemy, Pliny and Arrian to the *Periplus of the Erythraean Sea)* and Brahmi inscriptions. Tamil documents were used from the original text, while Sinhala sources were utilized in translation. Chief attention is given to the kingdoms of the Pandiya and Chola dynasties. The second, third and sixteenth chapters discuss commodities noted as significant in the southern trading networks, chiefly pearls, conch shells,cinnamon, pepper and related spices, gold, and gemstones, while succeeding sections outline known historical references to the region by period and discuss individual trading ports. The principal application of archaeology in this dissertation is in the section on the ports of origin for the northern traders in Sind and Gujarat, as the author notes that "there have been no useful excavations of pre-Christian strata in the Tamil area or along coastal Ceylon." (p. xlvi) His awareness of the need for substantial exploration is most forcefully stated in his observation that "not a single systematic archaeological excavation has been conducted along that long coast, though there is no lack of potential sites." (p. 191) Researchers will find this dissertation useful as a summary of the state of archaeological work done in this section of India by the early 1960's.

104. Mukherjee, S.N. *Sir William Jones: A Study in Eighteenth-Century British Attitudes to India.* Cambridge, University Press, 1968.

The shorter of the two extant biographies of Sir William Jones, founder of the Asiatic Society of Bengal and considered by many to have laid the groundwork for scientific investigation of the Indian past. Researchers unfamiliar with the early years, activities and publications of the Society will find detailed coverage of these events in the fifth and sixth chapters. A bibliography is provided for further study. For a fuller treatment of Jones' career, readers should consult Garland Cannon's 1990 work *The Life and Mind of Oriental Jones: Sir William Jones, the Father of Modern Linguistics.*

105. Soundara Rajan, K.V. "The Changing Face of Archaeology," *Puratattva* 1 (1967/68): 24-30.

A discussion of recent technological and theoretical developments in archaeology, and the potential for their application in India. The absence of skeletal remains of early man (to be addressed by renewed investigation of cave sites), the destructive role played by India's climate on the preservation of open-air sites, and the expansion of field work to include the retrieval of traces of past behavior patterns beyond the simple amassing of artifact types, and new dating techniques are noted. Perhaps the most telling observation made is that on the isolation of archaeology from social anthropology within India." The anthropologist in India is perhaps the one that is likely to overtake (and perhaps overrun) the Prehistoric archaeologist in the task of systematising the rudiments of Stone Age Culture-reconstruction soon, unless the Prehistorian is assiduously widening his parameter, and integrating his inferences with those of the anthropologist." (p. 25)

106. Sinha, K.K. "The Use of the Terms Prehistory & Protohistory in Indian Archaeology," *Puratattva* 1 (1967/68): 39-41.

The text of a paper read at the Indian Science Congress held in Varanasi in January, 1968, examining the European origins and local interpretations of two terms frequently used to subdivide the Indian past. A primary complicating factor in applying the broad idea of "prehistoric" to the Indian context has been how to categorize the Harappan culture, whose writing has not yet been translated. A definition of prehistoric as before 1300 B.C., with protohistory defined as the period 1300-600 B.C., is suggested.

107. Wheeler, Robert Eric Mortimer. *Early India and Pakistan to Ashoka*. London, 1969.

Another of the interpretive books by the Director of the Archaeological Survey of India aimed at reviewing the results of fieldwork for a general auduience, this volume appeared as part of the series *Ancient Peoples and Places*. The preface notes the increased complexity of the Indian archaeological record as then known and defines its selected topics as "representative of the cultural trends in the arterial valleys and on the great plains and plateaux, where the major developments took place." (p. 13) Individual chapters cover the Stone Age tool industries of northern, central and Southern India, the question of whether the subcontinent passed through three Paleolithic stages as occurred in Europe, the civilizations of the Indus and Ganges valleys, the megalithic cultures of south India, and the major sites of central India. Fifty-seven high quality black and white photographs offer the reader an excellent range of artifacts from stone tools to the streets of Mohenjo-daro, silver bar coins from Taxila and the lion capitals of Ashoka's columns. Each chapter is provided with a bibliography for further reading. Although somewhat dated, the work remains a useful introduction due to its scope and clarity of argument.

108. Taddei, Maurizio. *The Ancient Civilization of India*. London: Barrie and Jenkins, 1970.

An English version of the author's work, this short and well-illustrated volume is part of the popular archaeological series *Ancient Civilizations*. He notes that "unlike classical archaeology, Indian archaeology has never shown a weakness for abstract systems of classification…nor has it ever…lost sight of its own first objective, that of writing the history of man." (p. 15) Three lengthy chapters begin with the appearance of the Indus civilization and trace development in the subcontinent through the Iron Age, the Mauryan Empire, Greek influence and the flowering of Buddhist art in Gandhara (with the creation of the stupa and its evolution treated separately), and the Kushan age. The text presupposes some knowledge of Indian history and previous archaeological field work, and lacks an adequate bibliography for further study.

109. Fairservis, Walter A. *The Roots of Ancient India*.New York: Macmillan, 1971.

The author, an archaeologist whose specific area of expertise is the northwest borderlands of India, describes this highly readable work as "a review of the findings of archaeology on the South Asian subcontinent relating to the vast, essentially prehistoric, period before the Buddha." (p. xxiii) Emphasizing in his presentation the necessity of comprehending the complex web of environmental influences within which all ancient cultures arose and functioned, the first chapter sets forth the three major physiographic divisions of the region: the Himalaya and associated mountain chains, the vast river plains and the rocky mass of the Deccan plateau, flanked by the varied coastal strips. Successive chapters report on the Stone Ages, the rise of urban settlements (examples cited being Amri, Kot Diji, and the Kulli culture of Baluchistan), the rise and eclipse of the Harappan civilization, and the varied regional cultures such as Malwa. A collection of twelve appendixes presents data on a wide variety of subjects including regional archaeological sequences in Iran, radiocarbon dates, and Middle Stone Age sites in India. Researchers will find Fairservis' lengthy bibliography a useful review of the diverse approaches being applied in Indian archaeology at this time.

110. Ghosh, Asok K. "Hand Adzes in the Palaeolithic Culture of India," *Asian Perspectives* 15 (1972): 158-166.

In 1943, Hallam Movius introduced the concept of the "hand adze" to the literature of Palaeolithic archaeology, basing this category "entirely on the form and technique of the tools themselves." (p. 159) This article takes the criteria of this category and applies them to Indian stone tool technology, defining and illustrating three types based on the raw materials used (pebbles, cores and flakes), noting that "despite its presence, the hand adze has gone unnoticed in the Indian context." (p. 160) These tools were first reported from the Sabarmati Valley of Maharashtra and have been found across an area stretching from Madras to Rawalpindi.

111. *Proceedings of the Seminar on Ochre-Coloured Ware and Northern Black Polished Ware* edited by Dr. Y.D. Sharma *Puratattva* 5 (1971-72): 1-103.

The fifth issue of *Puratattva* was completely devoted to reporting in full the presentations and speeches given at a special seminar sponsored by the Indian Archaeological Society on May 11, 1971 at the National Museum in New Delhi. Thirty-five scholars participated, virtually every major Indian prehistoric archaeologist then active. The subject of discussion was "the OCP culture and the crucial role that it played in bringing the Harappa culture into contact with the...Ganga basin." (p. *ii*). At the time the seminar was held, much of the publication on the Chacolithic period of Indian prehistory had been centered on discoveries in western India and the Deccan at such sites as Navdatoli, while "knowledge of the Copper Age cultures of the Punjab and Haryana remained confined to the field archaeologists." (p. *ii*) Each ceramic was considered in a separate forum, whose texts make up the bulk of this monograph. Nine appendixes review five field projects where Ochre Coloured Ware was found, a geochronological study, technical notes on the Northern Black Polished Ware (all reprinted from journals such as *Ancient India* and *Man*, as well as contemporary works on Indian archaeology), and two lengthy bibliographies on each pottery type. A map showing the distribution of Ochre-Coloured Ware in the Upper Ganga Valley and drawings of vessel shapes and decoration from sites used as examples in the discussions are included.Collective opinion was that, given the data then available, it was not possible to sufficiently resolve issues of nomenclature, age and diffusion of the two distinctive types of Chalcolithic pottery.

112. *Ecological Backgrounds of South Asian Prehistory* edited by Kenneth A.R. Kennedy and Gregory L. Possehl. Ithaca, New York: Cornell University South Asia Program, 1973.

This collection of fourteen papers contains ten given at the title symposium held during the annual meeting of the American Anthropological Association in New Orleans on December 2, 1973, with four additional submissions from leading scholars in the field of palaeoecology. Topics center on interdisciplinary studies of ancient demographic factors such as migration, nutrition and disease, and "other facets of ancient lifeways which have given form to the bio-social evolution of human populations in South Asia." (p. iii) Selected papers have been separately entered in this bibliography.

113. Malik, S.C. "The Role of Theory in the Study of Archaeology in India," *Puratattva* 6 (1972/73): 1-11.

The title of this article is somewhat misleading, in that the author spends most of his time discussing the general role theoretical considerations can play in archaeology by balancing the interpretation of field excavation data. Regarding Indian archaeology in specific, he acknowledges the use of three interpretive models, "unilinear evolution, descriptive-historical and ...diffusionist." (p. 8) His chief objection to the then-current use of theory is an absence of conscious analysis of these models, an implicit acceptance rather than explicit definition prior to field work. "We take for granted what India is or was...whatever we employ we must explain and relate explicitly to our own material and data." (p. 9)

114. Misra, V.N. "Ecological Adaptations during the Terminal Stone Age in Western and Central India," in *Ecological Backgrounds of South Asian Prehistory* edited by Kenneth Kennedy and Gregory Possehl. Ithaca, New York: Cornell South Asia Program, 1974: 28-51.

This paper presents a survey of the Mesolithic cultures of Gujarat, Rajasthan, Madhya Pradesh and the Ganges Valley in Uttar Pradesh. The history of archaeological research on the Late Stone Age in each state is summarized in detail, with major excavations noted and notable findings assessed. Sites discussed are Langhnaj, Bhimbetka, Tilwara, Bagor, Morhana Pahar, Lekhahia, and Sarai Nahar Rai. Available data on the adaptation to and exploitation of a range of ecological zones by Stone Age man, reflected in patterns of settlement location and resource utilization, is reviewed. Maps of known microlithic sites are included.

115. *South Asian Archaeology* edited by Norman Hammond. London: Duckworth, 1973.

The twenty-one papers collected in this volume were originally presented at the First International Conference of South Asian Archaeologists, held at Cambridge in July, 1971. Readers will note that Afghanistan is included as well as more traditional regions within India. Individual papers have been entered under their respective geographic regions. Of interest to the development of the field is the editor's preface which details planned scholarly work and publishing. An index is provided by site name and investigator.

116. *South Asian Archaeology 1973* edited by J.E. Van Lohuizen-De Leeuw and J.B.M. Ubaghs. Leiden: E.J. Brill, 1974.

This collection presents fifteen papers given at the Second International Conference for the Promotion of South Asian Archaeology in Western Europe, held at the University of Amsterdam in 1973. Items specifically related to India include discussion of the prehistoric geographic limits of the Indian Desert, archaeozoology as applied to the breeding of Indian cattle, and individual buildings at Sonkh and Mukundara. The relevant papers have been separately entered by geographic region.

117. Clason, A.T. "Archaeozoological Study In India: Aspects of Stock-Breeding and Hunting in Prehistoric and Early Historic Times," in *South Asian Archaeology 1973* edited by J.E. Van Lohuizen-De Leeuw and J.B.M. Ubaghs. Leiden; E.J. Brill, 1974: 78-89.

Clason begins this excellent background essay by setting forth the climatic and vegetation zones of the subcontinent, noting that "the first archaeozoological studies in India...were the direct result of the discovery and subsequent excavation...of Moenjo Daro and Harappa." (p. 78) His study examines materials recovered at ten sites in western India. States represented are Maharashtra (Inamgaon and Nevasa), Madhya Pradesh (Navdatoli) and Rajasthan (Kayatha).

Comparison of the skeletal remains, chiefly of cattle and other domestic animals but including elephant and rhinoceros, is made with available textual sources.

118. Allchin, F.R. "Problems and Perspectives In South Asian Archaeology," in *South Asian Archaeology* edited by Norman Hammond; London, Duckworth, 1973: 1-12.

A general essay outlining the history of archaeology in India and the major areas of research in the early 1970's. These were the palaeolithic glacial sequences and the geology of the rivers of India, the Late Stone Age (covering the domestication of plants and animals), the origins of the Indus Valley civilization, continuing analysis of Indus remains from new theoretical viewpoints (similar to the work done by Robert Redfield), the question of the Aryan arrival, the rise of urban centers in northern India, and the Iron Age megalithic grave complexes of southern India.

119. Sankalia, H.D. "Prehistoric Colonization in India," *World Archaeology* 5(1) (June 1973): 86-91.

A survey of sites from periods of Indian prehistory where new cultural assemblages are found which cannot be traced as deriving from earlier groups known from the archaeological record. The author suggests using the idea of colonization as a model for explaining such events, a position more fully set out in several of his books. Type sites noted range from the Palaeolithic to the Neolithic and Chalcolithic in date.

120. Agrawal, D.P. and Sheela Kusumgar. *Prehistoric Chronology and Radiocarbon Dating in India.* Delhi: Munshiram Manoharlal, 1974.

This volume presents a different perspective on the issue of establishing reliable chronologies for the various periods of Indian prehistory, as its authors are the operators of the radiocarbon laboratory created in 1962 at the Tata Institute of Fundamental Research in Bombay. Rather than discussing individual sites in detail, they begin with a brief overview of the dating technologies available (including thermoluminescence and archaeomagnetism) and work to create chronological frameworks for the Early, Middle and Late Stone Ages, and the Neolithic, Chalcolithic and Iron Age cultures known at the time of publication. A final summary synthesizes previous arguments into a general timeline for the subcontinent.

121. *South Asian Archaeology 1975* edited by J.E. Van Lohuizen-de Leeuw. Leiden: E.J. Brill, 1979.

This volume contains the full texts (in English and French) of fifteen papers presented at the Third International Conference of South Asian Archaeologists in Western Europe held at the Centre National de Recherche Scientifique in Paris. Subjects covered include discussions of copper weapons from southern India, the ancient carnelian and agate industries of western India and Pakistan, and reports from the site of Mehrgarh. Selections from this collection have been entered in the present bibliography.

122. Allchin, Bridget. "The Agate and Carnelian Industry of Western India and Pakistan," in *South Asian Archaeology 1975* edited by J.E.van Lohuizen-de Leeuw. Leiden: Brill, 1979: 91-105.

A smoothly-written synthesis of archaeological, ethnographic and written historical information on the collection and mining of agate and carnelian stone in western India and Pakistan since Harappan times. The author's extensive fieldwork in the region permitted her to observe firsthand then-current bead manufacturing in Cambay and to visit the mining community of Ratnapura. Topics covered are the various stages of bead shaping and finishing, mine construction, and aspects of the industry requiring further research.

123. Maloney, Clarence. "Archaeology in South India: Accomplishments and Prospects," in *Essays on South India* edited by Burton Stein. Honolulu: University Press of Hawaii, 1975: 1-40.

Covering the archaeological sequence of Southern India from Palaeolithic times to A.D. 300, the opening section of this essay examines claims for the existence of significant civilization during the Sangam period (comprising the first three centuries A.D.) for Tamil Nadu and Kerala. A definition of "civilization" incorporating such elements as a specialized agricultural base, urbanization, formalized religion and political organization, and writing is applied to the available evidence, supporting the claim. Sri Lanka is seen as "the source of inspiration of much that was incorporated into the early civilization of Tamil Nadu." (p. 22) The known history and archaeology of Karnataka, Andhra Pradesh and Kerala are also discussed, with a separate examination of excavated (and potential) coastal sites.

124. "Art and Archaeological Theft in India," in *The Protection of the Artistic and Archaeological Heritage, A View From Italy and India*. Rome: United Nations Social Defense Research Institute, 1976: 193- 259.

Based upon a study by the director of the Central Bureau of Investigation of India, this report presents a highly detailed picture of the trade in illegally obtained antiquities (from archaeological sites, temples and regional museums) as it was operating during the 1970s. Beginning with a list of examples of items stolen, various factors are adduced to explain the existence of this activity, including an erosion of public reverence for such objects and the role of private collectors as salesmen and middlemen. Case histories from Madras, Orissa, Madhya Pradesh, Maharashtra and Uttar Pradesh reveal a history of at least fifty years of reported thefts of this nature with a consistently adapting *modus operandi*. Factors hindering prevention and retrieval of stolen materials are noted as woefully insufficient security staff, delays in reporting thefts to police, and the fact that precise descriptions of most items, vital to positive identification, are rarely available. Of particular value to researchers is the section headed "Instrumentalities of Prevention and Control" (p. 226) which covers "legal norms (special and general; penal and civil); administration of the archaeological patrimony and international norms and recommendations." (p. 226) The specific pieces of legislation enacted since 1872 covering topics as varied as treasure trove, monument preservation, and the legal trade in antiquities are reviewed. The "archaeological patrimony" section notes that "3,744 monuments and sites throughout the country are under the authority and care of the Archaeological Survey of India,"(p. 235) with the real problems seen to lie in the areas of implementation of Indian law through insufficient manpower and the inadequacy of extant international law in this area. An appendix provides the full text of editorials and news reports which appeared in the Indian press in 1972 and 1973 on various incidents. The states noted as being most heavily affected by such thefts are Uttar Pradesh, Tamil Nadu, Rajasthan, Mysore, Madhya Pradesh, Gujarat and Andhra Pradesh "as these are ...best known for the quantity and artistic quality of their temples, shrines and places of pilgrimage." (p. 201)

125. Chattopadhyaya, B.D. "Indian Archaeology and The Epic Traditions," *Puratattva* 8 (1975/76): 67-72.

The "epic traditions" considered here are the *Mahabharata* and the *Ramayana,* while the focus of argument is initially to review Indian archaeology's involvement with these ancient classics through excavation at sites identified as cities mentioned in them, with Hastinapura used as illustration. More valuable for the researcher unfamiliar with the precise texts of the epics is Chattopadhyaya's analysis of the assumptions made about the identity of specific features of the hunting and agrarian societies described in verse and how these have been translated into approaches to excavation. Complicating factors include the time span of the epics, their relative chronologies, regional archaeological cultures of Uttar Pradesh and northern Bihar and their variance with expected Mahabharata states, and the spread of agriculture. The Vedas are seen to have preserved a clearer reflection of early societies in the Ganga Valley than the later epics, both of which were elaborated over the centuries. Field workers are tartly cautioned to keep their scientific goals clearly in mind, as "one would have expected ...excavations to rest on...academic considerations and the current state of research...not on a decision to resolve certain emotional hang-ups regarding a particular epic hero or an archaeological site." (p. 71)

126. Champaklakshmi, B.K. "Archaeology and Tamil Literary Tradition," *Puratattva* 8 (1975/76): 110-122.

Beginning by observing that most of the excavations carried out to date in the Tamil country have centered on the river valleys and sites named in the Sangam literature, the author then explores the question of whether it is feasible "to check the reliability of historical tradition through excavated data." (p. 110) Ongoing and completed field work done at sites both within the Kaveri Valley, chiefly Karur,

Uraiyur and Kaveripumpattinam, as well as Tamil sites located elswehere in the region (among which are Arikamedu and Kanchipuram) is reviewed, followed by an assessment of the correlation of black-on-red ware, iron use and irrigation agriculture with the spread of megalithic construction across southern India. Further investigation is called for into the appearance of this uniform protohistoric culture.

127. Parpola, Asko. "Bibliographical Aids for the Study of the Indus Civilization: A Critical Survey," *Puratattva* 8 (1975/76): 150-156.

One of the few evaluations of available bibliographical information relating to any aspect of Indian archaeology to appear as a separate article, Parpola's essay examines ten compilations in print as of 1976 which contain coverage of Indus-related research publications. They include the *Annual Bibliography of Indian Archaeology*, Louis Renou's 1931 *Bibliographie vedique* and the three volumes of R.N. Dandekar's *Vedic Bibliography* (1946-1973) which continues its work, and B.M. Pande and K.S. Ramachandran's *Bibliography of the Harappan Culture* (1971). Numerous errors in citations and duplications of entries are noted. Researchers unfamiliar with any of the bibliographic tools regarded as standard in the field of Indian archaeology will find this analysis a useful guide and caution.

128. Brooks, Robert R.R. and Vishnu S. Wakankar. *Stone Age Painting In India*. New Haven: Yale University Press, 1976.

A readable introduction to the rock art of India as it was known in the mid-1970s. Subjects covered include the distribution of art sites, the tribal cultures which continued to produce them from the Mesolithic era until relatively recent times, problems of dating (using the techniques of superposition, content and associated artifacts when present) and similarities with rock paintings elsewhere in the world. Particularly useful is a map showing the eighteen sandstone and four granite regions of central and southern India where paintings were known. The lavish color and black and white photographs and detailed line copies of selected paintings substantially enrich the text. A bibliography of related literature is included. Researchers wishing a slightly later survey should consult Ernst Neumayer's 1983 volume *Prehistoric Indian Rock Painting*.

129. Wheeler, Mortimer. *My Archaeological Mission To India and Pakistan*. London: Thames and Hudson, 1976.

In August, 1943, Sir Mortimer Wheeler was invited by the India Office and Lord Wavell, the Viceroy, to direct the complete reorganization of the Archaeological Survey of India. This lucid memoir recounts the high points of his work between 1944 and 1948. Topics addressed include the beginning of field work in India with the first excavations at Charsada in 1902, the creation of the Taxila School of Archaeology in 1944 where many of the later leaders in Indian archaeology received their basic training, the Roman trading station at Arikamedu near Madras, the *Periplus of the Erythraean Sea* with its sailing directions for ancient merchants crossing the Indian Ocean, the megaliths of southern India and the discovery of the Indus Valley civilization. This last is illustrated with data drawn from the excavations at Mohenjo-daro. As personal accounts of the development of archaeology in the subcontinent are few in number, this reminiscence places a human face on the last years of archaeology under the Raj. A brief bibliography is appended.

130. Mathpal, Yashodar. "Rock Art of India," *Journal of Indian History* 54(1) (April 1976): 27-51.

In 1880, the first known rock paintings to be found in India were discovered at Mirzapur in Uttar Pradesh, beginning the investigation of a new aspect of the subcontinent's prehistory. This article opens with a detailed review of the early publications in this field from 1883 to the first decades of the twentieth century. The author notes that "in India, there are several thousand rockshelters containing paintings situated in more than 150 sites" (p. 28) which have been classified into nineteen major areas, Central India (in particular the Vindhya and Kaimur Hills) having the greatest concentration. Most of this article is a lengthy survey of each region and the major rock art sites located there. Issues of dating the paintings according to contents (such as the depiction of vanished species), overlapping inscriptions in scripts ranging from Brahmi to Kharoshthi, and association with stone tools are considered in the final section. The five-page bibliography of major writings on Indian rock art will prove useful to the researcher seeking to locate the older scientific reports on this topic. No illustrations are provided.

131. Chakrabarti, Dilip K. "Distribution of Iron Ores and the Archaeological Evidence of Early Iron in India," *Journal of the Economic and Social History of the Orient* 20, Part 2 (1977): 166-184.

The author begins his analysis by pointing out flaws in the literature written on the development of Indian iron usage to date, rejecting all *a priori* diffusionist arguments(including the legend of a Hittite monopoly on this technology) suggesting instead that "it may just be sensible to discuss an archaeological-cultural phenomenon in an area first in its own terms." (p. 167) Citing the formerly widespread local smelting of iron from a wide variety of low-grade sources not suitable for mass commercial exploitation, Chakrabarti then notes some twenty regions of India where iron ores are found, including both the type of pre-industrial smelting for which evidence exists, "virtually ...the whole of India outside the major alluvial stretches." (p. 171) Archaeological evidence from the six major centers of iron working in India dating earlier than the first half of the first millennium B.C. as then known is presented. Regions cited are Baluchistan, the Swat Valley and its tributaries, the divide between the Indus and Ganges valleys and the Upper Ganges itself, the Middle Ganges Valley, the Malwa plateau area of Uttar Pradesh in Central India and the site of Hallur in Karnataka.

132. *Ecology and Archaeology of Western India* edited by D.P. Agrawal and B.M. Pande. Delhi: Concept Publishing Company, 1977.

Subtitled "Proceedings of A Workshop Held at the Physical Research Laboratory, Ahmedabad, February 23-26, 1976," this collection of twenty-eight papers, while focused principally on the states of Gujarat and Rajasthan, also includes research on Quaternary climates and geological events in Central India as well as general discussions of factors affecting palaeoclimates. The nine articles directly related to archaeology are found in the second section on "Human Settlement and Palaeoenvironment."

133. Sankalia, H.D. *The Prehistory of India*. New Delhi: Munshiram Manoharlal, 1977.

Written for "the educated layman interested in the development of Indian culture from its earliest beginnings to the dawn of history," (p. 1) this volume is an excellent example of the type of popular literature produced on archaeology within the subcontinent. Individual chapters outline basic concepts in the study of prehistory then review specific eras from palaeolithic times to the Iron Age. A chapter on "Colonization and the Beginning of Civilization" is a good summary of this theoretical model of the origins of regional cultures. Forty-five black and white photographs and line drawings are included. Researchers will find the maps on the distribution of the Neolithic-Chalcolithic sites (in particular the South Indian Neolithic, with 145 sites listed) useful for reference. A better treatment of the same subject is D.P. Agrawal's 1982 work *The Archaeology of India*.

134. Allchin, Bridget, Andrew Goudie and Kauranarkara Hegde. *The Prehistory and Palaeogeography of the Great Indian Desert. London, Academic Press, 1978.*

Based upon six seasons of field work between 1969 and 1976, this report examines "the development of early man during the latter part of the Pleistocene in the region between the Indus River and the Aravalli Hills," (p. v.) stressing the evidence for past climatic conditions uncovered in this survey. Beginning with a chapter on the general geography of the desert and its biotic zones, the history of previous research into ancient climates in the Thar is reviewed. Types of data examined range from lake pollen cores taken in Rajasthan, palaeosols, the stratigraphy of the river terraces of Gujarat, and fossilized dunes. Researchers unfamiliar with previous studies of Thar prehistory will find the third chapter "the Prehistoric Context" valuable background, with illustrations of known stone tool types provided. Individual sections provide more detailed coverage on the Pushkar Basin and Central Rajasthan, western Rajasthan, the Luni Valley, Gujarat and the lower Indus Valley. Data analysis indicates the Thar to be an ancient regional structure and not a recent creation during the Holocene. A lengthy bibliography completes the volume.

135. *A Source-Book of Indian Archaeology* edited by F. Raymond Allchin and Dilip K. Chakrabarti. New Delhi: Munshiram Manoharlal, 1979.

The first volume in an envisioned set, this title provides an invaluable service to the historian of Indian archaeology through gathering and reprinting in one place many of the scattered important writings of major figures influential in the development of the field. Beginning with Sir William Jones' 1788 discourse on the program of research of the Asiatic Society of Bengal and reaching into the early 1960s, four sections present background documents, discussions of early field investigative methods, the interplay of geography and climate with early man, and the domestication of plants and animals. Selections from this collection have been entered separately in the present bibliography.

136. *South Asian Archaeology 1977* edited by Maurizio Taddei. Naples: Instituto Universitario Orientale, 1979. 2 volumes.

Continuing evidence of the growth of interest in subcontinental archaeology within the scientific community, this set of two volumes presents the full text and illustrations of all papers given at the Fourth International Conference of the Association of South Asian Archaeologists in Western Europe, held at the Instituto in Naples July 4-8, 1977. The first volume covers prehistory and the third millennium B.C., while the second covers historical archaeology. Selected entries from this collection may be found in the present bibliography under the geographic region where the original research was carried out. All papers are provided in English.

137. Jacobson, Jerome. "Recent Developments in South Asian Prehistory and Protohistory," *Annual Review of Anthropology* 8 (1979): 467-502.

A highly readable overview essay of the state of archaeological knowledge and ongoing research on India's prehistoric and protohistoric eras as it existed at the end of the 1970s. Changes in theoretical approaches toward more frequent use of anthropological theory in formulating questions to be answered by excavation and an increasing environmental orientation of many projects are noted. Among the general results cited is the rejection of the model of Himalayan glaciations offered in the 1939 study by de Terra and Patterson, dating of rock paintings and pictographs, applications of ethnoarchaeology to the analysis of both house forms and patterns of plant use, technological studies of stone tools, and syntheses of available data on burial practices. The body of the essay is organized by time period into lower,middle and upper Palaeolithic and the Mesolithic (with extensive citation of data from the site of Sarai Nahar Rai in Uttar Pradesh). Discussion of more detailed topics such as the appearance of early villages and domestication, recent work on the origin, decline and nature of the Harappan civilization, the relationship of archaeology to traditional literatures such as the Vedas, and the possible independent occurrence of Indian iron technology completes the review. An extensive bibliography is included. Researchers may also wish to consult Kenneth Kennedy's article on the prehistoric skeletal remains known from South Asia in the 1980 *Annual Review of Anthropology* as a complement to the Jacobson piece.

138. Mohapatra, G.C. "Neolithic of Western Sub-Himalaya," *Puratattva* 10 (1978/79): 20-24.

A summary of the state of knowledge of the Neolithic age in the sub-Himalayan regions of India (defined by site locations in Jammu, Himachal Pradesh, the Punjab amd the Siwalik Hills.). First noted at Dehragopipur in the Beas Valley, the fifteen sites so far identified occur chiefly in areas previously associated with the Soan palaeolithic stone tool industry, suggesting that the established chronology of cultural succession within the subcontinent lacks the Mesolithic stage in these areas. Six major types of stone artifacts (axes, chisels, picks, axe-hammers, ring-stones and grinders) are seen as diagnostic markers of the Neolithic and are described in detail. Comparison of site distribution patterns with settlements of the earliest protohistoric peasant cultures indicates the use of a different ecological niche, with the larger Neolithic sites occurring on alluvial terraces of rivers of medium size draining the Himalayan massif. None of the Neolithic sites had been excavated as of the time of writing.

139. Dhavalikar, M.H. "New Archaeology and the Indian Situation," *Puratattva* 10 (1978/79): 33-38.

A review and assessment of the paradigm shift in archaeology in the 1970s towards a methodology which would assist in the retrieval of cultural process (initiated by Lewis Binford and David Clarke), and the need for expanding the field methods of Indian excavators beyond the approaches popularized by Sir Mortimer Wheeler in the 1940s. Dhavalikar cites his own successful application of the new techniques at the sites of Inamgaon and Walki, and calls upon his colleagues to experiment with this method, rather than "take pride in digging two or three sites every season." (p. 36)

140. *South Asian Archaeology 1979* edited by Herbert Hartel. Berlin: Dietrich Riemer Verlag, 1981.

On July 3-7, 1979, the Fifth International Conference of South Asian Archaeologists in Western Europe met at the Museum fur Indische Kunst in Berlin, at which time forty papers were presented. Thirty-five of them are published in this collection. Topics discussed include ongoing excavations in the Bannu Basin of Pakistan, the development of specific elements of Buddhist iconography, and regional reports from Afghanistan. Researchers will find selected papers entered under their respective geographic regions in this bibliography. All texts are in English.

141. McIntosh, J.R. "The Megalith Builders of South India: A Historical Survey," in *South Asian Archaeology 1979* edited by Herbert Hartel. Berlin: Dietrich Rimer, 1981: 459-468.

Since the first notice was taken of their existence in the early nineteenth century, the megalithic constructions found in many regions of southern India have been the subject of much speculation. This concise essay reviews the varied explanations put forward as to their origin, ranging from the presence of a migratory population of "Celto-Scythians" to influences from ancient Egypt. This diffusionist view attributing the construction of the megaliths to one particular group was supplanted by the 1950s with an appreciation of "the fact that the megalithic culture was characterized by a number of distinct elements …architecture and the associated funerary rites, Black-and-Red ware pottery, ironworking, horses and horse-trappings, and the Dravidian language." (p. 465)

142. Kennedy, Kenneth A.R. "Prehistoric Skeletal Record of Man In South Asia," *Annual Review of Anthropology* 9 (1980): 391-432.

This uniquely valuable survey of the physical traces of prehistoric hominids and *Homo sapiens* known from the South Asian region opens with the comment that "archaeological evidence rather than skeletal remains has documented the existence of Pleistocene man in the immense landmass …of India…Pakistan…and island Sri Lanka." (p. 391) Topics discussed are the hominid fossils known from the Siwalik Hills sites (principally Haritalyangar and Chinji) which include *Ramapithecus*, human remains associated with Mesolithic hunters and gatherers, the herding and farming cultures of northwestern India, Harappan civilization sites, the Chalcolithic and Neolithic populations of south and central India, and the Iron Age megalithic cultures of south India. Each section presents all known finds in chronological order and whether the specimens are known to be still in existence. Generic problems of conservation,osteology ,palaeodemography and questions of affiliation with modern ethnic groups are also considered. The massive bibliography gathers together an extremely scattered literature. Essential reading for all researchers unfamiliar with this aspect of South Asian archaeology.

143. Lal, B.B. "The Banganga-Beas Paleolithic Industry: A Look Back," *Puratattva* 11 (1979/80): 1-10.

In June, 1955 the author conducted investigations within the valleys of the Beas and Banganga Rivers, identifying on their terraces a previously unknown stone tool industry characterized by unifacial choppers, bifacial chopping tools and an almost total absence of handaxes and cleavers. Further explorations indicated this pattern of tool making was distributed over a wide area of Himachal Pradesh,Jammu, Punjab and Haryana. This detailed paper reviews the growth of knowledge about this palaeolithic culture over a quarter century, including the chief objections set forth as to its distinct identity and relationship to a series of sites in Haryana and Punjab near the front range of the Siwalik Hills where a separate industry marked by cleavers and handaxes has been found. Lal calls for further investigations for "as matters stand…there are not sufficient data from excavation which would help us in working out an evolution of this industry" (p. 5) although the hypothesis is offered that the handaxe element represents a new culture moving into the region.

144. *South Asian Archaeology 1981* edited by Bridget Allchin. Cambridge: The

University Press, 1984.

This volume contains the full texts of the forty-nine papers presented at the Sixth International Conference of the Association of South Asian Archaeologists in Western Europe held at Cambridge July 5-10 1981. The established format of these proceedings is continued through the emphasis on ongoing research on the Potwar Plateau of Pakistan and the sites of Mehrgarh and Shahr-i Sokhta, as well as protohistory, early historic and Buddhist archaeology, medieval architecture and Vijayanagara, and the relationship of bordering areas such as Thailand and Nepal to South Asian cultural developments.

145. Lal. B.B. "Archaeology in India Since Independence: Some Random Thoughts," *Puratattva* 12 9 (1980/81): 17-21.

The text of this address to the Indian Archaeological Society by a longtime veteran of Indian fieldwork offers a valuable perspective on the changes which have occurred in the discipline since Partition in 1947. Among them are the loss of the primary sites of Harappa and Mohenjo-daro to Pakistan (occasioning a survey which yielded new sites of the Indus culture), expansion of knowledge of the Stone Age Sohan Culture, the discovery of the painted caves and rock-shelters of Bhimbetka, improvement of dating techniques and the chronological placement of the Copper Hoard, Malwa and Jorwe cultures. Areas seen as requiring new (or renewed) energy are epigraphy,the use of extant ancient texts as supplements to field data, underwater archaeology, and development of expertise in the neglected archaeology of regions with which India had contact in past times (including even South East Asia). Lal is also sharply critical of two habits he views as destructive, "excavating sites without any specific problem in mind...just because funds are available and there is an ancient site in the neighborhood" (p. 18) and the inadequate preservation of many sites once excavations have been completed. Examples cited of the latter are the major tank system at Sringaverapura and the urban plan of Kalibangan.

146. Lal, Makkhan. "Copper Hoard Culture of India: A Reassessment," *Puratattva* 12 (1980/81): 65-77.

This brief article summarizes available data on the Copper Hoard culture as known at the time of publication, updating a similar listing made in 1951 by B.B.Lal. Since that time, the number of known sites has increased to eighty-six, the majority in Uttar Pradesh and Bihar. Topics reviewed are the major types of copper implements and their possible uses (celts, harpoons, the famous "antennae swords," anthropomorphic figures and double axes) and the results of metallurgical analyses done on sample objects. Of greatest value for the researcher unfamiliar with this period is the map showing all Copper Hoard sites in India and a table listing all sites by location, the types of artifacts found and the museums where they have been deposited.

147. Agrawal, D.P. *The Archaeology of India*. London: Curzon Press, 1982.

Stating that "the need for an archaeological review written with a multidisciplinary perspective has long been felt... in a situation where archaeological activity is fairly prolific, but publications rare," (p. 1) the author synthesizes a vast body of material into a readable account of India's past. Topics addressed include the palaeolithic of the subcontinent (by region), the Mesolithic, prehistoric art (chiefly rock paintings), agriculture's origins, and the Indus Valley civilization and related cultures in Baluchistan. The diverse array of Chalcolithic sites known as the Jorwe, Malwa, Banas and Kayatha cultures are examined as a group. Each chapter is lavishly illustrated with both line drawings and black and white photographs. A bibliography is included.

148. *Indian Archaeology: New Perspectives* edited by R.K. Sharma. Delhi: Agam Kala Prakashan, 1982.

This volume contains complete texts of the thirty-eight papers presented at the joint seminar on the protohistoric chronology of central India held at Bhopal March 16-18, 1980. Sponsoring organizations were the Indian Archaeological Society and the Indian Society for Prehistoric and Quaternary Studies. Four sections focus on prehistory, proto-history, central India and some specific questions chiefly concerned with sculpture and architecture. Much of the information here centers on the states of Madhya Pradesh, Maharashtra, Gujarat and Kerala. Selected papers from this conference are entered under their individual states.

149. *Madhu: Recent Researches In Indian Archaeology and Art History*. Edited by M.S. Nagaraja Rao. Atlantic Highlands, New Jersey: Humanities Press, 1982.

This assemblage of fifty-nine articles was created as a tribute to the retirement of Shri M.N. Deshpande as Director General of the Archaeological Survey of India in 1978. His historic interests in and research on rock-cut cave temples are reflected in some of the contributed papers, which emphasize pre- and protohistory and architecture in addition to sculpture and art, numismatics, conservation and historical archaeology. Individual works have been entered in the present bibliography under specific sites and regions.

150. Chakrabarti, Dilip K. "The Development of Archaeology in the Indian Subcontinent," *World Archaeology* 13 (2) (Spring 1982): 326-344.

This examination of the history of archaeology in India begins earlier than many other treatments of the same topic, with the first accounts of active coastal temples in the writings of Pietro delle Valle in 1664, which often included ground plans. Among the sites recorded were the complexes at Elephanta, Kanheri and Ellora. Activities in the mid-eighteenth century centered on the precise measurements of these three temples and collection of the mythology associated with them. The theoretical approaches to India's past, the geographic and the historical, are briefly summarized. Discoveries made between 1784 (the year of foundation of the Asiatic Society of Bengal) and 1830 during the site surveys of Colonel Colin Mackenize and Francis Buchanan are noted, followed by coverage of the period 1830-1861.

During the latter, emphasis was placed upon exploring the northwest and the north Indian plain. The contributions of James Prinsep, Alexander Cunningham, James Burgess and John Marshall, the development of prehistoric studies of microlithic and Neolithic implements, and Mortimer Wheeler's role in restructuring archaeology are then examined. Post-Independence and Partition work and the major expansions of prehistoric researches, natural scientific analyses, and university participation complete the text.

151. Neumayer, Ernst. *Prehistoric Indian Rock Paintings.* Delhi: Oxford University Press, 1983.

An album of two hundred and ten drawings (some colored) and fifteen black and white photographs with accompanying text covering Indian rock art of the Mesolithic, Chalcolithic and historic periods. The introductory essay summarizes the involvement of archaeologists with rock art in India, beginning with the first discovery in 1880-81 by Archibald Carlleyle in the northern Vindhyas. All illustrations are provided with detailed captions.

152. *South Asian Archaeology 1983* edited by Janice Schotsmans and Maurizio Taddei. Naples: Istituto Universitario Orientale, 1985.

A two-volume set containing the full text of forty-six papers given at the Seventh International Conference of South Asian Archaeologists in Western Europe, held at the Musees Royaux d'Art et d'Histoire in Brussels, Belgium July 4-8 1983. Topics addressed include analysis of various aspects of the major Neolithic site of Mehrgarh in Pakistan, ethnoarchaeology in South Asia, dating issues of objects ranging from coins to megaliths, regional manifestations of the Harappan culture, and the Vijayanagara project. Selections from these proceedings have been entered separately in the present bibliography. A notable feature of this collection is a lengthy obituary of Johanna van Lohuizen-de Leeuw, a leading authority on Indian art and first director of the Institute of South and Southeast Asian Archaeology in Amsterdam.

153. Yule, Paul. "On the Function of the Prehistoric Copper Hoards of the Indian Subcontinent," in *South Asian Archaeology 1983* edited by Janice Schotsmans and Maurizio Taddei. Naples: Istituto Universitario Orientale, 1985: 495-508.

Dating to the second millennium B.C., some seventy-five hoards of copper artifacts have been located in several regions of India. This paper centers attention on the finds from Haryana, the Ganges-Yamuna river systems, eastern Chota Nagpur and the central highlands of Madhya Pradesh. A limited range of artifact types may be discerned : harpoons, anthropomorphic figurines, lance heads, swords and axes. Full-page illustrations and photographs of representative artifacts from each region are included. This essay is based upon a broader study by the author published in 1985 as *Metalwork of the Bronze Age in India.*

154. Cribb, Joe. "Dating India's Earliest Coins," in *South Asian Archaeology 1983*

edited by Janice Schotsmans and Maurizio Taddei. Naples: Istituto Universitario Orientale, 1985: 535-554.

The utility of coin finds as site dating aids to Indian archaeologists is thus far limited, "as the designs of many ancient Indian coins have yet to be fully understood and interpreted." (p. 535) This essay discusses the available evidence for the forms and denominations of the first coinages of India variously dated to between 1100-400 B.C., the different forms of coin manufacture in use (punch marked as opposed to the cast coin technology of Greece and Rome) and markings. The applicability of additional sources of data such as literary references from the Vedas and cross-correlations with dated Greek and Iranian coins are evaluated. The author interprets the punch marked coins as an Indian response to the example of Greek coinage and places their appearance in fourth century B.C.

155. McIntosh, Jane R. "Dating the South Indian Megaliths," in *South Asian Archaeology 1983* edited by Janice Schotsmans and Maurizio Taddei. Naples: Istituto Universitario Orientale, 1985: 467-493.

A summary of the author's doctoral dissertation, this essay begins by setting forth the problems surrounding the dating of the megalith groups widely found across southern India. Chief among them is the absence of easily datable material associated with the monuments and the limited number of radiocarbon dates available, permitting an assignment only within the Iron Age (1100-300 B.C.). McIntosh takes issue with prior dating attempts and presents a division of the megalithic culture into six periods based upon comparative dating for distinctive megalithic artifacts, together with grave morphology, funeral rites and geographic distribution.

156. *Srinidhih: Perspectives in Indian Archaeology, Art and Culture*. Madras: New Era Publications, 1983.

This collection of sixty-six papers was assembled as a commemorative festschrift for K.R. Srinivasan, a botanist who began his career with the Archaeological Survey of India under Sir Mortimer Wheeler and subsequently coordinated the Temple Survey Project. The first seven papers in the volume cover the site of Domeli in the Punjab, the Malwa culture of Maharashtra, painted grey ware from Allahapur, and pre-iron cultures of Karnataka, as well as the role of art museums in India and electrolytic restoration. Selected items from this section have been entered in the present bibliography. Researchers interested in the life and career of Srinivasan will find the section of reminiscences which closes the volume illuminating.

157. Rajendran, P. "The Coastal Mesolithic Industries of South India," *Journal of Indian History* 61 (1-3)(April, August, December, 1983): 25-29.

The coastal regions of Maharashtra, Karnataka, Kerala, Tamil Nadu and Andhra Pradesh and the state of archaeological knowledge regarding their Mesolithic stone tool industries at the time of publication are summarized in this overview. The southern tools are seen to have a distinct identity of their own in the areas of raw materials (chiefly quartz and chert), prominent use of flakes, bifacial points and small choppers, and a common range of length, breadth and thickness. Five black and white photographs illustrate samples of each class mentioned.

158. Agrawal, D.P. "Metal Technology of the Harappans," in *Frontiers of the Indus Civilization* edited by B.B.Lal and S.P. Gupta. New Delhi: Books and Books, 1984: 163-167.

A general review of the state of knowledge of Harappan metallurgy as it existed in the early 1980's. Topics addressed are the metals used (chiefly gold, silver, tin and copper), techniques of manufacture (smelting, forging, casting, and welding) and sources of the ores used. Identification of these last is centered upon copper, with the author supporting Harappan exploitation of Indian ore veins rather than imported materials.

159. Dhavalikar, M.K. "Sub-Indus Cultures of Central and Western India," in *Frontiers of the Indus Civilization* edited by B.B. Lal and S.P. Gupta. New Delhi: Books and Books, 1984: 243-251.

The phrase "Sub-Indus cultures" was coined by Sir Mortimer Wheeler to describe those archaeological assemblages clearly influenced by various phases of the Harappan civilization but not part of it. This paper focuses chiefly on two, the Kayatha (dated to ca. 2000-1800 B.C. at its type site [on a tributary of the Kali Sindh river in central India] and first excavated in 1966-1967), and the site of Prabhas in Gujarat. Extensive discussion of the Kayatha ceramic industry, its stylistic affiliation with Early Harappan, and the 1800-1200 B.C. evolution of the Prabhas culture from clearly linked Harappan styles of pottery, copper axes, chert weights, seals and faience beads comprise the bulk of this article. Brief consideration is also given to the available Sub-Indus data from Maharashtra.

160. Dikshit, N.K. "Late Harappa In Northern India," in *Frontiers of the Indus Civilization* edited by B.B.Lal and S.P. Gupta. New Delhi: Books and Books, 1984: 253-269.

Focusing specifically on the last defined phase of the Indus civilization, the author attempts "to describe, state-wise, the process of disintegration or devolution of this civilization in northern India." (p. 253) The specific political units of modern India referred to are Jammu and Kashmir, Punjab, Haryana and western Uttar Pradesh. Three maps of all known Harappan sites in these areas are included. Cultural elements used to define these local and regional variations from the central Indus heartland include settlement patterns, ceramics, trade contacts and burial customs. Readers should use this valuable overview article as background for the numerous individual site reports listed in the bibliography.

161. Kennedy, Kenneth A.R. et.al. "Principal-Components Analysis of Prehistoric

South Asian Crania." *American Journal of Physical Anthropology* 64 (2) (June 1984): 105-118.

A multivariate analytical study of one hundred and seventeen human crania obtained from fifteen archaeological sites spanning an area from Sri Lanka to Kashmir. Results suggest changes in facial architecture which challenge the typologies derived from racial classifications and historical reconstruction for the ancient peoples of South Asia. Sites contributing skeletal materials to this sample are Bellanbandi Palassa (Sri Lanka), Adittanalur, Brahmagiri, Tekkalakota, Yeleswaram, Nevasa, Lothal, Langhnaj, Harappa and Mohenjo-daro in Pakistan, Timargarha and Burzahom (both in Kashmir), Mahadaha, and Sarai Nahar Rai.

162. *Studies in the Archaeology and Palaeolanthropology of South Asia* edited by Kenneth A.R. Kennedy and Gregory L.Possehl. New Delhi: Oxford and IBH Publishing Company, 1984.

A gathering of thirteen papers centered on the field of prehistoric archaeology within India and Pakistan, including as well investigation and assessment of evidence for the presence of hominids in the subcontinent. Specific archaeological issues discussed are the use of ethnoarchaeology, Indus Valley settlement patterns and problems of relating the Ganges Valley cultures to the rest of India. Selections from this collection have been entered in the present bibliography.

163. *Archaeological Perspective of India Since Independence* edited by K.N. Dikshit. New Delhi: Books and Books, 1985.

A full reprint of twenty papers delivered at the International Seminar held during the fourteenth conference of the Indian Archaeological Society in New Delhi on October 25-27, 1982. The status and history of archaeological investigation into all periods of India's past, from the palaeolithic and mesolithic to the medieval and historical eras, is reviewed, as are the applications of specialized fieldwork technologies and contemporary issues such as atmospheric pollution. Selected entries have been entered in the present bibliography.

164. Mohapatra, G.C. "The Lower Palaeolithic in India," in *Archaeological Perspective of India Since Independence* edited by K.N. Dikshit. New Delhi: Books and Books, 1985: 1-8.

This essay presents in some detail the problems of defining a Lower Palaeolithic sequence for peninsular India, centering on the absence of both artifacts found *in situ* and the then-unclear geology of the Neogene-Quaternary boundary outside the western Himalayan region. Special attention is given to the study of the Kasi River Basin in West Bengal as an instance where regional geological relationships have been clarified. The Soan stone tool industry of the western Himalaya is contrasted with the Acheulian tools known from caves and river deposits across the peninsula, its development noted and correlations made with similar tools made by *Homo erectus* in Africa and Europe during the Middle Pleistocene. Readers will find having a map of India available for reference useful when scanning this text.

165. Soundararajan, K.V. "Middle Palaeolithic in India," in *Archaeological Perspective of India Since Independence* edited by K.N. Dikshit. New Delhi: Books and Books, 1985: 9-14.

An evaluation of the general acceptability of transferring the concepts of Early, Middle and Late Stone Ages to a consideration of India's past. The author suggests that "the regional study of the faunal, floral, climatic and raw material source components ...of the early Palaeolithic becomes an imperative exercise through multidisciplinary teams." (p. 11) A table utilizing geological and climatic data as a basis for sequencing then-known Early and Middle Stone Age cultures of southern India is presented.

166. Murty, M.L.K. "Upper Palaeolithic Culture in India," in *Archaeological Perspective of India Since Independence* edited by K.N. Dikshit. New Delhi: Books and Books, 1985: 15-25.

A concise assessment of the state of knowledge of the Upper Palaeolithic period of Indian prehistory in the mid-1980's. Following a summary of the history of field investigation from its beginnings in the late nineteenth century, the three major lithic industries (flake-blade, blade tools and burins) are defined. Bone tools from several cave sites, a general chronology (roughly 40,000 to 10,000 years B.P.) and known palaeocological data complete the chapter. Of special interest are the three tables which list twenty-nine Upper Palaeolithic sites and note the major features of each.

167. Varma, Radhakant. "The Mesolithic Cultures of India," in *Archaeological Perspective of India Since Independence* edited by K.N. Dikshit. New Delhi: Books and Books, 1985: 27-36.

Stating that "till the fifties of the present century almost nothing was known about the Mesolithic industries and their associated cultural equipment," (p. 29) the author begins by reviewing the geological field work which verified the existence of an Indian counterpart to the European Upper Palaeolithic. The microlithic stone tools of the Mesolithic found during excavations at such key sites as the Singrauli Basin of Uttar Pradesh, Langhnaj in Gujarat and Birbhanpur in Bengal are shown to have evolved out of this earlier stage. Questions of Mesolithic subsistence (including domestication of animals), structures, pottery and burials, religious beliefs and personal ornamentation are considered in light of available data.

168. Dhavalikar, M.K. "Chalcolithic Cultures: A Socio-Economic Perspective," in *Archaeological Perspective of India Since Independence* edited by K.N. Dikshit. New Delhi: Books and Books, 1985: 63-80.

The major cultures of Chalcolithic India (dating to betwwen 2000 and 700 B.C.) covered in this paper are the Kayatha and Ahar, Malwa, Prabhas, Rangpur and

Jorwe, with the absence of extensive lateral site excavation noted. The author approaches this massive assemblage of data by considering common factors related to these early farming communities: settlement patterns, subsistence, social and political organizations, technology, exchange networks and religious beliefs.

169. Deo, S.B. "Historical Archaeology: Review and Perspective," in *Archaeological Perspective of India Since Independence* edited by K.N. Dikshit. New Delhi: Books and Books, 1985: 87-95.

Cautioning that "during the last three decades, the emphasis of investigations shows a predilection more for protohistoric ...rather than...the historical," (p. 87) this essay focuses on the process of urbanisation, agreement between literary and archaeological sources, settlement patterns, trade, and levels of technology during various historical periods. Fourteen areas of the subcontinent are reviewed in detail as to the state of historical archaeological knowledge, ranging from the heavily explored regions of Maharashtra, Andhra Pradesh, Tamil Nadu, Uttar Pradesh and Karnataka to lesser known areas such as Assam.

170. Mehta, R.N. "Mediaeval Archaeology," in *Archaeological Perspective of India Since Independence* edited by K.N. Dikshit. New Delhi: Books and Books, 1985: 97-102.

Drawing on field research in villages and towns of western India, the author explores the potential contributions of archaeology to the study of the medieval era in the subcontinent. Noting that "archaeological study was not and is not used to any great extent" (p. 98) by specialists in this period, he reviews data from a survey done of the city of Surat, tracing fortifications and successive locations of the city. The importance of recognizing the value of local traditions and folklore (requiring a knowledge of both dialects and the languages used in a particular region over time) is seen to be a weakness of many field investigators dealing with medieval material. The overall trends of medieval Indian history (native, Islamic, European and Chinese/South East Asian) are also briefly summarized.

171. Sinha, B.P. "Indian Tradition and Archaeology," in *Archaeological Perspective of India Since Independence* edited by K.N. Dikshit. New Delhi: Books and Books, 1985: 103-109.

The central issue addressed in this essay is the degree to which archaeological excavations have been able to prove the factual authenticity of traditional Indian epics such as the *Mahabharata* and *Ramayana*.This topic was added to subcontinental archaeology rather late, following an initial emphasis by Cunningham on Buddhist sites and the explosion of Indus fieldwork occasioned by the discovery of Mohenjo-daro. Fieldwork done at the *Mahabharata* sites of Hastinapura and Ayodhya indicating a date for events in the *Ramayana* later than the war chonicled in the *Mahabharata* (a reversal of accepted literary and historical traditions) is discussed.

172. Mittre, Vishnu et.al. "Pollen Stratigraphy of India," in *Archaeological Perspective of India Since Independence* edited by K.N. Dikshit. New Delhi: Books and Books, 1985: 115-122.

Beginning with an overview of the state of palynology and its usage in constructing local and regional models of past subcontinental climates which can then be corrrelated with known glaciations, this paper presents a first pan-Indian model of environmental change. A sequence of alterations in vegetation from before 700,000 B.C. to five hundred years before the present is offered as both a synthesis of prior work and a starting point for refinement. Radiocarbon dating is "perhaps the only means to build up pollen stratigraphy of this vast country...tying up contemporary events of vegetational change ...in distant regions." (p. 115)

173. Bhardwaj, H.C. "Studies in Ancient Indian Technology: A Review," in *Archaeological Perspective of India Since Independence* edited by K.N. Dikshit. New Delhi: Books and Books, 1985: 139-148.

The title of this article misleads, in that the author predominantly focuses his attention on the technologies involved in copper/ bronze, iron and steel metallurgy, adding short sections on pottery analysis and glass production. Readers will find this piece a useful assessment of the state of this aspect of Indian archaeology but should consult Bhardwaj's 1979 work *Aspects of Ancient Indian Technology* for a fuller treatment of the subject.

174. *South Asian Archaeology 1985* edited by Karen Frifelt and Per Sorensen. London: Curzon Press, 1989.

The full texts of forty-seven papers presented at the eighth international conference of the Association of South Asian Archaeologists in Western Europe, held at Moesgaard, Denmark July 1-5, 1985. Papers are included on the site of Mehrgarh in Baluchistan, Indus civilization urbanism and art, investigation of ancient landscapes in Rajasthan, and the interplay of environmental factors and the archaeological record in Kashmir. Selected items are entered under their regions in the present bibliography.

175. Poster, Amy G. *From Indian Earth: 4,000 Years of Terracotta Art*. Brooklyn, New York: The Brooklyn Museum, 1986.

Written to accompany the exhibition of the same name held at the Brooklyn Museum January 17-April 14,1986, this catalog traces the development and florescence of terracotta art forms in India from the Indus Valley era through the twentieth century. One hundred and forty-three black and white plates illustrate figurines (many representing deities, especially the mother goddess), plaques from temple facades (frequently depicting incidents from the life of the Buddha or adventures out of Hindu mythology or the *Ramayana*) molds, and models of ordinary objects such as carts. Geographic regions represented are north and northwestern India and Pakistan, eastern India and the Deccan. Five accompanying essays provide an overview of Indian terracottas, the social milieus within which they were created, the origin and diversification of styles of brick temple construction, uses of terracotta in nineteenth and twentieth century Indian culture, and technical questions requiring further study. A bibliography of related literature is appended.

176. Soundara Rajan, K.V. *Invitation to Indian Archaeology*. Atlantic Highlands, New Jersey: Humanities Press, 1986.

A short and highly thematic volume, first published in India, centering on the "major developments of human cultures in India" (p. 89) and written for a general audience. Emphasis here is on cultural processes, with individual sites noted as examples of each period from prehistoric times to the Early Historic era but not treated in depth.

177. Chakrabarti, Dilip K. "The Pre-Industrial Mines of India," *Puratattva* 16 (85/86): 65-71.

This essay presents a synthesis of the scattered sources of information on the history and methods of pre-industrial mining of copper,tin,lead,silver,gold,iron and zinc in India, "a thoroughly neglected field among Indian archaeologists and historians till now." (p. 65) The bulk of the paper treats the archaeological remains of mines then known, with the few available radiocarbon dates noted as derived from samples obtained by random collection, most being medieval, with copper mining traceable to 1260 B.C. Nineteenth century accounts of extractive techniques are cited to round out the picture of actual mine operations.

178. Bhattacharya, S.K. "Buddhist Relic Caskets in Indian Museums," *Puratattva* 17 (1986/87): 43-49.

The "relic caskets" of the title refer to the practice of enshrining physical objects or body parts belonging to either the Buddha or Buddhist saints beneath a stupa within specially constructed (often nested) boxes of precious metals. Bhattacharya observes that although numerous such objects have been recovered over the past decades "so far there is no single publication wherein one…could ascertain their provenance." (p. 43) This article attempts to begin that task, noting eleven locations in Madhya Pradesh, Andhra Pradesh, Maharashtra, Uttar Pradesh, West Bengal and Tamil Nadu where reliquaries have been found or are presently being conserved. These range from the site museums at Sanchi and Nagarjunakonda to individual vihara and the Asiatic Society Library in Bombay. Details as to the finding, condition and dates of the caskets are provided.

179. *South Asian Archaeology 1987* edited by Maurizio Taddei. Rome: Istituto Italiano per Il Medio ed Estremo Oriente, 1990.

This two-volume set reprints the texts of sixty-seven papers given at the Ninth International Conference of South Asian Archaeologists in Western Europe, held in Venice in 1987. Topics relating to India, Pakistan and Sri Lanka include renewed field surveys seeking Palaeolithic sites, regional variations of the Indus culture, the Vijayanagara research project, and detection of disease in the available skeletal record. Selections from this collection have been entered under the appropriate geographical area in the present bibliography.

180. Kennedy, Kenneth A.R. "Reconstruction of Trauma, Disease and Lifeways of Prehistoric Peoples of South Asia from the Skeletal Record," in *South Asian Archaeology 1987* edited by Maurizio Taddei. *Naples: Istituto Universitario Orientale, 1990: 61-77.*

An evaluative paper analysing available ancient human skeletal remains from South Asia to determine whether the hypothesis that "acquisition of food-production lifeways demanded a biological cost" (p. 61) is valid for this region. The limited known Pleistocene skeletal assemblage from an area ranging from Afghanistan and Pakistan through India to Sri Lanka is reviewed. Morphometric comparisons of pre- and post-Neolithic skeletons indicate modifications of overall sexual dimorphism, an increase of lesions due to infection and possible genetic abnormalities, more dental caries and osteoarthritis.

181. *Studies in the Archaeology of India and Pakistan* edited by Jerome Jacobson. Warminster, England; Aris and Phillips, 1987.

A collection of twenty-six papers focusing on the work done in South Asia by archaeologists based in the United States, some with the assistance of the Smithsonian Institution. Field projects covered include the Adittannalur skeletons of Tamil Nadu, palaeoecology, several aspects of the Indus culture ranging from its pictographic script to faunal exploitation, and the Soan stone tool assemblages of the Palaeolithic. Selections from this collection have been entered separately in the present bibliography. Reseachers interested in the history of involvement by American archaeologists in the area will find the preface to this volume a valuable summary.

182. Clark, Desmond and Martin A.J. Williams. "Palaeoenvironments and Prehistory in North Central India: A Preliminary Report," in *Studies in the Archaeology of India and Pakistan* edited by Jerome Jacobson. Warminster: Aris and Phillips, 1987: 19-41.

This article reports on an interdisciplinary project carried out for two and one-half months in the winter of 1980 in the eastern Vindhyas of southern Uttar Pradesh and northern Madhya Pradesh, centering on the middle Son valley. Objectives were to establish a sequence of palaeoclimatic events by examining the geomorphology of the valley, defining a local archaeological profile (including determining chronology, site location and spatial distribution) and developing behavioral models for each site. Following a detailed outline of Son geology and its correlation with previous work in the Belan valley in an adjacent region of the Vindhyas, a succession of occupations from lower Palaeolithic times to the

Neolithic is presented. Preliminary conclusions support the model of a drier and cooler climate during the last glaciation.

183. Ray, Himanshu Prabha. "Early Historical Urbanization: The Case of the Western Deccan," *World Archaeology* 19 (1) (June 1987): 94-104.

A clear and cogent survey of the development of urban settlements in the western Deccan Plateau between the first century B.C. and third century A.D. Analysis is based upon an assemblage of radiocarbon dates and begins with the rise of small centers in the Upper Ganges Valley in the sixth century B.C. Discussion touches upon the mineral resources being worked in each area (initially iron and salt, later expanded by trade in gold and precious stones) ,the placement of cities in light of regional topography, the role of external trade with the Roman Empire, and the relationship between these settlements and the rock-cut Buddhist monasteries which often shared resources with them. A map showing sites referred to is included. Useful as background reading for students unfamiliar with this period of Indian history and its archaeological remains.

184. Paddayya, K. "Prehistoric Research in India: As Viewed By Two Senior American Archaeologists," *Puratattva* 19 (1988-89): 77-79.

An interview with J. Desmond Clark and Lewis Binford, both of whom had worked in or visited India between 1980 and 1987. Within the field of prehistoric research in the subcontinent, Clark cites the historic emphasis on the retrieval of palaeolithic materials from redeposited areas such as river gravels and the absence of a firm chronology as the reasons why, for India, "there is not much awareness about our prehistory among archaeologists in the west." (p. 77) Binford calls for more intensive surface surveys of rain-collecting basins to delineate further Stone Age sites. The work being done in the Hunsgi Valley by Paddayya is noted as an example of the type of local investigations needed across the country.

185. *South Asian Archaeology 1989* edited by Catherine Jarrige. Madison, Wisconsin: Prehistory Press, 1992.

A collection of fifty-seven papers presented at the Tenth International Conference of South Asian Archaeologists in Western Europe, held in Paris July 3-7 1989. Topics reviewed include settlement patterns in Sri Lanka, the Soan stone tool industry of Pakistan, several sites of the Indus civilization, historical archaeology and aspects of ancient regional trade. Selected papers have been entered in the present bibliography.

186. Allchin, Bridget. "South Asian Archaeology in Western Europe: Its Relation to Conservation," in *South Asian Archaeology 1989* edited by Catherine Jarrige. Madison, Wisconsin: Prehistory Press, 1992: 1-3.

A presentation by one of its leaders of a "state of the discipline" review as of 1989, noting that in some European countries the fields of study supporting South Asian archaeology are being deprived of fiscal and teaching support. Her primary observations on conservation roles which may be played in their host nations by South Asian archaeologists and prehistorians include contributing their in-depth knowledge of local environments to development agencies to guide in planning suitable options for preservation and serving as resources for conservation technology information.

187. Raven, Ellen M. "Candragupta III: Tracing the Coins of a Gupta King," in *South Asian Archaeology 1989* edited by Catherine Jarrige. Madison, Wisconsin: Prehistory Press, 1992: 441-448.

A technical paper in numismatics illustrating one of the original approaches to the retrieval of Indian historical information. The author notes sufficient variation in style and attributes among the coins assigned to the two known monarchs of the Gupta dynasty who bore the throne name of Candra to posit a third ruler bearing this title as well.

188. Yule, Paul and Andreas Hauptmann. "The Copper Hoards of India: New Finds, New Results," in *South Asian Archaeology 1989* edited by Catherine Jarrige. Madison, Wisconsin: Prehistory Press, 1992: 465-467.

Acknowledging that "until recently, all discussions of the hoards focused on the Ganges-Yamuna doab...the existence of the eastern hoards has been all but ignored for decades," (p. 465), the author presents analyses of copper objects from Madhya Pradesh, Orissa, Haryana, Rajasthan and Uttar Pradesh. With the completion of a catalogue of all materials from the known hoard deposits, questions of their metallurgy and purpose may now be considered.

189. Cannon, Garland. *The Life and Mind of Oriental Jones: Sir William Jones, the Father of Modern Linguistics.*Cambridge: University Press, 1990.

The first lengthy biography of the man considered to have founded and supported the first forum for scientific investigation of Indian culture and all aspects of its past, the Asiatic Society of Bengal, in 1784. While much of the text deals with Jones' interest in Sanskrit and other ancient languages, this work is a valuable source of data on the purposes of the Society and the creation of the intellectual climate within which researches on India first began to be conducted by Western scholars. Readers wishing a more concise treatment of Jones should consult the 1968 biography by S.N. Mukherjee.

190. *An Encyclopedia of Indian Archaeology* edited by A.Ghosh. Leiden: Brill, 1990. 2 volumes.

This work is without question the most comprehensive reference source available to both specialists and the general public on the archaeology of the subcontinent.The twenty articles of the first volume cover such major component subjects as the domestication of animals, coins and seals, archaeobotany, dating, major pottery types, settlement patterns, rock art, technology, weapons, and writing. Information on the basic geological formations and soils of the subcontinent is also included. Only this volume is indexed. The second volume, subtitled *Gazetteer of the Explored and Excavated Sites*, is an essential resource for any reader wishing to make sense of the sea of articles, field surveys and site reports which form the body of Indian archaeological literature. Entries (listed alphabetically by the formal name of record) begin with the exact latitude and longitude of the site, followed by a summary of fieldwork done there, the significance of findings, and a representative bibliography of related literature.

191. *Rome and India, the Ancient Sea Trade* edited by Vimala Begley and Richard Daniel. Madison, Wisconsin: University of Wisconsin Press,1991.

A collection of thirteen papers originally presented at a December, 1986 colloquium with the same title held during the annual meeting of the Archaeological Institute of America in San Antonio. Topics explored range from analysis of classical texts through an examination of the Ptolemaic ports of the Red Sea, although stress is laid upon reportage from excavations in India and Sri Lanka. Sites represented by the latter include Arikamedu, Kolhapur, and Mantai, as well as a discussion of pottery from Gujarat. Individual papers from this volume have been entered separately under their respective regions of India.

192. Casson, Lionel. "Ancient Naval Technology and the Route to India," in *Rome and India, the Ancient Sea Trade* edited by Vimala Begley and Richard Daniel. Madison, Wisconsin, University of Wisconsin Press, 1991: 8-11.

An interesting analysis of the merchant traffic on both the eastern and western coasts of India during Roman times from the view of available shipbuilding capabilities. The mortise and tenon technology of the major vessels sailing to the western coast is contrasted with the more modest local craft which operated in the Bay of Bengal year round. The finds at Arikamedu are cited as evidence of both a foreign presence and the type of small trading center which would have been characteristic of the east coast. Researchers should also consult the published literature on the *Periplus of the Erythraean Sea* for background on this subject.

193. Sidebotham, Steven. E. "Ports of the Red Sea and the Arabia-India Trade," in *Rome and India: The Ancient Sea Trade* edited by Vimala Begley and Richard Daniel. Madison: University of Wisconsin Press, 1991: 12-38.

A two-part discussion covering both the seven principal Roman trading ports of the Red Sea involved in imperial commerce with India, their archaeological remains, and the types of goods involved. Of particular interest are the sections on the organization of the road systems between the Nile and the Red Sea and the documented presence of Indian traders within the Roman sphere of influence. An extensive bibliography is provided.

194. Deo, S.B. "Roman Trade: Recent Archaeological Discoveries in Western

India," in *Rome and India: The Ancient Sea Trade* edited by Vimala Begley and Richard Daniel Madison; University of Wisconsin Press, 1991: 39-45.

A brief summary of the types of identifiably Mediterranean artifacts recovered from excavations in Gujarat, Maharashtra, and parts of Andhra Pradesh. These include ceramics, coinage (ranging in age from Imperial Roman to Byzantine), terracotta and metal "bullae," bronze mirrors, glass and miscellaneous relief carvings done in the Roman style. A bibliography of related literature is appended.

195. Stern, E.Marianne. "Early Roman Export Glass In India," in *Rome and India: The Ancient Sea Trade* edited by Vimala Begley and Richard Daniel. Madison: University of Wisconsin Press, 1991: 113-124.

An unusual exploration of the role played by glass in the ancient trade network with India. The text first notes those sections of the *Periplus of the Erythraean Sea* which cite glass as either produced or traded at specific locations, then notes those sites in India where evidence of glass use or manufacture has been found. The latter include Ter and Nevasa on the western coast as well as the massive finds at Arikamedu in the southeast. The author points out a disparity in information between the two regions, the western coast fully described in the *Periplus* but having yielded little evidence of the glass trade, while "the east coast of south India is exactly the opposite...There is no written evidence but finds from excavation are abundant." (p. 117) Items of trade included raw glass for local bead industries as well as dishes and wine bowls. Samples of all type finds are illustrated.

196. Begley, Vimala. "Ceramic Evidence for Pre-Periplus Trade on the Indian Coasts," in *Rome and India, The Ancient Sea Trade* edited by Vimala Begley and Richard Daniel. Madison, University of Wisconsin Press, 1991: 157-196.

This article discusses the ceramic evidence for contact and trade between India and the West prior to the compilation of the *Periplus of the Erythraean Sea*. Specific vessel types noted are the moldmade ware from the coasts of Gujarat and Maharashtra and the "rouletted" pottery of the southeastern coasts and inland Tamil Nadu sites. Each group is illustrated and analysed as to its distinctive features (and possible parallels with classical Hellenistic and Roman potteries.) Maps showing their distribution within peninsular India and Sri Lanka are included. Results indicate contact in the second century B.C.

197. Lahiri, Nayanjot. *The Archaeology of Indian Trade Routes Up To ca. 200 B.C.: Resource Use, Resource Access and Lines of Communication*. New York: Oxford University Press, 1992.

This study's intent is "to understand the utilization of certain specific raw materials by the archaeological cultures in different periods, delineation of the probable areas which could have supplied the raw materials, and...the essential direction of trade routes in,and across, distinct zones." (p. 3) Opening with a brief review of the extant literature on the archaeology of trade (and recent examples where materials analysis has not been applied), available data from the known cultures antedating the Harappan civilization, the Harappan sites themselves, Neolithic and Chalcolithic cultures outside the immediate area of Harappan urbanism, and the Iron Age and early historical periods (ca.1000-200 B.C.) are then evaluated. An extensive bibliography of both archaeological and mineralogical literature is appended. The many clearly drawn and labeled maps and charts make this a basic source for any research involving aspects of ancient India's commerce.

198. Narasimhaiah. B. "Restoration of Angkor Vat (Cambodia): Indian Crusade," *Puratattva* 22 (1992/92): 109-113.

In early 1980, the government of Cambodia issued a call for assistance from the international community for the continued preservation of the twelfth-century temple complex of Angkor Wat, which had been interrupted by the departure of a French team in 1970. Given the close historic ties between South East Asia and India due to India's status as the birthplace of Buddhism, the Archaeological Survey of India agreed to take on the task of conservation and restoration, with the first team arriving in November 1980 and a second in 1982. This article reports on the substantial work accomplished since 1986, which has chiefly taken the form of dismantling and reconstructing sections of the gateways and surrounding embankments and restoring architectural members of standing but threatened portions of the temple to their correct alignments

199. Neumayer, Ernst. *Lines On Stone: The Prehistoric Rock Art of India*. New Delhi: Manohar, 1993.

The most comprehensive treatment of the subject available in one volume, this lavishly illustrated work covers the rock art of the entire Indian subcontinent. A brief history of rock-art research in India, beginning with Carlleyle's 1867 discoveries in the Vindhya Mountains, provides a useful introduction to the topic. Separate chapters discuss the environment of the rock-art sites (ranging from the granite hills of the Southern Deccan to the quartzite regions of Central India), the conditions of preservation,and problems of establishing chronologies. The most lengthy sections cover the pictures left by early hunters and gatherers and the later agricultural peoples. Excellent maps delineating all major rock art regions of India, the Central Vindhyas and the Mahadeo Hills, the Bhopal and Chambal regions, the Northern Vindhya Hills, the Southern Deccan plateau, and a bibliography of related literature are included. Seven hundred and twelve detailed line drawings permit comparison of style and content.

200. Tripathi, Vibha and Amit Tripathi. "Iron Working In Ancient India: An Ethnoarchaeological Study," in *From Sumer To Meluhha:Contributions to the Archaeology of South and West Asia in Memory of George F. Dales, Jr.* edited by Jonathan Mark Kenoyer. Madison, Wisconsin: University of Wisconsin Department of Anthropology, 1994: 241-251.

The practices of iron production on the local level were carried out in various regions of India up to the beginning of the twentieth century. This paper examines the diverse evidence for this technology known from the archaeological record from sites ranging from the city of Ujjain (Madhya Pradesh) to Khairadih (Uttar Pradesh) and Naikund (Maharashtra). Ethnographic data on mining techniques, ore dressing, and smelting drawn from virtually all regions of the subcontinent are reviewed and a model derived for the social structure of the ancient industry.

201. Allchin, Bridget. ed. *Living Traditions: Studies In The Ethnoarchaeology of South Asia*. New Delhi: Oxbow Books and Oxford and IBH Publishing Company, 1994.

The nineteen papers collected in this volume were originally delivered at a symposium held at Cambridge in September, 1991. The history and application of the ethnoarchaeological approach within the study of the Indian past are clearly set forth by Bridget Allchin in her opening essay, "South Asia's Living Past," while regions as disparate as Orissa, Rajasthan, the Andaman Islands, Gujarat, West Bengal and Sri Lanka are represented through field work. Each paper includes a listing of related literature. Selected entries have been entered under the appropriate geographical division within the present bibliography.

202. Allchin, Bridget "South Asia's Living Past," in *Living Traditions: Studies In the Ethnoarchaeology of South Asia*. New Delhi: Oxbow Book and Oxford and IBH Publishing Company, 1994: 1-11.

This essay serves as the preface to a collected volume of papers on various applications of ethnoarchaeology to India'a artifactual record. Using surviving practices in animal husbandry, agriculture, social structure and religion to explain and illuminate the region's past was noted as a viable idea by Sir Alexander Cunningham in 1873, while James Fergusson noted in his *History of Indian Architecture*(1876) that, due to the numerous traditional survivals observed, "every art has its living representative." (p. 1) Subsequent applications also included John Marshall's references to contemporary construction methods during his work at Mohenjo-Daro in the 1930's and evidence of ploughing techniques noted in a field outside the ancient city of Kalibangan during the 1960's. Allchin then offers examples of approaches to the use of this technique, specifying both the documentation of a specific traditional practice and its associated use of buildings and other structures to achieve a complete picture.

203. Chakrabarti, Dilip K. and Nayanjot Lahiri. "The Iron Age in India: The Beginning and Consequences," *Puratattva* 24 (1993/94): 12-32.

Stating that "this paper is a brief statement of the current state of research on the Indian Iron Age" (p. 12), the authors then present an overview of the archaeological evidence from this period (roughly accepted to have been in full flower by 1000 B.C.) known as of 1994. Beginning with the distribution of iron ore across the subcontinent and the roots of iron technology in the copper technology of the Chalcolithic era, profiles of the known early iron-using areas and their cultures are presented, with major relevant sites noted. These include Kashmir, Baluchistan, the Gandhara Grave Culture, Ahar (Rajasthan),Lothal (Gujarat), Nagda (Malwa), the megalithic site of Hallur,Atranjikera and Mangalkot (West Bengal). Continuities in agricultural products, local systems of trade and cultural institutions are seen as sufficient to challenge "the notion of the Iron Age representing a major social and economic transformation." (p. 32)

204. Allchin, F. Raymond. *The Archaeology of Early Historic South Asia: The Emergence of Cities and States*. Cambridge: Cambridge University Press, 1995.

In this work, the definition of early historic archaeology is expanded to include data on "domestic architecture, city planning...the construction of secular and religious monuments, development of various branches of art...epigraphy and early use of writing in South Asia, the standardization of weights and measures and the use of coinage." (p.10) As used here, South Asia is taken to include all nations of the subcontinent as well as Nepal. Topics addressed are the history of archaeology in India, the question of whether urbanism was interrupted following the Harappan era or continued, the city-states of the time of the Buddha, and the urban past of Sri Lanka and the Ganges Valley. Exploration of the Mauryan Empire and its legacy comprise approximately one quarter of the book. Researchers unfamiliar with the history of South Asia will find this work essential before consulting more specialized research such as Chakrabarti's *The Archaeology of Ancient Indian Cities* (1995).

205. Chakrabarti, Dilip K. *The Archaeology of Ancient Indian Cities*. Oxford, 1995.

Originally written as a doctoral dissertation at the University of Calcutta in 1972, this investigation is described by its author as "a systematic evaluation of archaeological data on the early urban history of India." (p. 1) Following an introductory chapter on the background of the Indus civilization, separate chapters address the distribution of Harappan settlements and community development in the Neolithic/Chacolithic era (using examples from Rajasthan, Kashmir, Maharashtra and the Upper Gangetic Valley and eastern India). Early historical cities such as Taxila and Charsada from all major regions of the subcontinent are next considered as a group. Thirty-two figures present site plans of twenty-seven cities, many drawn from the pioneering surveys and reports of Sir Alexander Cunningham and Sir Mortimer Wheeler. Sixty-seven major urban centres are represented in this study. A concluding section notes the issues of settlement distribution, landscape analysis, incompletely published data (a problem more characteristic of historic sites than of the Indus valley cities), site identification, and questions regarding the origin and spread of Indus culture as requiring further study. Researchers unfamiliar with the massive literature created by urban excavations in India will find this an excellent beginning.

206. Hassan, Fekri A. "The World Archaeological Congress in India: Politicizing the Past," *Antiquity* 69 (1995): 874-877.

On December 2, 1992, the sixteenth-century Babari mosque at Ayodhya was razed by a mob, which then set up Hindu statuary at the site. Grounds for this action were said to lie in a putative discovery by B.B. Lal of evidence for a former Hindu shrine underlying the mosque. This article profiles the attempted politicization of the third World Archaeological Congress's meeting, held in Delhi in 1994 on the second anniversary of the Ayodhya action, around the issue. The author severely criticizes the political involvement of Lal (whose delayed release of evidence allegedly supporting the Hindu claim to Ayodhya is perhaps the sorest point) and other Indian archaeologists, noting that "the destruction of monuments, sites and artefacts in the distant past ...provide no ground for 'retaliation' or a justification for wanton destruction today...in this context, the presence or absence of the remnants of a medieval Hindu temple below the Babari mosque...is immaterial." (p. 876)

207. Barnes, Gina L. "An Introduction To Buddhist Archaeology," *World Archaeology* 27 (2) (October 1995): 165-182.

A background essay providing both a history of the origin, spread and diversification of Buddhist philosophies and teachings and the accompanying physical structures characteristic of each phase. Geographical coverage reaches from India and Sri Lanka to Central amd South East Asia, China,and Japan. Useful for students of Indian archaeology unfamiliar with the details of Buddhist culture.

208. "Glossary of Selected Terms." *World Archaeology* 27 (2) (October 1995): 183-184.

A concise listing of Buddhist terminology covering structures, points of doctrine and individual titles. Valuable for anyone reading the literature of Indian archaeology, much of which presupposes familiarity with these concepts. Note is taken of the contribution of both Pali and Sanskrit to the technical language of this religion.

209. Chakrabarti, Dilip K. "Buddhist Sites Across South Asia As Influenced By Political and Economic Forces," *World Archaeology* 27 (2) (October 1995): 185-202.

Considering Buddhism within the archaeological record of the rise of urbanism across South Asia, this paper focuses on the sixth century B.C. to the thirteenth century A.D. Factors presented are the historic chronology of the life of the Buddha, the political setting within which he taught and traveled, and the definition of a "Buddhist" site archaeologically. Architecturally, "one or all of the following three elements should be present...the *stupa*, the *chaitya* worship hall containing a *stupa*, and the *vihara* or monastery." (p. 192) Fifty sites mentioned in the text are illustrated with a map. The reign of Asoka, cave monasteries and teaching centers, and the range of social classes represented by dedicated offerings are also reviewed.

210. Morrison, Kathleen D. "Trade, Urbanism and Agricultural Expansion:

Buddhist Monastic Institutions and the State in the Early Historic Western Deccan," *World Archaeology* 27 (20) (October 1995): 203-221.

The Early Historic era of the title, as defined in South Asia, lasted from 500 BC to 500 A.D. This essay explores complex questions on the economic structure of the Western Deccan, a region which, although intensively settled by Buddhist monastic establishments and with a long tradition of settled communities had been treated as a mere adjunct to the Ganges plain. The evolution and history of local settlement patterns from the Chalcolithic through the Satavahana era is traced, with the interplay of agricultural factors, political development and long-distance trade (reflected in both excavation results and in official documents such as the *Arthasastra*) seen as insufficient to account for the rise of urbanism documented in the archaeological record. The monastic centers and their role in local economic systems must be added as a factor in any expanded analysis of the Deccan, while trade in nonperishable goods with the Ganges plain has yet to be demonstrated.

211. Johnson, Gordon, ed. *Cultural Atlas of India: India, Pakistan, Nepal, Bhutan, Bangladesh and Sri Lanka*. New York: Facts On File, 1996.

Part of a series of reference works intended for popular audiences, this lavishly illustrated volume begins by presenting the physical and cultural background of the subcontinent, then moves to consider the history of specific nations. Material related to the archaeology of India is contained in the essay "Prehistory and Early History," while the sites of Sanchi, Vijayanagara, Mohenjo-Daro and Khajuraho are profiled in the section on "Special Features," as are the class of "Rock-cut Monuments." A map of the known settlements of the Indus Valley civilization is also included.

212. *Tradition and Archaeology: Early Maritime Contacts in the Indian Ocean* edited by Himanshu Prabha Ray and Jean-Francois Salles. New Delhi: Manohar, 1996.

This volume contains the full texts of eighteen papers delivered at the international seminar on "Techno-Archaeological Perspectives of Seafaring in the Indian Ocean 4th Century B.C.- 15th Century A.D," held in in New Delhi February 28-March 4, 1994. Topics investigated range from the archaeology of several coastal regions of India to details of ship construction and the role of trade with Arabia and Southeast Asia. Selected articles have been entered under their geographic regions in the present bibliography.

213. Ray, Himanshu Prabha. "Maritime Archaeology of the Indian Ocean: An Overview," in *Tradition and Archaeology: Early Maritime Contacts in the Indian Ocean* edited by Himanshu Prabha Ray and Jean-Francois Salles. New Delhi: Manohar, 1996: 1-10.

A discussion of the principal areas within Indian Ocean archaeological research requiring further elaboration and investigation. They include demarcation of indigenous trading networks using ceramics, non-local pottery as a possible indicator of transportation containers, expanding the definition of "ports" and their relationship to interior exchange networks, shipbuilding techniques, and the importance of pilgrimage (Buddhist, Hindu and Muslim) as a factor influencing the pattern of the archaeological record. Researchers unfamiliar with the major issues of maritime archaeology in the lands bordering the Indian Ocean will find this essay highly instructive.

214. Subbarayalu, Y. "Chinese Ceramics of Tamilnadu and Kerala Coasts," in *Tradition and Archaeology: Early Maritime Contacts in the Indian Ocean* edited by Himanshu Prabha Ray and Jean-Francois Salles. New Delhi: Manohar, 1996: 109-114.

While long known as an item of medieval trade with India from textual sources, "in Indian archaeology, pottery after the Early Historical period is generally ignored as of not much consequence." (p.109) This article reviews both chance finds of porcelains and test excavations along the coasts of Tamil Nadu and Kerala at the sites of ports known to have been active in foreign trade. Analysis of the ceramics found reflects major activity during the thirteenth and fourteenth centuries. A map showing known find sites is a useful reference to the archaeology of these two Indian states.

215. Deloche, Jean. "Iconographic Evidence on the Development of Boat and Ship Structures in India (2nd C. B.C.-15th C. A.D.): A New Approach," in *Tradition and Archaeology, Early Maritime Contacts in the Indian Ocean* edited by Himanshu Prabha Ray and Jean-Francois Salles. New Delhi: Manohar, 1996: 199-224.

A review of the available sources of evidence for the reconstruction of the history of nautical technology in India, chiefly written texts, carved reliefs and monuments. Two periods of development, between the second century B.C. and the seventh century A.D., and the eleventh to fifteenth centuries A.D. are explored, illustrated with copies of the more important original depictions. Archaeological data is seen to be lacking as yet, partly due to the difficulty of identifying ancient ports and the unfortunate fact that "not a single ancient shipwreck has been discovered near the Indian shores in the Arabian Sea or in the Bay of Bengal." (p. 199)

216. Kenoyer, Jonathan Mark. "Early City-States in South Asia: Comparing the Harappan Phase and Early Historical Period," in *The Archaeology of City-States: Cross-Cultural Approaches* edited by Deborah L. Nichols and Thomas H.Charlton. Washington, D.C.: Smithsonian Institution Press, 1997: 51-70.

"This chapter will focus on new discoveries and interpretations about the physical structure and growth of three major Harappan-phase urban centers and how the organization of these cities can be correlated with general models of social and political organization." (p. 51) In the absence of contemporary textual materials such as exist for other major ancient civilizations, the reconstruction of social forms for the Harappan culture must rely upon analogy with possible models from later eras of Indian history.The sites referred to are Harappa, Mohenjo-daro, and the regional center of Dholavira in Gujarat. Beginning with an overview of the geographical setting of the Indus Valley culture and its general chronology as then known, the pattern of settlement at the five largest Indus sites (the three sites named above, plus Ganweriwala and Rakhigarhi) is noted. Specific data on Harappa, Mohenjo-daro and Dholavira and their system of organization is then presented. Models of the state extant in northern and northwestern India between the seventh and fourth centuries B.C. (drawn from the *Arthashastra* of Kautilya, the *Astadhyayi* of Panini, and various Jain and Buddhist texts) are offered as applicable to the Indus Valley cities. Regional integration is seen as based on economic factors rather than military force.

217. Schopen, Gregory. *Bones, Stones and Buddhist Monks: Collected Papers on the Archaeology, Epigraphy and Texts of Monastic Buddhism in India.* Honolulu, University of Hawaii Press, 1997.

This collection of twelve papers gathers together a scattered scholarly production which challenges many of the standard assumptions of the field of Buddhist studies and creates "the basis for a new historiography of Buddhism." (p. x) Emphasis is placed upon the utilization of archaeological evidence equally with epigraphic data, whether in manuscript or inscription form. Given the early focus of Indian archaeological field survey initiated by Sir Alexander Cunningham on locating the sites of major Indian Buddhist centers, this volume provides a contemporary perspective on this continuing research focus. Useful as a supplement to the present bibliography for those readers unfamiliar with the structure of Buddhism.

218. Schopen, Gregory. "Archaeology and Protestant Presuppositions in the Study of Indian Buddhism," in *Bones, Stones and Buddhist Monks: Collected Papers on the Archaeology, Epigraphy and Texts of Monastic Buddhism in India.* Honolulu, University of Hawaii Press, 1997: 1-23.

Beginning with the observation that "the way in which the history of Indian Buddhism has been studied by modern scholars is decidedly peculiar," (p. 1.), the author analyses the underlying intellectual framework used by this discipline and its approach to the evaluation of archaeological information. A review of the history of Buddhist scholarship reveals a tendency to regard archaeology strictly as a tool for supporting the (presumably) universally known and prescriptive texts which are assumed to have guided actual daily life and religious practice. Dedicatory inscriptions from buildings and railings at Bharhut, Sanchi and Nagarjunakonda among other sites are cited indicating the possession of wealth by individual Buddhist clergy and the possible manufacture of coinage. The history of this devaluation of actual archaeological evidence in tracing the history of a religion is noted as also being present in the study of Christianity and is ascribed to a survival of a mindset from the Reformation. It is notable that the primary investigations of Sir Alexander Cunningham, who used Buddhist sources as guides to site location, are cited among the types of evidence considered as contradictory to pure scriptural realities.

219. Guha-Thakurta, Tapati. "The Museumised Relic: Archaeology and the First Museum of Colonial India," *The Indian Economic and Social History Review* 34(1) (1997): 21-51.

The focus of this article is on the objectives, philosophies and evolution of the idea of the museum in colonial India and the role played by the developing science of archaeology, both as influence and as a subject for exhibits. The discussion begins with the founding of the Asiatic Society in Calcutta in 1784 and its recognition of the need for "a learned material archive" (p. 24) whose philosophy was one of collection of antiquities rather than their display. Natural history (broadly defined) was the central interest of India's first museums, initially botany and zoology. The influence of the first Crystal Palace Exhibition, held in London in 1851, as an impetus to the collecting of Indian craft objects as a distinctive class of materials, and subsequent developments within museology are followed using the Indian Museum in Calcutta (founded in 1814) as example. The need for systematically organized sections for ethnology and archaeology in the Museum was acknowledged upon the Museum's severance from the Asiatic Society in 1866. Historians of Indian archaeology will find the section on "Archaeology in Late-nineteenth-century India: The Urge to Conserve and Document" of particular value for understanding the stated goals of the science and the manner in which it affected field research. The creation of the Curatorship of Ancient Monuments in 1880 is noted and its interaction with excavation traced. Documentation projects carried out after 1869 and their use of the new medium of photography are presented in some detail, among them James Burgess' large 1897 album *The Ancient Monuments, Temples and Sculptures of India*. Among the ideas discussed is the concept of all of India as a great open-air museum, within which major ancient structures could be conserved and protected, the value of transferring original remains from their sites to museums for care (spotlighted by the cases of the *stupas* of Amaravati and Bharhut) and the philosophies of exhibit construction. The educational value of artifacts is seen to have been hampered by the varied nature of the "publics" (ranging from the scholarly to the illiterate) the Indian Museum was attempting unsuccessfully to serve.

220. Biswas, Sachindra Sekhar. *Protecting the Cultural Heritage-National Legislations and International Conventions*. New Delhi :Vedams, 1999.

This work offers for both the general reader and specialist a detailed review of all the antiquarian law and legislation promulgated in India since 1878, with each of the eight measures examined in a separate chapter. The first section covers the Indian Treasure Trove Act of 1878, the Ancient Monuments Preservation Act of 1904, the Antiquities Export Control Act and the Antiquities Export Control Rules (both passed in 1947),the Ancient Monuments and Archaeological Sites and Remains Act of 1958 (and the rules passed in 1959 for its implementation), the 1972 Antiquities and Art Treasures Act, and the Antiquities and Art Treasures

Rules of 1973. The second major portion of the volume presents all then-extant international conventions governing the international movement, sale and export of cultural property, beginning with the Hague Convention of 1954. Researchers unable to obtain actual copies of the original legislation will find Biswas's volume a useful supplement to this aspect of Indian archaeology.

Andaman Islands

221. Cooper, Zarine. "Abandoned Onge Encampments and Their Relevance in Understanding the Archaeological Record in the Andaman Islands," in *Living Traditions; Studies in the Ethnoarchaeology of South Asia* edited by Bridget Allchin. Columbia, Missouri: South Asia Publications, 1994: 235-264.

A report on an ethnoarchaeological study of the Andaman Islands based upon data from excavated shell middens. Types of encampments, their internal arrangement, and the possible cultural origins of the vertebrate and faunal remains and bone, shell and stone artifacts found in the middens are compared with historic patterns of occupation and resource use by the Onge.

222. Cooper, Zarine. "Archaeological Evidence of Maritime Contacts: The Andaman Islands," in *Tradition and Archaeology: Early Maritime Contacts in the Indian Ocean* edited by Himanshu Prabha Ray and Jean-Francois Salles. New Delhi: Manohar, 1996: 239-245.

An overview of the known archaeological data from the Andaman archipelago reflecting external trade and contacts by the indigenous population. Shell middens (none dated prior to 2000 B.C.), the use of ceramics, the origins and history of pigs as domestic animals and of iron usage, and the types of water transport available are included. The excavation of Hava Beel Cave is also summarized.

Andhra Pradesh

223. Burgess, James. *Notes on the Amaravati Stupa.* Delhi: Indological Book House, 1972.

A facsimile reprint of the original 1882 report on the investigation and mass clearance of debris from the stupa at Amaravati in eastern Andhra Pradesh. The first pages quote extensively from correspondence dealing with the unauthorised clearance ordered by the Duke of Buckingham, with the scientific community stressing that "the work of the examination and survey of an ancient monument of such unique value should be entrusted only to some competent archaeologist and scholar." (p. 1) Unfortunately, the wholesale removal of earth virtually wiped out any chance of reconstructing the appearance of the central stupa. Stone elements were noted and numbered in the survey, and each is described in the text. Seventeen plates provide reproductions of sculptures, inscriptions and a general plan of the site as it existed in 1880. Useful as an illustration of the beginning of archaeology in Andhra Pradesh and India in general.

224. Burgess, James. *The Buddhist Stupas of Amaravati and Jaggayyapeta in the Krishna District, Madras Presidency, Surveyed In 1882.* Varanasi: Indological Book House, 1970.

A reprint of the 1886 report by Burgess on the salvage work carried out the site of Amaravati, whose central stupa had been essentially eradicated by a government project in 1880. The text of this report begins with an examination of all known accounts of Amaravati, both in ancient accounts such as that of Hsuan Tsang and since its rediscovery by Colin Mackenzie in 1797. Individual chapters discuss all excavations carried out at Amaravati (both in search of treasure and for archaeological purposes), the sculptures and elements of the encircling outer and inner rails, friezes and remains of the central stupa and inscriptions. Remains of a smaller stupa at Jaggayyapeta some thirty miles north west of Amaravati are also briefly treated in the final chapter. Sixty-six illustrations present photographs and highly detailed line drawings of all sculptural elements and slabs from both stupas, inscriptions from Amaravati and Jaggayyapeta and the Ashokan edicts from Dhauli.

225. Yazdani,Ghulam. *The Temples of Palampet.* Calcutta: Superintendent of Government Printing, 1922.

The sixth *Memoir* of the Archaeological Survey of India, this concise text reports on the small group of ornate medieval temples built by the Kakatiya dynasty northwest of Hanamkonda in Andhra Pradesh as they existed in the early twentieth century. The first section describes the main temple and its four satellite shrines while the second presents a translation of an inscription recording a gift to the temple in 1213 A.D. Six pages of black and white photographs of external and inner architectural and sculptural features of the complex and an overall plan are appended.

226. Cammiade, L.A. "Prehistoric Man in India and the Kurnool Bone Caves: A Neglected Field of Inquiry," *Man In India*, v.7 (1) (March 1927): 1-11.

In 1925, the author was posted to the Kurnool district of Andhra Pradesh, where Robert Bruce Foote had in the 1870's explored several caves which yielded stone tools in association with the bones of extinct fauna. The absence of human remains of palaeolithic man from the subcontinent is noted as being partly due to the non-calcareous nature of the soils of many of the places (such as open plains) where settlements might have been made. Foote's work at Kurnool is faulted, as the contemporary caves which he investigated would in ancient times have been the innermost reaches of inhabited spaces and too small to hold anything but wildlife. Excavations are suggested in the modern canyons outside the caves, which represent the full extent of older rock structures now collapsed. Cammiade notes that "for the glory of India I hope someone will be able to carry to a successful issue the exploration of the Kurnool bone caves." (p. 11)

227. Cammiade, L.A. and M.C. Burkitt. "Fresh Light On the Stone Ages In

Southeast India," *Antiquity* IV (1930): 327-339.

This report on the occurrence of stone tools in southeastern India as known at the time of publication opens with a note that the first such implement noted was found some sixty years before at Pallavaram in northeastern Tamil Nadu. During his government service, Cammiade had made a survey along the Eastern Ghats, resulting in the discovery of a sequence of four distinctive stone tool assemblages. Sites noted are Chodavaram, Giddalur and a section of the cliffs of the Bhavanasi River in the Nallamalai Mountains of southwestern Andhra Pradesh. The earliest industry is characterized by quartzite handaxes, succeeded by flake tools, burins and microliths. Illustration is provided by line drawings and black and white photographs. The stimulus for this essay appears to have been the then-recent discoveries of palaeolithic tools made in South Africa, Kenya and Uganda by Louis Leakey and others. The authors end by calling for "a small, well-equipped expedition to re-examine the whole problem in the Peninsula of India." (p. 339)

228. Ramachandran, T.N. *Nagarjunakonda 1938*. Delhi: Manager of Publications, 1953.

The rocky valley of Nagarjunakonda, "dotted with numerous hillocks and mounds covered with jungle" which "represent the sites of former Buddhist monuments" (pp. 3-4) was first noted by the Archaeological Survey of India in March 1926. Between 1926 and 1931, a series of excavations revealed one large stupa, four monasteries, several smaller stupas, six apsidal temples, a palace and a stone-built wharf on the Krishna River. Over five hundred splendidly-carved bas-reliefs in a style previously noted at Amaravati were also recovered. Inscriptions identified the sites as a focus of activity by the Ikshvaku dynasty (second to third centuries A.D.), then known as Vijayapuri. The present report, covering excavations carried out by the author and his team between 1938 and 1940 (at two stupas and what proved to be a three-sided monastery built about an open courtyard) opens with a brief but lyrical review of the history of Andhra Pradesh and the valley of Nagarjunakonda. Details of the excavation of each structure, plans and associated artifacts are set out in the text. Two appendixes set out the *Mandhatu Jataka* tale (illustrated on eighteen of the Nagarjunakonda panels) and outline the thirty-two sects of Buddhism. Thirty-eight black and white plates provide views of the site and each structure cleared, and samples of the carved reliefs, inscriptions and pottery and coinage recovered. The report was issued as the seventy-first *Memoir* of the Archaeological Survey of India.

229. Yazdani, Ghulam. "Hyderabad," in *Revealing India's Past: A Co-Operative Record of Archaeological Conservation and Exploration in India and Beyond*. London, India Society, 1939: 253-262.

Written as part of the assessment of the progress of archaeology in what were at the time independent Indian states under the rule of traditional systems of government allied to the Raj, the author of this piece was the first Director of Archaeology for the Nizam of Hyderabad. A separate Archaeological Department was inaugurated in this region of Andhra Pradesh in 1914, and its accomplishments in conservation and preservation of various sites are noted. Among these are the improvement of access to the famed frescoes of Ajanta, clearance and reconstruction of several structures at the cave temples of Elura, Pitalkhora, Ghatotkach and Aurangabad, major Muslim mosques and masjids in the cities of Bidar, Gulbarga and Hyderabad, and the Qutb Shahi tombs of Golconda. Yazdani observes that "perhaps in no part of India is there a greater abundance and variety of forts than in the Nizam's Dominions" (p. 259) and relates this fact to the region's dissected topography. Of particular interest to the historian of archaeology are the sections of the report noting the recording, translation and publication of several hundred Brahmi, Sanskrit, Telugu, Marathi, Arabic and Persian inscriptions and the rapid growth of the new museum in Hyderabad, founded in 1931.

230. Aiyappan, A. *The Manley Collection of Stone Age Tools*. Delhi: Manager of Publications, 1942.

The title of this publication is slightly inaccurate, as the actual catalogue of quartzite and chert artifacts collected by Dr. Frank Manley of the American Baptist Telugu Mission in the Nellore district of Andhra Pradesh does not occupy the entire volume. Aiyappan's preface records his journey in 1939 to visit many of the sites collected at by Manley and includes detailed topographical descriptions based on his earlier fieldwork. Questions on the raw materials used, typology, and analogies with then-known European and African Palaeolithic tool complexes are explored. This is the sixty-eighth *Memoir* of the Archaeological Survey of India.

231. Wentzel, Volkmar. "India's Sculptured Temple Caves," *National Geographic* 103 (5) (May, 1953): 665-678.

A photographic essay with brief text centered on the cave temple complexes of Ajanta and Ellora, done as part of a two-year survey of India for America's National Geographic Society. Special note is made of the excellent condition of the varied surviving Ajanta frescoes and the creation of the Kailasa shrine to Siva at Ellora from a single massive block of stone carefully cut from above.

232. Yazdani, Ghulam. *Ajanta: The Colour and Monochrome Reproductions of the Ajanta Frescoes Based on Photography*. London: Oxford University Press, 1930-1955.

The eight volumes of this set represent the result of a massive project (spanning a quarter century) to comprehensively record and annotate the major frescoes of the Ajanta cave temple complex. Each part is composed of two sections, a textual review and detailed explication of the location of each painting, its subject, technique and significance, and a folio of photographic plates illustrating each panel. Coverage includes Cave I, the frescoes of Cave II, the back wall of the veranda of Cave XVII and the entire interior surface of the *vihara*. An essential resource for any research dealing with the archaeology and preservation of this major site. A reprint was issued in 1983.

233. Soundara Rajan, K.V. "Studies In The Stone Age of Nagarjunakonda and Its Neighbourhood," *Ancient India* 14 (1958): 49-113.

"Due largely to its inaccessible and indeed forbidding nature, the jungle-clad valley of Nagarjunakonda did not attract the attention of archaeologists till the middle twenties of the present century." (p. 93) This article discusses the palaeolithic, microlithic and neolithic occupations of the area, data being obtained through surface collections, location of an *in situ* deposit at Karempudi by the author ancillary to ongoing work elsewhere in the valley (which was scheduled to be flooded by the Nagarjunasagar Dam), and from excavations of a Neolithic site. The bulk of this text is devoted to a detailed analysis of tool types (based on a sample of one hundred and thirty specimens) and their relationship to similar materials known from Europe and Africa, as well as the adjoining Kurnool district in western Andhra Pradesh.

234. Allchin, F.R. *Neolithic Cattle-keepers of South India: A Study of the Deccan Ashmounds.* Cambridge: University Press, 1963.

The ashmounds of burnt cow dung widely distributed across the Deccan which are the subject of this monograph were sampled through excavations at Utnur in eastern Andhra Pradesh in September 1957, although their existence had been noted in the early nineteenth century. Robert Bruce Foote visited one of them in 1872 and first raised the hypothesis that they were Neolithic in date. Later excavation of the Neolithic site of Piklihal had indicated that this period was characterized by pastoralism based on Indian humped cattle. The 1957 season had as its aim both the in-depth investigation of a specific mound and the visiting of a representative number of similar formations. Topics presented by individual chapters are a profile of the excavations and ashmounds in four other districts, the range of objects from the dig (including pottery, Neolithic blade tools, worked bone and human remains), the relationship of place names and traditional knowledge (both local and more general) to the subject of ash, and modern pastoralism and its influence on folk religion. Results of the Utnur season verified that the ashmounds were indeed Neolithic cattle pens, where the accumulated dung was periodically burnt. The place of this phenomenon within a more general Neolithic context and in later Indian history is considered in the final chapter.

235. Sarkar, H. "Kesarapalle 1962," *Ancient India* 22 (1966): 37-74.

A problematic aspect of the excavations at Nagarjunakonda was the establishment of an accurate chronology of cultural superimposition in this region of Andhra Pradesh. To address this question, excavations were carried out in 1961-62 at Kesarapalle, Krishna District, Andhra Pradesh. The goals of this season were to find a site where megaliths were close to a contemporary settlement (as was not the case at Nagarjunakonda) tracing the relationship of the megalithic culture of the Krishna Basin to the later Neolithic and Chalcolithic cultures, establishing a chronology of megaliths in relation to the Ikshvaku era (third to fourth century A.D.) and attempting to explain the absence of rouletted ware from the historical deposits at Nagarjunakonda. A sequence of three cultures was clearly established by taking two cuttings through the Kesarapalle mound, their dates ranging from the eighth century B.C. to late medieval times. An extensive and heavily illustrated analysis of the pottery recovered and a discussion of seven classes of smaller artfacts (including Neolithic polished stone axes, beads, terracotta objects and fifteen iron pieces (one a spearhead) complete the report. Researchers should consult other published work on Nagarjunakonda to provide a context for the Kesarapalle data.

236. Karthikeya Sarma, I. "A Coin-Mould Piece from Nagarjunakonda Excavations: New Light on the Silver Coinage of the Satavahanas," *Journal of the Economic and Social History of the Orient* 16 (1) (1973): 89-106.

The detailed publication of a baked clay mold for the production of a coin of the Satavahana dynasty ruler Vasishthiputra Pulumavi from the earliest historical layers of Nagarjunakonda, stated to be "first of its kind" (p. 89) known from a controlled excavation. Much of the discussion is devoted to arguments over the interpretation of the Telugu legend on the coin and general consideration of the palaeography of Satavahana coinage.

237. Murty, M.L.K. "A Late Pleistocene Cave Site in Southern India," *American Philosophical Society Proceedings* 118(2)(April 1974): 196-230.

The limestone caves near Betamcherla in the Kurnool district of Andhra Pradesh were first identified as sites of ancient human occupation in the late nineteenth century. Excavations by Robert Bruce and Henry Bruce Foote at Billa Surgam retrieved some two hundred bone tools and implements, although a complementary stone tool industry (taken as the hallmark of the Upper Palaeolithic elsewhere in the Old World) was not located. This article reports on the excavation of another cave in the same area, Muchchatla Chitamanu Gavi, which provided evidence of the extensive use of flake and blade tools. Most of the text is a detailed presentation and analysis of both stone and bone tool types, illustrated by black and white photographs and line drawings.

238. Murty, M.L.K. and K.Thimma Reddy. "The Significance of Lithic Finds in the Cave Areas of Kurnool, India," *Asian Perspectives* 18 (2) 1976: 214-226.

The question of an Indian parallel to the Upper Palaeolithic of Europe, in particular the bone tool technology, is reviewed. Preservation of similar artifacts is reported almost exclusively from cave sites where such data is available for the subcontinent. This report covers fresh excavations carried out in the exposed cave deposits of Billa Surgam in the Kurnool district of Andhra Pradesh in an effort to provide data on the types of stone tools associated with the bone technologies so as to provide a method of correlation with open-air sites lacking bone remains. Results included blade artifacts in the cave and a microlithic and flake tool assemblage from the surface deposits. This data permits the initial finds of bone tools to be placed more securely in the Stone Age sequence. For a report on the excavation of another cave in the Billa Surgam group, researchers should consult the 1980 article by K.Thimma Reddy.

239. Krishna Murthy, C. "Unique Megalith from Kaditiraya Cherevu, Andhra Pradesh," *Journal of Indian History* 54 (2) (August 1976): 239-241.

A descriptive note of an unusual megalithic construction noted in Chittoor district of Andhra Pradesh among a larger group of twenty stone cist burials, eleven of which were relatively intact. Two of the circles were extremely elaborate in plan, one having the cist contained within six concentric rings of upright slabs, the other similar but with only four rings. A full map of the larger group and black and white photographs of its general location are included.

240. Reddy, K. Thimma. "Billasurgam: An Upper Palaeolithic Cave Site in South India," *Asian Perspectives* 20(2) (1980): 206-227.

The group of limestone caves at Billasurgam in the Kurnool district of Andhra Pradesh have been known as possessing Stone Age materials since their discovery in 1844 and subsequent investigations begun in 1884 by Robert Bruce Foote. A report of the results of excavation of a cave not worked by Foote, accompanied by an analysis of the 1356 stone tools (chiefly blades, but including burins, points, arrowheads, borers, scrapers and knives) and the more limited bone tool industry makes up the majority of the text. Faunal remains from the Billasurgam area are analysed, indicating a wetter climate during the Late Pleistocene.

241. Srinivasulu, K. "Acheulean Situations In Andhra Pradesh," *Man In India* 63 (4) (December, 1983): 351-360.

This summary article reviews in detail the range of stone tool types assigned to the Acheulean phase of the Palaeolithic and their sites of ocurrence within Andhra Pradesh as known in the early 1980s. Areas yielding this industry are the Godavari Valley and several of its tributaries, the Nellore district, the Paleru Valley, and the Krishna Valley around Nagarjunakonda. Sites profiled are Rajupalem, Cherla, Lankalapalem, Pamidipadu and Karempudi. Exploitation of a variety of ecological niches by the ancient population is discussed. Readers should be aware that many of the technical descriptive terms used are borrowed from the Palaeolithic archaeology of southern Africa and Europe.

242. Ghosh, N.C. *Excavations at Satanikota 1977-80*. New Delhi: Director General, Archaeological Survey of India, 1986.

The decision to construct a hydroelectric project at Srisailam on the river Krishna in southern India triggered a massive program of archaeological survey and salvage excavation from the late 1960s to the middle 1970s. Of the eighty-five sites located in the potentially submerged areas, ten were selected for excavation, Satanikota being one and having yielded remains ranging from Stone Age to medieval in date. This report (covering field work carried out from 1977 to 1980) opens by reviewing prior archaeological work in Andhra Pradesh, Orissa and the southern parts of Madhya Pradesh, followed by a brief profile of the physical situation of the site and its known history. Data on the occupation of Satanikota and its environs during the Stone Age are next examined, beginning with the established stratigraphy of this era and available data on Middle Palaeolithic and Mesolithic activities. The fourth and fifth chapters treat the megalithic cultures of southern India as expressed at Satanikota and the early historic and medieval periods. This latter is the most extensively analysed, with material culture (especially pottery) discussed at length. Sixty-two black and white photographic plates are appended and illustrate a variety of excavated objects in terracotta, pottery types, ground plans of the historic era fort, burials at the foot of the megaliths, and Middle Palaeolithic tools.

243. Rao, Nandini. "Subsistence and Associated Settlement Patterns In Central India: An Ethnoarchaeological Analysis," in *Living Traditions; Studies in the Ethnoarchaeology of South Asia* edited by Bridget Allchin. Columbia, Missouri; South Asia Publications, 1994: 143-168.

An analysis of contemporary and recent historic settlement patterns and economic activities in the Adilabad district of Andhra Pradesh carried out by the historic Gond tribe, which are then correlated with the distribution of archaeological remains surrounding the Kuntala waterfall. Data on a similar reconnaissance of the Narmada Valley of Maharashtra are also presented.

Bengal

This particular regional name has been variously used in the history of twentieth century India. This section covers field work done in the former British territory of Bengal, divided into West Bengal and East Pakistan (later Bangladesh) at Partition in 1947. Reports done during the existence of the latter two states will be found under those headings in the present bibliography.

244. Dikshit, K.N. *Excavations At Paharpur, Bengal*. Delhi: Manager of Publications, 1938.

Issued as the fifty-fifth *Memoir* of the Archaeological Survey of India, this report presents both the history of investigations of the cruciform temple at Paharpur and an analysis of the remains obtained between 1923 and 1934. First noted in 1807, the site consisted of a large mound of bricks, representing the ruins of a single large temple dating to the eighth and ninth centuries A.D., and adjoining monastic living quarters. The most notable type of find made here was some eight hundred terracotta plaques depicting both Buddhist and Hindu religious figures, with two thousand more remaining in their original wall positions. Following an introductory chapter placing Paharpur (the ancient Somapura) within regional history, data on the main temple, the monastery, the stone and terracotta artifacts found, minor antiquities (chiefly inscribed copper plates and stone pillars), and the preliminary clearance of the site of Satyapir Bhita are presented. A detailed plan and elevation of the temple are followed by sixty-six high quality black and white photographs tracing all phases of the excavation and illustrating numerous sculptural elements. Researchers will find citations to related scientific literature within the text of the report.

Bihar

245. Ghosh, Manoranjan. *Rock-Paintings and Other Antiquities of Prehistoric and Later Times.* Calcutta: Government of India Central Publications Branch, 1932.

This twenty-fourth *Memoir* of the Archaeological Survey of India was written by the curator of the Patna Museum, and reports on ancient remains as then known from four areas; the Chakradharpur area near Singhbum in southern Bihar, the rock shelters of Singanpur west of Raigarh in extreme southeastern Madhya Pradesh, Hoshangabad in Madhya Pradesh and the Son Valley near Mirzapur in Uttar Pradesh. This last is the longest section of text, with most discussion being devoted to the rock art of the region, first noted in 1880. Each region is presented in detail, accompanied by catalogs of surface collections of artifacts. Twenty-eight black and white plates provide several site plans while emphasizing the types of pottery decorations found.

246. Law, Bimala Churn. *Rajagriha in Ancient Literature.* Delhi: Manager of Publications, 1938.

Issued as the fifty-eighth *Memoir* of the Archaeological Survey of India, the intent of this study was "to give an exhaustive...account of one of the most important ancient Indian cities, from all the available literary sources." (p. 1) Rajagriha (contemporary Rajgir) was the capital of the kingdom of Magadha, and figured prominently in the life of the Buddha. After two opening sections exploring the varied names assigned to the city, their origins, and the topography of its five hills, the significance of the city in regional political and Buddhist religious history is documented, including a visit by the Chinese pilgrim Fa Hsien in the fifth century A.D. Two black and white plates illustrating a section of the city walls, a gateway and fragments of sculpture are appended. Researchers interested in following up the interplay of Indian archaeology with the body of historical literatures available for the subcontinent may wish to consult the author's other works on Sravasti (1935) and Kausambi (1939).

247. Ghosh, A. "Rajgir 1950," *Ancient India* 7 (January 1951): 66-78.

Rajgir, the ancient city of Rajagriha, capital of the kingdom of Magadha, lies in a valley some sixty miles southeast of modern Patna. Prior to February 1950, most scientific investigation at the site had been focused on identifying sections of ruins with structures closely associated with the life of the Buddha. This report presents data obtained through the clearing and recording of a twenty-foot stratigraphic cut made across one edge of the city by a local river. The resulting sequence offers the first profile of occupation for the city. Thirty-four types of pottery are illustrated and analysed. On the basis of cross-references to other known sites, Rajgir's life began sometime before 500 B.C. Text notes provide valuable citations to prior work, beginning with Sir Alexander Cunningham's visit in the 1870's.

248. Broadley, A.M. *Ruins of the Nalanda Monasteries at Burgaon, Sub-Division Bihar, Zillah Patna*. Calcutta: Bengal Secretariat Press, 1872.

In October, 1871, the author began an excavation of the central tumulus in the ruins of the monastery complex of Nalanda in Bihar. This twenty-four page essay begins by presenting the history of the site as then known, drawing on the accounts of the ancient pilgrims Fa Hsien and Hsuan Tsang. Emphasis is laid upon the contribution of the teachers of Nalanda to the spread of Buddhism throughout southern Asia. The detailed description of the site as it existed during Hsuan Tsang's year of residence (637-38 A.D.) is immediately followed by Broadley's discussion of the state of the ruins (together with notes on sculptures and ornamental elements collected by him) and the results of his clearance of the the central mound, which contained the remains of an impressive temple. Two appendixes present the seventy-one carvings recovered and a Devanagari transcription and translation of a ninth century inscription retrieved during the excavations.

249. Sastri, Hirananda. *Nalanda and Its Epigraphic Material*. Delhi: Manager of Publications, 1942.

Issued as the sixty-sixth *Memoir* of the Archaeological Survey of India, this monograph was prepared by the government epigraphist and deals with the numerous copper plates, seals and stone inscriptions discovered during archaeological survey and excavation of the ancient Buddhist monastery and teaching center of Nalanda since 1916. The first nineteen pages review known references to Nalanda in Tibetan, Hindu and Jain literature as well as citations in the traditional Buddhist canon, including the vivid description left by the Chinese pilgrim Hsuan Tsang. The majority of the text is devoted to the varied assemblage of baked clay seal impressions. While most were issued by the different viharas at Nalanda, others record the names of local rulers, monastic and other officials, and villages. Descriptions of type seals from each class are provided in considerable detail. The section on "Inscriptions" discusses the notable finds of this nature and presents transliterations and translations of both stone and copper plate texts.Nine high quality black and white photographic plates provide examples of all classes of seals and votive inscriptions. Researchers should use this volume with Mary Stewart's 1989 work *Nalanda Mahavihara* for updated information.

250. Lal, B.B. "An Examination of Some Metal Images From Nalanda," *Ancient India* 12 (1956): 53-57.

This brief article focuses on a metallurgical analysis of eighteen of the more than five hundred bronze images known from the important Buddhist monastery center of Nalanda. A summary of traditional "lost wax" casting techniques is followed by data indicating that both bronze and brass were used, the ore being drawn from adjacent local mines. The author observes that this note is the first such study of the Nalanda material to be published.

251. Allchin, F.R. "The Neolithic Stone Industry of the Santal Parganas," *Journal of the Economic and Social History of the Orient* 25 (1962): 306-330.

The author states that this "present paper carries forward my plan of studying the major collections of neolithic tools housed in European museums and remaining incompletely published" (p. 306) by examining a set of stone tools from the Santal Parganas district of Bihar. Originally gathered by a Norwegian missionary and local villagers between 1900 and 1930 on the ridges comprising the southern edge of the Rajmahal hills, the total number of pieces is an astounding 2,620. The assemblage exhibits what Allchin describes as "a remarkable homogeneity," (p. 308) with the vast majority being axes, celts, adzes,hammers and varieties of these four basic forms. Similarities of the axes to other Neolithic sites in the Deccan are noted. Researchers unfamiliar with the development of analytical models for the Indian Neolithic will find the discussion of the three "traditions" of stone tool designs identified up to the time of publication a valuable and interesting summary. High quality line drawings and black and white photographs of type samples are included.

252. Chakrabarti, Dilip K. "Rajagriha: An Early Historic Site In India," *World Archaeology* 7 (3) (February 1976): 261-268.

The author states his intention is "to assess what is archaeologically known about Rajgir as it existed during the time of the Buddha…this has never been clearly attempted," (p. 261) despite the city's well-documented association with Buddhism as the former capital of the kingdom of Magadha. All major structures within the valley of Rajgir are reviewed, and the archaeological evidence for their dating to Buddha's time found to be questionable. Particular emphasis is placed on the need for further excavation and survey of the defensive walls. Chakrabarti notes that Rajgir is an excellent example of the problems facing historical archaeology in India.

253. Bhattacharya, Gouriswar. "The Newly Discovered Buddhist Temple at Nalanda," in *South Asian Archaeology 1983* edited by Janice Schotsmans and Maurizio Taddei. Naples: Istituto Universitario Orientale, 1985: 719-740.

The extensive ruins of the Buddhist religious and educational center at Nalanda were explored and excavated between 1915 and 1953. In 1975-76, further work by the Archaeological Survey of India exposed a rectangular brick temple complex within one of the mounds of the previously cleared area. The article begins with a description and plan of this new Buddhist shrine, marked by the remains of a massive standing figure of the Buddha in the sanctuary and a unique series of surviving paintings, the latter depicting in addition to the Buddha the Seven Jewels

(*Sapta Ratnani*) of Buddhist canonical literature. These last are compared with miniature text illustrations dating to the late tenth century A.D. in style and format. An inscribed stone slab formerly attached to the front wall of the temple referring to a great image of the Buddha is analysed in the closing section and dated by textual style to the sixth century A.D. Said date accords well with the literary description of Nalanada in 637 A.D. by the Chinese pilgrim Hsuan Tsang.

254. Stewart, Mary. L. *Nalanda Mahavihara: A Study of an Indian Pala Period Buddhist Site and British Historical Archaeology, 1861-1938*. Oxford: B.A.R., 1989.

This detailed monograph (based on the author's 1988 thesis for the School of Oriental and African Studies at the University of London) is perhaps the best single volume summary of data on the Buddhist university and teaching center of Nalanda available. Using the official documentation produced by the Archaeological Survey of India in the course of its excavations and surveys at Nalanda since its identification by Sir Alexander Cunningham in 1861 and purchase by the Survey in 1916, the question of interpreting the context of decades of field work and analysis is raised. "There needs to be a way of evaluating and interpreting the historical archaeology of Nalanda in terms of the thinking and procedures of its...period...the placement of the archaeology of Nalanda in its historic and intellectual context to see what the basic assumptions regarding Buddhism, its artefacts, literary sources and monuments were." (p. 20) The first section of text addresses religious, art historical and historical literary contexts of the early field campaigns, while the second follows scientific attention to Nalanda from the first visitors in 1812 through the Survey's twenty-two years of activity at the site from 1916 to 1939. The account left by the Chinese pilgrim Hsuan Tsang who visited Nalanda is compared with two other accounts available to archaeologists but never examined, those of I-tsing and Ki Ye, in an effort to determine the extent of the *vihara* and interpret specific groups of monuments. The final chapter reports that "because the archaeologists were preoccupied with verifying the Chinese literary accounts of Nalanda, they concentrated their efforts primarily on the restoration of the monasteries," (p. 246) and suggestions for further historical analysis of the site are made. Detailed plans of Nalanda at various stages of clearance by the Archaeological Survey, together with cross sections and reproductions of specific structures and copper dedication plates, are interspersed throughout the text. A lengthy bibliography is appended.

255. Chakrabarti, Dilip. K "Archaeology of the Chhotanagpur Plateau and the Bengal Basin," in *From Sumer To Meluhha: Contributions to the Archaeology of South and West Asia in Memory of George F. Dales, Jr.* Madison, Wisconsin: University of Wisconsin Department of Anthropology, 1994: 253-259.

A detailed synthesis of available archaeological data on the Chhotanagpur Plateau of southern Bihar, which is considered as a unit with the Bengal basin due to longstanding cultural interactions. Known sequences reaching from the Palaeolithic era through historic times are presented and discussed. Researchers will find referring to a map of the state useful when reading this article.

Delhi

256. Hearn, Gordon Risley. *The Seven Cities of Delhi*. London: W. Thacker and Company, 1906.

Originally written as a combination guidebook and historical work, this volume is divided into three sections. The first two chapters present a description of the major monuments of then-contemporary Delhi and the surrounding plains, while the third summarizes the city's history from the Muslim conquest in the late twelfth century through the Raj and Indian Mutiny of 1857 to modern times. Chapters three through seven are collectively entitled "Detailed Descriptions of the Cities and Their Monuments." By tradition there have been seven cities on the site of Delhi, beginning with the mythical Indraprastha. Hearn reviews the sites and remaining structures of Old Delhi, Siri, Tughlaqabad, Jahanpanah, Firozabad, the Delhi built by Sher Shah, and Shahjahanabad. The text is illustrated with several excellent maps and twenty-four photographic plates. While dated, this text provides the reader unfamiliar with the most recent eight centuries of Delhi's history with background. A brief appendix of works consulted shows that the author drew upon the publications of the Archaeological Survey of India, the *Journal of the Asiatic Society of Bengal* and the *Journal of the Archaeological Society of Delhi* among other sources.

257. Waddington, Hilary. "Adilabad: A Part of the 'Fourth' Delhi," *Ancient India* 1 (January 1946): 60-75.

Within the space presently occupied by India's capital, no fewer than seven cities built by a succession of rulers are attested by tradition. This article focuses on initial excavations carried out in 1944-45 at the fortress of 'Adilabad, part of the fourth city constructed by Emperor Ghiathuddin Tughlaq in 1321 and abandoned in 1327. The article opens with a summary of the known history of the period, followed by discussion of Tughlaqabad, composed of the walled city itself, the emperor's tomb and the fortress. An aerial photograph, unusual for the time in India, shows the city plan and modern occupation. The primary emphasis in the first season was on creating plans of both city and fortress, clearing the west gate of 'Adilabad and obtaining a pottery typology of this precisely dated site to assist in dating other medieval sites. Photographs and line drawings present the plain and glazed wares found in some detail.

258. Naqvi, S.A.A. "Sultan Ghari, Delhi," *Ancient India* 3 (January, 1947): 4-10.

"The oldest Muslim tomb known to exist in India lies unnoticed in a remote corner of Delhi province." (p. 4) This colorful phrase introduces a report on the tomb of Prince Nasiruddin Mahmud, built in 1231. The tomb and its three phases of associated occupation debris (chiefly houses from the fourteenth, seventeenth and eighteenth centuries) are presented through precise architectural sections and plans. All inscriptions on the structure are translated and the history of the town set into its regional context. Black and white plates illustrating the external faces of the tomb, the *mihrab* and dome of the prayer chamber, the mosque of Firoz Shah and some of the late Mughal era houses are appended.

259. Thapar, B.K. "The Buried Past of Delhi," *Expedition* 14 (2) Winter 1972: 21-26.

"According to popular belief there have been eight imperial cities of Delhi." (p. 21) This article reports on a second season of excavations carried out at the mound of Purana Qila within the modern city limits. Following up on earlier soundings done in 1955, a series of step cuts was made to obtain a complete sequence of occupation of the site and examine portions of each level. Results indicate use since the Mauryan period of the third century B.C. through the Sunga, Saka-Kushana, Gupta, Post-Gupta, Rajput and Delhi Sultanate eras. Sample artifacts from each level are illustrated.

260. Mani, B.R. "Excavations at Lal Kot 1991-92 and Further Explorations in Delhi," *Puratattva* 22 (1991/92): 75-87.

A combined report covering both field work at the fortress of Lal Kot and a survey of formerly known mounds within the urban area. Lal Kot was selected "to locate the citadel area...study the layout and settlement pattern of the palaces and other allied structures...and confirm the literary evidences about the location and the shifting of the royal seat to Delhi." (p. 79) The village survey was done to "spot out the sites of archaeological importance in the map of Delhi as the growing constructions and levelling of old mounds have effected the whole of the city." (p. 83) The range of mounds is seen by the author as a series of independent villages associated with the city of Indraprastha, traditionally the first city of Delhi. Nine sites are noted and their condition assessed. Readers unfamiliar with Delhi archaeology will find the preface to the reports useful for historical background.

Ganges Valley

261. Smith, Vincent A. "The Copper Age and Prehistoric Bronze Implements of India," *Indian Antiquary* 34 (October, 1905): 229-244.

The major question of whether and how the progression from stone tools to the successively more complex metallurgical technologies of copper, bronze and iron established for western Europe might have occurred in India is addressed in this essay. Beginning with the flat statement that "India had no Bronze Age" (p. 229), the author then focuses on the differences between northern and southern India, the latter seen as having shifted directly from stone tools to iron when such technology became available. Copper implements are noted from twelve locales, eight of which (Rajpur, Mathura, Mainpuri, Fathgarh, Niorai, Bithur, Itawa, and Kosam) lie in the Ganges drainage. A major hoard of 424 hammered copper implements and 102 silver plates found at Gungeria in the Central Provinces is also discussed. The assemblage of shapes and forms from all sites is grouped into seven classes: flat and bar celts, "swords" and daggers, distinctive pronged harpoons, arrowheads, rings and anthropomorphic figures. In the brief final section, Smith reviews the six objects of bronze then known, only three of which qualify as true bronze according to metallurgical standards. Researchers should note that virtually none of the artifacts which form the basis for this report can be securely dated, all having been found by surface collection. An interesting feature of the essay are the frequent parallels drawn with the better known bronze technology of Ireland. For further information on a major collection of similar artifacts, readers may consult Robert Bruce Foote's 1901 publication *Catalogue of the Prehistoric Antiquities, Government Museum, Madras*.

262. Lal, B.B. "Further Copper Hoards From The Gangetic Basin and A Review of the Problem," *Ancient India* 7 (January, 1951): 20-39.

Beginning in 1822, finds had been made of groups of copper implements at various locales within the valley of the Ganges River, with the first comprehensive survey of such materials published in 1905. This article reports on several collections of such artifacts not previously recorded from museums in Allahabad and Banaras and newly-acquired items from the State Museum in Lucknow. Hypotheses advanced by investigators such as Stuart Piggott, drawing parallels between the Ganges finds and similar metallurgy from Persia, are challenged on the basis of the distribution of such distinctive forms such as the pronged harpoon, anthropomorphic figurines and "antennae" swords, none of which is found west of the Ganges basin. A map illustrating the then-known distribution of copper implements is included, as are high quality line drawings and photographs of materials from each of the new collections.

263. Roy, T.N. *The Ganges Civilization: A Critical Archaeological Study of the Painted Grey Ware and Northern Black Polished Ware Periods of the The Ganga Plains of India*. New Delhi: Ramanan Vidya Bhawan, 1983.

Originally prepared as the author's 1977 doctoral thesis, this work has as its background the discovery of a stratum of black slipped pottery at the site of Prahladpur in 1963. Given the finding of similar pottery at other sites in eastern Uttar Pradesh and Bihar, and its consideration as one attribute of one of the earliest Iron Age cultures known in India, debate on their value as cultural markers has been longstanding in Indian archaeology. Roy uses as his data set information gathered during the vertical excavation of sixty sites in the Ganga Plains and attempts a re-examination of the sequence question, working backward from the historic Kushan era and considering the total artifactual assemblage rather than one single pottery type as chronological markers. Evidence is offered supporting human presence in the Ganges valley from Neolithic times onward. Individual chapters examine the ecological setting of the Ganges Valley and its implications for human culture, excavated Iron Age sites by region, the chronology of the painted grey and northern black polished wares as then known, and their associated material cultures. Researchers will find the "Conclusions" section a clear and useful summary of arguments on specific areas. A bibliography and one dozen black and white plates are also included.

264. Falk, Harry. "Copper Hoard Weapons and the Vedic *vajra*," in *South Asian Archaeology 1993* edited by Asko Parpola and Petteri Koskikallio. Helsinki: Suomalainen Tiedeakatemia, 1994: 193-206.

In the *Rigveda*, a weapon of the gods made of cast copper is described, termed the *vajra*. While attempts have been made to equate this item with products of the Copper Hoard Culture whose center lay in the Ganges and Yamuna regions, no successful identification has yet been achieved. This article takes up the debate, suggesting that this archaeological assemblage represents not the Rigveda era "but rather corresponds to the Middle Vedic texts and schools and to the political units known by the namems of the Kurus and Pancalas." (p 194) Three types of copper artifacts are examined as candidates for the *vajra*: harpoons, anthropomorphic figures and bar-celts. Readers unfamiliar with the texts of the Vedas will find the interweaving of textual materials with field work a useful frame of reference. The author regretfully admits that, at the time of publication, "we still know next to nothing about Vedic archaeology." (p. 205)

Goa

265. Mitterwallner, G. von. "Two Natural Caves and 11 Man-made Cave Excavations of Goa, India," in *South Asian Archaeology 1979* edited by Herbert Hartel. Berlin: Dietrich Riemer Verlag, 1981: 469-511.

One of the few surveys extant on the archaeology of the former Portuguese enclave of Goa, this well-illustrated essay examines in detail thirteen cave- and niche-temples carved from the region's laterite rock. Plans of each structure and photographs of notable features such as lingas and associated artifacts are provided for each site.

266. Sharma, A.K. "Exposing and Conserving A World Heritage Monument," *Puratattva* 19 (1988-89): 64-67.

The monument referred to in the title of this article is the complex of buildings comprising the Church of St. Augustine, erected in Old Goa in 1602 and active until the suppression of the order in India in 1835. The results of one season's excavation of the main sanctuary are reported, emphasizing the scope of the project and the degree of conservation of badly weathered laterite stone and plaster architectural elements. A plan and section elevation are provided. Tombs within the floor of the sanctuary are noted as dating back to 1612.

Gujarat

267. Burgess, James and Henry Cousens. *The Architectural Antiquities of Northern Gujarat*. London: Bernard Quaritch, 1903.

An excellent example of the approach taken to the ancient buildings of the subcontinent by the colonial British scientific establishment in the first year of the revitalized Archaeological Survey of India, this lavish volume treats "antiquarian remains...within the dominions of Baroda" (p. v), a native state within the present political boundaries of Gujarat. The data on which the work is based were compiled by the authors at various times, with Burgess (who was deceased by the time this publication appeared in 1903) touring the region in 1869,1872 and 1875, with Cousens surveying and photographing the area in 1886-87 and 1889-90. Background geographical and historical data on Baroda is given in the first of fourteen chapters, with a discussion of regional architectural styles (chiefly Jain) and problems of preservation covered in the second. The remaining twelve chapters focus on local towns and villages within Baroda where significant constructions and inscriptions were to be found at that time, detailing for each their natures as then known. The one hundred and eleven photographic plates are interspersed throughout the volume and provide invaluable data on the condition of these structures and edifices at the opening of the twentieth century, with further illustration provided by drawings of architectural elements, plans and sections. Researchers dealing with later Gujarati archaeology should consult this work as the beginning of their local professional literature.

268. Sankalia, Hasmukh D. *Investigations Into the Prehistoric Archaeology of Gujarat, Being The Official Report of the First Gujarat Prehistoric Expedition 1941-42*. Baroda State Press, 1946.

Although the first traces of human occupation in Gujarat (stone tools found by geologist Robert Bruce Foote in the bed of the Sabarmati River) had been known since 1893, until 1940 no coherent plan of investigation was envisioned to obtain further data. In that year K.N. Dikshit, Director General of Archaeology, referred to the apparently long gap between palaeolithic and neolithic cultures in Gujarat in his address to the Anthropological Section of the Science Congress held in Madras. Coming at a time when the discovery of the Indus civlization and the establishment of a glacial sequence for Kashmir had brought the need for linking up available data on the historic, proto-historic and prehistoric eras of Indian archaeology into prominence, his speech provided a focus for research.

This volume presents the results of the First Gujarat Prehistoric Expedition conducted from December 1941 to February 1942. Its aim was to carry out a survey of the river valleys of the state to identify possible sites for excavation, to conduct trial excavations at some of them, and attempt to establish correlations between this data and the known microlithic sites lying outside the river drainages. Following an introductory chapter discussing the basic geography and geology of

Gujarat (with particular attention to the Sabarmati and Orsang Valleys), data on the palaeolithic industry is given. The more lengthy of the four chapters cover the surface exploration of microlithic sites (and the digs at Hirpura and Langhnaj) and compare the Gujarat palaeolithic and microlithic artifacts with then-known industries from other parts of India, Sri Lanka, southeast Asia and southern Africa. Eight appendixes provide a detailed catalogue of the microlithic finds, implements recovered from the Langhnaj and Hirpura excavations, analyses of soil and bone samples and a comparison of the loess beds of Gujarat with those of Europe. Five colored maps illustrate the Sabarmati valley, the distribution of the loess hills in central and northern Gujarat where many of the microlithic sites are located, while thirty-one plates (nineteen black and white photographs and twelve line drawings) show stratigraphic sections and general aspects of several sites and type specimens of both excavated and surface collected stone tools. A brief unannotated bibliography is also provided. Researchers dealing with any subsequent field work in Gujarat archaeology will be obliged to consult this massive report.

269. Rao, S.R. "Excavation at Rangpur and Other Explorations in Gujarat," *Ancient India* 18/19 (1962/63): 5-207.

The majority of this lengthy article is devoted to the results of excavations carried out at the mound of Rangpur on the river Bhadar in central Gujarat between 1953 and 1956, first identified as a possible outpost of the Harappan culture in 1934. The current excavation was done as a consequence of the need to locate accessible Harappan sites following Partition. Beginning with a review of the previous seasons' field work, this text then outlines the goals of the project, chiefly to confirm the Harappan affinities of the site and establish the local cultural sequence. Three levels of occupation were found: a microlithic culture lacking pottery, the Harappan phase, and a later regional assemblage referred to as the Lustrous Red Ware Culture. Individual sections cover type artifacts of each stage, the nine stratigraphic trenches and their profiles, architectural remains as identified, animal and plant data, pottery styles and objects of terracotta, stone, shell and metal. The third section reports on the exploration of the Kathiawar amd Kutch peninsulas for traces of further use or occupation during the Harappan era. Sites discussed in this section include the port of Lothal, Rojdi, Desalpur, Prabhas, and the southernmost Indus Valley site then known, Bhagatrav, with a complete list of all protohistoric sites in Gujarat provided in the Appendix. The author's conclusions as to the survival of the Harappan culture in a local form following damaging floods about 1500 B.C. and its evolution into the later Lustrous Red Ware culture should be evaluated against subsequent field investigations in the region. Numerous high quality black and white photographs and line drawings add to the value of this report.

270. Allchin, Bridget and Andrew Goudie. "Dunes, Aridity and Early Man in Gujarat, Western India," *Man*, v.6, n.2 (June 1971): 248-265.

During 1970 and 1971, the authors of this piece carried out a survey of the fossil dune fields in Gujarat in an attempt to address the chronology of climate fluctuations. Four major types of wind-related landforms are described, with attention then centering on those associated with the Chota Udaipur escarpment. The microlithic sites at Pavagarh, Mitli and Visadi are discussed and compared with stone tools found during the excavations at Langhnaj. Sample tools from Visadi only are illustrated. Researchers wishing a fuller discussion of the question of archaeology and climate in this part of India should consult the 1976 work by the authors, *The Prehistory and Palaeogeography of the Great Indian Desert.*

271. Rao, Shikaripur Ranganatha. *Lothal, A Harappan Port Town* (1955-1962). New Delhi; Archaeological Survey of India, 1979-1985.

Following the partition of the subcontinent in 1947, the majority of known Indus Valley civilization sites lay outside the political borders of India. To recover this area of study, the Archaeological Survey expanded its investigation of the areas immediately east of the Indus to locate new sites for excavation and to better delineate the area of cultural occupation. The author conducted excavations at the Gujarat site of Rangpur in 1953-54, confirming its identity as Harappan. This discovery was followed by a village by village survey of Kathiawar which led to the identification of forty more archaeological sites, six of them of the Harappan period, the most important of which was Lothal. This two-volume set is the definitive report on the seven-year program of excavation carried out there between 1955 and 1962.

The first volume opens by placing the site within regional environmental geography before focusing on specific aspects of the mound itself and the results of field work. Fourteen chapters trace the cultural sequence as then known, discuss the chronology of Harappan civilization and present the stratigraphic sections of the mound. The seventh chapter analyses the structural remains located (including an impressive dock facility) while the extensive cemetery revealed joint inhumation as a local custom. Other areas addressed are the decipherment of the Harappan script, trade and transportation (with links to Mesopotamia via overseas trade noted through the occurrence of Sumerian seals, stone weights, copper objects, beads and pottery) and evidence of religious practices. The second volume contains technical reports on the anthropology, botany, zoology and chemistry of various artifact classes from Lothal. Illustrations are provided by one hundred and twenty seven maps and black and white plates appended to the first volume.

272. Possehl, Gregory L. *Indus Civilization In Saurashtra*. Delhi: B.R. Publishing Corporation, 1980.

This publication is an extensively revised version of the author's doctoral dissertation accepted at the University of Chicago in 1980, and takes as its focus the "study of change and variation in the Harappan civilization" (p. 5), using data obtained from a survey of settlement patterning in the state of Gujarat. Possehl notes that the accumulated information on the end of the Indus culture amassed to date is so scanty that theories advanced thus far are unclear as to the precise process and sequence of events they attempt to account for. Gujarat was chosen both for its clearly defined geographical limits and the large number of documented Harappan period sites known. The central argument of this work is that, in outlying provincial regions of the Indus culture, "changes which affected the civilization as a whole would be sensitively recorded...without the masking effect likely to be present in the more central zones." (p. 8) Two phases of Harappan development are delineated, the "Mature" and "Post-Urban," and the continuity of cultural practices in Gujarat after the decline of the cities of Harappa and Mohenjo-Daro is noted.

The three objectives of the study were to more fully document the "Post-Urban" phase of the Harappan era, challenge the idea that this era represents a time of cultural decline, and offer an interpretation of the role of Lothal (the only site within Gujarat comparable to the larger urban centers of the north) as an interface between settled communities and the hunter-gatherer cultures archaeologically documented from North Gujarat. Five chapters present an historical overview of excavations in Gujarat and the definition of the archaeological sequence known at the time of the initial survey, detailed information on the natural regions and microenvironments of Gujarat, a profile of settlement patterns (revealing an emphasis on riverine areas and regions of "black cotton" soils) and a summary challenging the long-accepted model of homogeneous cultural evolution previously used in discussions of the Indus civilization.

273. Mehta, R.N. "Champaner: An Experiment in Medieaval Archaeology," in *Madhu: Recent Researches in Indian Archaeology and Art History* edited by M.S. Nagaraja Rao. New Delhi, 1981: 119-128.

This paper reports on the initial stages of excavation and mapping of the medieval city of Champaner in eastern Gujarat. Following a review of the available literary references, the reconnaissance, survey and photography, and results of the limited excavation are presented. The entire project was seen as an experiment to determine useful methods for further use in Indian urban archaeology.

274. Sonawane, V.H. "Tarsang-A First Excavated Mesolithic Rock-shelter of Gujarat," in *Indian Archaeology: New Perspectives* edited by R.K. Sharma. Delhi: Agam Kala Prakashan, 1982: 59-64.

A survey of the granite hills of the Panchmahala district of Gujarat revealed numerous rockshelters with evidence of human use in various historical periods, chiefly as religious centers. The shelter at Tarsang, however, was notable for its evidence of occupation during the Mesolithic, dated to 5000-2000 B.C. on the basis of similarities with other regional sites. This report summarizes the results of test excavations, including details of the massive number of flaked stone tools and the manufacturing sections of the site.

275. Rissman, Paul. "The Oriyo Test Excavation and the Study of the Harappan Tradition

in Gujarat," in *South Asian Archaeology 1983* edited by Janine Schotsmans and Maurizio Taddei. Naples: Istituto Universitario Orientale, 1985: 345-355.

In 1981, the Gujarat Prehistoric Project was formed as a joint effort of the Gujarat State Department of Archaeology and the American Institute of Indian Studies "to address the gaps in our knowledge of Harappan culture change in Gujarat and to concentrate specifically on the economic factors contributing to culture change." (p. 345-346) This article reports on the results of excavation at the mound of Oriyo Timbo in Bhavnagar District, whose results indicate a flexible pastoral economy jointly based upon agriculture and domestic herds of goats and cattle. This model is then applied to known data for the later Harappan era as a possible explanation of economic shifts during the final period of regional occupation in which known Harappan sites drop dramatically in number.

276. Soundararajan, K.V. "Kutch Harappan – A Corridor of the Indus Phase," in *Frontiers of the Indus Civilization* edited by B.B. Lal and S.P.Gupta. New Delhi: Books and Books, 1984: 217-226.

A summary discussion of the local form of Harappan culture known from the Kutch region of Gujarat, based upon data from the excavations at Desalpur and Surkotada. Stratigraphic profiles from each site are presented for reference.

277. Dhavalikar, M.K. "Kuntasi: A Harappan Port in Western India," in *South Asian Archaeology 1989* edited by Catherine Jarrige. Madison, Wisconsin: Prehistory Press, 1992: 73-81.

A summary of three seasons of excavation results since 1987 from the site of Kuntasi near the Arabian Sea in Gujarat, which bears evidence of primary Harappan occupation beginning about 2200 B.C. Analysis of the structures and associated deposits indicates the site served as both a center of small manufacturing (chiefly of pottery and beads of semi-precious stones) and a storage site for exports. A site plan and photographs of the workshop area and gateway are included.

278. Joshi, Jagat Pati. *Excavation at Surkotada 1971-72 and Exploration in Kutch.* New Delhi: Director General, Archaeological Survey of India, 1990.

The eighty-seventh *Memoir* issued by the Archaeological Survey of India, this massive detailed report covers two subjects, the results of excavation in 1971 and 1972 at the Harappan site of Surkotada in Kutch and a more general survey and assessment of the region's prehistoric cultural sequence. While prior fieldwork had indicated human activity in the area from the Stone Age onwards, only a few Harappan era sites were known in the two thousand square kilometer tract of Saurashtra. Three separate surveys carried out between December 1964 and January 1965 yielded over one hundred and twenty new sites of all periods, one of which was Surkotada. Questions addressed through its excavation were the expansion, diffusion, and decay of the Harappan civilization in a specific geographic region.The mound itself lies twelve kilometers northwest of Adesar in

Kutch and was first discovered by Joshi in December, 1964. Results of the two seasons work indicate "a sequence of three cultural subperiods well-within the span of Harappan chronology" (p. 17) and dating to 2300-1700 B.C. The majority of this text outlines the characteristics of these three eras according to architecture, pottery types in use (the largest section of the report, and illustrated with high quality line drawings and sections), burial patterns and artifacts ranging from stone tools through copper and bronze objects to shell bangles and a large number of carnelian beads, the latter possibly manufactured at Surkotada. Technical analyses of the animal bones, shell and plant remains found are appended. The regional "exploration in Kutch" referred to in the title is reviewed in the final section, with finds from the Stone Age to the historical period summarized. Among the field methods used was learning the usual routes followed by contemporary caravans crosing Kutch from east to west and tracing them to locate ancient sites. One hundred and twenty-one black and white photographs illustrate the Surkotada finds as well as the sites of Kotara, Kotadi and Pabumath.

279. Orton, Nancy Pinto. "Red Polished Ware From Gujarat: A Catalogue of Twelve Sites," in *Rome and India: The Ancient Sea Trade* edited by Vimala Begley and Richard Daniel. Madison: University of Wisconsin Press, 1991: 46-81.

The sites referred to in the title of this piece are Aledhar, Amreli, Baid, Bhoji-Kadwar, Chhara, Hubakvadi, Malsaram, Pariyadhar, Sutrapada, Umbari, Una and Vasxai, each illustrated by sections of the type of red ware found during surface surveys in the 1950's of some ninety sites. Later work by the author added over four hundred locations to the corpus of data on this pottery type. The more than 160 varieties of rim styles found, in her view, "indicate that there is no direct influence on Indian ceramics from the Mediterranean world as a result of contact with Roman traders." (p. 47)

280. Possehl, Gregory. "Govindbhai-no Vadi: A Modern Farmer's Garden in Gujarat and Its Ethnoarchaeological Significance," in *Living Traditions: Studies in the Ethnoarchaeology of South Asia* edited by Bridger Allchin. Columbia, Missouiri: South Asia Publications,1994: 193-204.

Babar Kot, "one of the few well-stratified Sorath Harappan sites," (p.,193) was originally discovered and investigated in 1955/56. This article reports on a 1990-91 project at the site aimed at obtaining information on plant and animal use, expanded through comparison of a simple but highly sophisticated irrigation system constructed by a neighboring farmer. Observations of its function are paralleled with the documented agricultural systems known from other Harappan sites such as Mohenjo-Daro.

281. Kenoyer, Jonathan Mark, Massimo Vidale and Kuldeep K.Bhan. "Carnelian Bead Production in Khambhat, India: An Ethnoarchaeological Study," in *Living Traditions: Studies In the Ethnoarchaeology of South Asia* edited by Bridget Allchin. Columbia, Missouri: South Asia Publications, 1994: 281-306.

The authors note that "the ethnoarchaeological study of Khambhat bead making has been an attempt to record a wide set of data on this traditional specialized industry before it is completely transformed by technological change." (p. 281) In the regional archaeological record, manufacturing of stone beads can be traced back to the period of the Indus civilization at such sites as Chanhu-daro and Mohenjo-daro. Results of this study include patterns in the different types of workshops, production of waste materials and finished objects, all of which may retrieved in excavation, indicating that "a vast amount of ...relevant information can be obtained through systematic ethnoarchaeological research of a traditional craft." (p. 283) Possible applications of this approach to other areas of Indian archaeology are reviewed.

282. Herman, Charles Frank, and K.Krishnan. "Micaceous Red Ware: A Gujarat Proto-Historic Cultural Complex Or Just Ceramics?" in *South Asian Archaeology 1993* edited by Asko Parpola and Petteri Koskikallio. Helsinki: Suomalainen Tiedekatemia, 1994: 225-243.

One of the distinctive pottery types identified for the Bronze Age era of Gujarat, micaceous red ware has, however, not received separate consideration until recently. This article presents a review and evaluation of the scattered literature on this ware, positing it as representing a local cultural phenomenon predating the Harappan entry into this region of India. Factors influencing the issue include the intensive search for Harappan era sites in post-Partition era Indian archaeology, a tendency to interpret local Gujarat materials in an Harappan context (given the discovery of the major site of Lothal), late recognition of this ware as a unique feature of Chalcolithic Gujarat in the early 1960's following the end of excavations at both Lothal and Rangpur, and the lengthy delay in issuing the Lothal site report. An associated cultural complex, "defined by a distinct interconnected body of material culture (architecture, potteries, small finds, metallurgy, etc.) from which specific spatial organization and socio-economic dynamics can be derived" (p. 235) is viewed as retrievable through a renewal of investigations at Lothal. A classification scheme for this ware is also presented.

283. Reddy, Seetha Narahari. *Plant Usage and Subsistence Modeling: An Ethnoarchaeological Approach to the Late Harappan of Northwest India.* Ph.D. dissertation, University of Wisconsin, 1994.

Based upon the author's participation in ongoing field projects at the sites of Oriyo Timbo and Babar Kot in Gujarat, this dissertation "examines the importance of millets in pastoral and settled farming communities during the Late Harappan (2100-1300 B.C.)." (p. 1) The broader theoretical issue of agriculture and pastoralism as complementary rather than exclusive economic systems in this era of Gujarat's prehistory (noted for the proliferation of settlements in arid regions) is also explored.Three types of data were combined in the research structure: ethnographic studies of contemporary crop processing methods (with a view toward establishing models of grain processing and its by-products applicable in an archaeological context), carbon isotope analysis of domesticated animal bones recovered from the excavations, and archaeobotany. The two sites showed a marked contrast in the character of their economies, with Oriyo Timbo exhibiting an absence of cultivation as oppposed the positive identification of millet cultivation at Babar Kot. Eight chapters set forth the historical background of regional archaeology in Gujarat, the theoretical approaches used in archaeology to study paleoethnobotàny and crop processing, ethnographic crop processing studies and the models based on them, archaeobotany of the two sites selected and the application of an integrated economic model within an archaeological context. A general discussion of the value of this approach to the analysis of Late Harappan completes the work.

284. Allchin, F.R. and Jagat Pati Joshi. *Excavations At Malvan*. New Delhi: Director General, Archaeological Survey of India, 1995.

As indicated by the subtitle, this ninety-second *Memoir* of the Archaeological Survey of India reports on the "collaboration of the Archaeological Survey of India and Cambridge University in 1970, on the Gujarat Plain." The chief problems underlying the choice of Malvan for excavation were "to investigate the southern limit of the Indus Civilization in Gujarat, to find out what if any links might have survived the withering Indus influence and how far these influences may have penetrated in a diffused form to the northern Deccan." (p. 3) The site itself is located in the lower estuary of the Tapti River, and was first discovered by the authors in December 1967 during a survey of the Gujarat coastal plain which visited thirty-two sites. The 1970 dig uncovered only two periods of occupation at the site, both post-Harappan in date and predating the arrival of iron.Individual chapters present the local geomorphology and geography of Malvan, stratigraphic sections, the types of ceramics found, stone,metal,shell and terracotta artifacts and beads, and analyses of pollen,sediment and animal skeletal samples. Twenty black and white photographs are included and illustrate overall views of the site, stratigraphic sections, and animal bone fragments. The long delay in publishing this report is explained in the preface.

Haryana

285. Francfort, F.C. "The Indo-French Archaeological Project in Haryana and Rajasthan," in *South Asian Archaeology 1985* edited by Karen Frifelt and Per Sorensen. London: Curzon Press, 1989: 260-264.

Reportage of two seasons of field work done in 1983 and 1984, testing the hypothesis that "protohistoric India developed artificial irrigation systems similar to those of Mesopotamia and Central Asia." (p. 260) Work was centered on an area west of Delhi in the drainages of the Ghaggar and Chautang Rivers. A geoarchaeological survey revealed canal systems of different periods. Site distribution reflected longterm usage of land areas outside the vanished rivers' banks, with a sharp reduction in the Late Harappan period. The construction, use and reuse of canal irrigation systems should thus be added as a factor when analysing the prehistory of this region of India.

286. Joshi, Jagat Pati et.al. *Excavation at Bhagwanpura 1975-76, and Other Explorations and Excavations 1975-81 in Haryana, Jammu, Kashmir and Punjab*. New Delhi: Director General Archaeological Survey of India, 1993.

The excavations at Bhagwanpura centered on the question of bridging the gap between the Harappan culture and the later culture characterized by the distinctive pottery type known as Painted Grey Ware, thought by some to represent the arrival of the Aryans. It was part of a more general series of investigations aimed at clarifying specific questions relating to India's "Dark Age," which involved re-examination of previously explored locations in eight districts of Haryana, the Punjab, Jammu and Kashmir. This latter survey is reported on in the final section of the text.

Bhagwanpura itself is a mound lying some twenty-four kilometers north of Kurukshetra near the Sarasvati River. The present thoroughly illustrated report summarizes in detail data indicating that the late Harappan culture was contemporaneous with the Painted Grey Ware complex in this region. The text opens with a general statement of research goals, a description of the site itself, and a useful "Summary of Results." Succeeding pages present evidence of daily life ranging from house plans to domesticated animals and religion. The largest section deals with the pottery types found. Separate sections on the highly varied terracotta artifacts, inscribed materials, analyses of the human skeletal remains and results of formal laboratory studies (ranging from thermoluminescence to soils, glass and metallurgy) of samples completes the study.

Himachal Pradesh

287. Vogel, Jean Philippe. *Antiquities of Chamba State*. V.1: Calcutta, Superintendent of Government Printing, 1911; v.2 New Delhi: Manager of Publications, 1957.

The state of Chamba lies among the western Himalaya in the northwestern reaches of Himachal Pradesh. This two-volume set had its inception in 1902, when Jean Philippe Vogel, then superintendent of the Northern Circle of the Archaeological Survey of India, made his first visit to Chamba, beginning what would prove to be a seven-year effort of collecting epigraphical material, eventually numbering one hundred and thirty inscriptions. Of these, fifty date to the period before the coming of Islam and eighty after that time. The first volume, entitled *Inscriptions of the Pre-Muhammadan Period* and issued in 1911, was the result. Its opening chapter sets forth in detail the geography of Chamba and its notable towns followed by discussion of the alphabets used and the dynasties which have ruled over the centuries. The fifty inscriptions are then presented in full followed by translations, thus creating a uniquely accessible body of data for this region of the Himalayas. Forty black and white photographic plates and rubbings are included depicting many of the inscriptions in their original settings. Four appendixes list other inscribed materials relating to the state. One interesting point made is that the large number of inscriptions from such a secluded place as Chamba only serves to point out the larger amount of similar materials formerly extant in more accessible regions such as Kashmir which have since been lost. Vogel originally intended to complete his analysis of the Chamba inscriptions, and had begun work on the second volume *Medieval and Later Inscriptions* but left it unfinished upon his return to the Netherlands. Prior to the disruption of most research in the subcontinent caused by World War II, Vogel contacted the Director General of Archaeology in India with a view toward having his interrupted work brought to completion. In 1939, the task was granted to B. Chand Chhabra, Government Epigraphist for India, who spent two months in Chamba examining the eighty-two copper-plate charters (representing twelve of Chamba's successive rulers) remaining to be published and making fresh transcripts. Chhabra's volume, finally published in 1957, continues the format established by Vogel, giving all inscriptions in full accompanied by translations. This two-volume set was republished in 1994 by the Archaeological Survey of India.

288. Lal, B.B. "Palaeoliths From The Beas and Banganga Valleys, Panjab," *Ancient India* 12 (1956): 58-92.

Following the partition of British India into the modern states of India and Pakistan in 1948, many palaeolithic sites associated with the Sohan culture became inaccessible to Indian excavators. This situation stimulated fresh survey within the new political boundaries for other sites. The present article reports on the discovery of four sites (Guler, Dehra, Dhaliara and Kangra) in western Himachal Pradesh in June, 1955. The summary discussion of choppers, chopping tools and handaxes and their significance will be useful for researchers unfamiliar with prior work on this topic in southern Asia.

289. Diserens, Helene. "Devi on the Lion Throne in the Kulu Valley (Himachal Pradesh), India," in *South Asian Archaeology 1985* edited by Karen Frifelt and Per Sorensen. London: Curzon Press, 1989: 372-379.

In June, 1983, the author was able to locate nine sculpted stone stelae depicting the goddess Devi at springs scattered across the Kulu Valley in Himachal Pradesh. Three types are distinguished and discussed, and the lion throne imagery related to similar carvings from contemporary temples. Dating is placed at between the ninth and twelfth centuries A.D.

Jammu and Kashmir

290. Kak, Ram Chandra. *Antiquities of Bhimbar and Rajauri.* Calcutta: Superintendent of Government Printing, 1923.

This fourteenth *Memoir* of the Archaeological Survey of India briefly reports on ancient remains in two districts in the province of Jammu as they existed in the first decades of the twentieth century. Based on a twenty-day field journey, the text notes a substantial number of *sarais* and mosques dating to the Mughal period, "but a discovery of still greater importance is the existence of the group of Kashmiri temples at Saidabad and Panjnara." (p. 15) Useful as a benchmark against which changes in the subsequent state of preservation of the various monuments on this main road to Srinagar may be measured. Twelve photographs show various caravan *sarais*, mosques and the medieval temples cited above, as well as ground plans of the sarais at Thanna, Saidabad, Chingus and the temple at Panjnara.

291. Kak, Ram Chandra. *Ancient Monuments of Kashmir*. London: The India Society, 1933.

Written by the director of the local archaeological survey from 1919 to 1929, this volume provides extensive reportage on forty-four sites within the Vale of Kashmir. The first three chapters provide detailed background on the physical geography, political history and architectural styles of Kashmir, whose name is derived from the term for saffron, long a major export of the region. The bulk of the text dealing with specific monuments lies in the fourth, fifth and six chapters, devoted to structures in and around the capital of Srinagar, those lying in the northwest portion of the Vale of Kashmir and those in the southwest. An examination of the listed sites indicates that the majority are either Buddhist or Muslim in nature, with a few exceptions such as the megaliths at Yandrahom. A section on the excavations conducted at Harwan by the author and discussion of the apsidal temple and extensive pavement of decorated tiles dating from the third century A.D. is included in the Srinagar section, noted as "the first time…an illustrated account of those excavations has been published." (p. xv) A portfolio of seventy-two black and white photographs and architectural drawings completes the work.

292. Kak, Ram Chandra. "Jammu and Kashmir," in *Revealing India's Past: A Co-Operative Record of Archaeological Conservation and Exploration in India and Beyond*. London: The India Society, 1939.: 279-288.

The first survey of the archaeological remains of Kashmir was done by the industrious Sir Alexander Cunningham, said account being published in the September, 1848 issue of the *Journal of the Asiatic Society of Bengal*. Little more was done except for study of the standing monuments until the reorganization of the Archaeological Survey of India in 1902 under Sir John Marshall. This essay was written by the former director of the state's local archaeological department from 1919 to 1929, focusing on work done since 1912. Major sites reviewed are Avatipur, Parihasapura, Ushkar, Pandrethan, Martand and Harwan. The corroboration of the historical information recorded by Kalhana in the *Rajatarangini*, the "River of Kings" chronicle, is noted. Problems of restoration (such as the difficulty of removing intrusive trees without demolishing the ancient buildings they have become integral to) are also discussed.

293. Pande, B.M. "Neolithic Hunting Scene On A Stone Slab from Burzahom, Kashmir," *Asian Perspectives* 14 (1971): 134-138.

Discussion and analysis of a stone slab recovered during excavations at Burzahom in the Srinagar district of Kashmir, where four occupation levels spanning the Neolithic, Megalithic and early historical periods have been identified, the former dating to the third millennium B.C. The slab had been reused as part of a rectangular structure and depicts two human figures hunting a stag. Its importance lies in the fact that it is "the first find of a graphic representation of neolithic life recovered from regular stratified excavations...the first indubitable example of neolithic art in India." (p. 137) Background information on the Northwestern Neolithic Culture and past excavations at Burzahom are included.

294. Sankalia, H.D. "New Evidence for Early Man in Kashmir," *Current Anthropology* 12 (4-5) (October-December 1971): 558-562.

In their survey of Ice Age glaciations in the Himalayas done in 1939, de Terra and Paterson "expressed surprise that no stone tools of early man had been found in the Kashmir Valley proper." (p. 558) Work done at the site of Pahlgam in the Liddar Valley in 1969 and 1970 by the author and colleagues yielded evidence of a tool industry characterized by massive flakes, choppers, scrapers, borers and handaxes. This article reports on each find in detail, illustrated by line drawings.

295. Basu, Arabinda and Anadi Pal. *Human Remains from Burzahom*. Calcutta: Archaeological Survey of India, 1980.

Issued as the eightieth *Memoir* of the Archaeological Survey, this publication presents analyses of the metric and non-metric features of the dentition, long bones and skulls of ten skeletons recovered from the Neolithic mound of Burzahom in Kashmir. Topics discussed include sex and age determination, trephination, stature and proportions of the individuals, all sections illustrated with black and white photographs of selected specimens. A bibliography of related literature in both physical anthropology and archaeology is included.

296. Agrawal, D.P. et.al. "Late Quaternary Environmental and Archaeological Changes in Kashmir," in *South Asian Archaeology 1985* edited by Karen Frifelt and Per Sorensen. London: Curzon Press, 1989: 271-276.

A summary of "the preliminary findings of the environmental changes witnessed by the Kashmir valley and the relationship of the archaeological settlements to these changes," (p. 271) Palaeoclimatic data was obtained through a variety of techniques including lake and bog pollen samples. Results indicate five distinct eras for the Kashmiri environment. The history of archaeological research in the valley (begun with excavations at Burzahom in the early 1960's) is next reviewed. Local chronology indicates an Upper Palaeolithic stone tool industry succeeded by settled Neolithic cultures during the climatic optimum between 5000-4000 B.C. and the Chalcolithic settlement of Semthan ca. 390 B.C. A systematic survey of the entire valley has been initiated to track palaeodemographic changes through time.

297. Saar, S.S. *Archaeology, Ancestors of Kashmir*. New Delhi: Lalit Art Publishers, 1992.

Written by a participant in the fieldwork at the mound of Burzahom north of Srinagar between 1961 and 1971,this text presents the major findings from the horizontal excavations in a manner suited to a popular audience. An updated occupation sequence from 2300 B.C. to the eighth century A.D. is proposed. Separate chapters present the aceramic and pottery-using Neolithic levels, the megalithic period and a note on historic era artifacts. A useful bibliography of cited sources (chiefly numbers of the *Indian Archaeological Reports* series) is appended. Researchers will find the two-page cross-section "Schematic Chronology" of the mound most useful of the illustrations.

Karnataka

298. Krishna, M.H. "Mysore," in *Revealing India's Past: A Co-Operative Record of Archaeological Conservation and Exploration in India and Beyond*. London: India Society, 1939: 262-269.

This essay is one of eight done for this volume assessing the state of archaeological work in what were at this time states under traditional rulers allied to the government of the Raj. The development of the extensive and detailed field work done in the limited physical area of Mysore state began in 1879 with the interest of B.L. Rice, employed as a local educational officer. In 1884 he became part-time Director of Archaeology, and assisted in constituting a formal Archaeological Department in 1890. He laid the foundations for later work through his collection of more than nine thousand inscriptions and their publication after 1886 in the twelve volumes of the series *Epigraphia Carnatica* and the compilation of the *Mysore Gazetteer*, where "information collected ...about the antiquities of various places in Mysore and their traditions was embodied in the notes." (p. 264) The full scope of his activities in collection and the preservation of state monuments is traced, followed by a review of the work of his successors in Mysore and the publication of their results. Special attention is also given to the development of the manuscript collections of the Oriental Library in Mysore city. Essential reading for anyone wishing a concise summary of the history of archaeology in this region of India, where "though archaeologists have been busily working...for nearly fifty years, scarcely a year passes without some new and interesting discovery." (p. 268)

299. Thapar, B.K. "Maski 1954: A Chalcolithic Site of the Southern Deccan," *Ancient India* 13 (1957): 4-142.

In an effort to continue tracing the sequence of prehistoric occupation of the Deccan previously identified in the excavations at Brahmagiri, the site of Maski (first noted in 1870 by Robert Bruce Foote) in northeast Karnataka was investigated between January and March, 1954. This lengthy report reviews the known geology of the region before offering a highly detailed analysis of the season's finds. Stratigraphy of the four cuttings and photographs of pottery type specimens of pottery recovered are reviewed. The two most extensive sections of the text are devoted to analyses of the ceramics and more than seven hundred microliths. The author also discusses the significance of the finds at Maski in light of then-current interest in the "chalcolithic" cultures of central and southern India.

300. Nagaraja Rao, M.S. and Kailash Chandra Malhotra. *The Stone Age Hill Dwellers of Tekkalakota*. Poona: Deccan College, 1965.

The granite hills of Tekkalakota near the Tungabadhra valley in eastern Karnataka were discovered in 1962 to possess relatively undisturbed cultural deposits dating to the Neolithic period. Excavations were begun on the middle spur of the hill range between November 1962 and March 1963 and their results form the subject of this publication. Two distinct cultures are identified with a beginning date of 2000 B.C. suggested by analogy with other similar sites. Rao first presents the region's geology and recent history, then reviews site stratigraphy and structural remains (including circular houses) and the seven burials located. The pottery, ground and polished stone artifacts, stone blades, copper objects, terracottas (ranging from lamps to portions of figures of bulls and humans) and animal remains recovered are presented in detail. This area was chosen for survey in the hope of finding sites linking the Neolithic of Karnataka with data obtained from sites of this period in the Deccan.

301. Seshadri. M. "Roman Contacts With South India," *Archaeology* 19 (4) (October, 1966): 244-247.

An analysis of a hoard of two hundred fifty-six Roman silver denarii found in 1965 during airport construction at Bangalore. The coins (which date to the reigns of Augustus and Tiberius) are analysed and placed in context with materials from others of the sixty-eight similar finds known at this time, fifty-seven of them from south of the Vindhya Mountains. Ancient trade patterns are then discussed, with pepper and semiprecious stones the chief commodities.A partial table of these sites is appended, beginning with the 1891 Yeshwantpur find, also in Bangalore. States represented in the assemblages include Andhra Pradesh, Kerala and Madras as well as Karnataka. Researchers will find the map of site distributions particularly valuable.

302. Nagaraja Rao, M.S. "New Evidence For Neolithic Life In India: Excavations in the Southern Deccan," *Archaeology* 20 (1) (January, 1967): 28-35.

Written by the director of excavations at the sites of Tekkalakota, Sanganakallu (first investigated in 1948) and the river valley site of Hallur, this article reviews data on the early Neolithic inhabitants of Karnataka as known from recent field work. Details of house construction, problems of dating, pottery and stone tool technology are included, as are photographs of sample artifacts and general overviews of all three sites. Researchers unfamiliar with the region's past should read this piece as a foundation for more technical works such as the author's 1965 volume *The Stone Age Hill Dwellers of Tekkalakota*.

303. Paddayya, K. "The Middle Palaeolithic Culture of the Shorapur Doab, Karnataka," *Journal of Indian History* 52 (1) (April 1974): 1-19.

This article presents an abridged version of the account of a group of sites discovered between 1965 and 1968 as part of a more general study of palaeolithic sites in this region of southwest Karnataka carried out as the author's doctoral project at Poona University. A brief review of local geography and geology is followed by profiles of nine sites yielding Middle Palaeolithic chert tool industries. Of the 1928 artifacts found only 328 are finished tools (scrapers, borers, points and multiple-use blades.) Further analysis of associated faunal materials is called for. A map showing the distribution of prehistoric sites in the Shorapur region is included, along with high quality line drawings of sample artifacts.

304. Sundara, A. "On the Megalithic Site at Rajawala: New Light on the Passage Chamber Tomb Tradition," *Journal of Indian History*, 53 (3) (December 1975): 361-365.

The site of Rajawala in east-central Karnataka was first noted in 1852 as possessing thirty-three chamber tombs. This paper reports on the re-examination of the tomb group in October 1971, reduced to twenty-five through the destruction of several structures by conversion to arable land. Rajawala's megalithic tombs all exhibit one distinctive plan of construction, the third site at which this type of passage tomb different from more widely recognized forms has been seen. Comparisons are drawn with the megaliths at Hallur and Kaladgi, and the new class is defined by construction features and geographic distribution, A provisional date of 900-700 B.C. is assigned to the Rajawala tombs.

305. Paddaya, K. "An Acheulean Occupation Site at Hunsgi, Peninsular India: A Summary of the Results of Two Seasons of Excavation (1975-76)," *World Archaeology* 8 (3) (February 1977): 344-355.

Detailed coverage of the first two seasons of excavation at a site in the Hunsgi valley of northern Karnataka, where a stone tool manufacturing site of the Acheulean period was uncovered. The author notes that the deposit of tools is "a cultural horizon preserved in its primary context...Such finds remain rare in the Indian subcontinent." (p. 346) Cleavers, handaxes, choppers, knives, scrapers, picks and polyhedrons are the principal object types among the 291 artifacts thus far recovered. The Hunsgi materials are set in the context of other Acheulean finds made to date in India.

306. Paddayya, K. "New Research Designs and Field Techniques in the

Palaeolithic Archaeology of India," *World Archaeology* 10 (1) (June 1978): 94-110.

In pursuing research on the Stone Age of India, much of the data has been limited due its sources in secondary deposits such as alluvial soils. The author presents data from a survey of the Hunsgi Valley in Karnataka which challenges the notion that primary occupation sites (such as butchering areas or tool workshops) of the Palaeolithic are difficult to identify in India. Field methods modeled on those used at Olduvai Gorge, involving the intensive examination of limited geographic areas already known as possessing archaeological materials and favoring preservation, are cited as making possible the retrieval of more detailed information than has hitherto been available on this phase of Indian history. Application of the method to the Hunsgi drainage has yielded a pattern of settlement limited to the valley and associated with permanent streams. Test excavations have uncovered a complex living surface, and ongoing analyses of the data are reviewed.

307. Allchin, F.R. "Textile Impressions From the South Indian Iron Age," in *P.E.P. Deraniyagala Comemmoration Volume* edited by Thelma Gunawardana et.el. Colombo: Lake House Publishers, 1980: 64-67.

A brief report on the recognition of fabric imprints on pottery from the Karnataka Chalcolithic sites of Narasipur and Piklihal. The traces are matched with an historically recorded manufacturing technique of a type of ceramic known as *thali* which uses a rag to shape and smooth the vessel. These traces are "the first archaeological evidence for the presence and probable manufacture of cotton cloth from…Karnataka during the first millennium B.C." (p. 64)

308. Fritz, John and George Michell. "The Vijayanagara Documentation and Research project: A Progress Report," in *South Asian Archaeology 1981* edited by Bridget Allchin. Cambridge University Press, 1984: 295-304.

A well-written history of the first two years of the comprehensive analysis and recording project begun at Vijayanagara in 1980. Emphasis was initially placed upon the retrieval of plans of all districts within the city (presaging the more extensive 1984 book *Where Kings and Gods Meet*), examination of standing structures from a conservation viewpoint, and study of building techniques. Examples of the high quality maps and section drawings are included.

309. Fritz, John M. George Michell and M.S. Nagaraja Rao. "Vijayanagara: The City of Victory," *Archaeology* 39 (2) (March/April 1986): 22-29.

A general presentation of this major Hindu urban site in northeastern Karnataka. Excellent as an introduction to this area of Indian archaeology. Researchers will find it useful to read this piece first before consulting the substantial literature on this period. Although first surveyed by Colin Mackenzie in 1799, formal archaeological fieldwork at this site did not begin until the late 1970s.

310. Fritz, John, George Michell and M.S. Nagaraja Rao. *Where Kings and Gods Meet: The Royal Centre at Vijayanagara, India.* Tucson: University of Arizona Press, 1984.

The documentation project upon which this book reports took as its aim the reflection of the relationship between ruler and divinity as expressed in the shaping of space at Vijayanagara. The authors focused on "the form and spatial organization of all visible features…we interpret these elements…as critical components in a system that established and maintained the authority of the imperial rulers." (p. 6) Eight chapters outline the scope of the project and define the various zones of the city, moving next to more detailed consideration of specific districts (the royal enclosures themselves, boundaries and routes, sacred art, platforms and palaces, and structures influenced by Islam) before the final summary. Illustrations are provided by high quality plans and sectional drawings of selected structures. A brief bibliography is included.

311. Blurton, T. Richard. "Palace Structures at Vijayanagara: The Archaeological Evidence," in *South Asian Archaeology 1985* edited by Karen Frifelt and Per Sorensen. London: Curzon Press, 1989: 426-440.

A discussion and analysis of the variety of secular structures found in the enclosures of the "Royal Center" of the medieval Hindu capital of Vijayanagara. These buildings are of special value for the knowledge of pre-Muslim architecture in India, as most other examples were constructed of wood and have since vanished. Attributes studied by the present survey are alignment and plan, platform decorations and ornaments, functions and decoration of internal chambers, varieties of columns and piers utilized, upper storeys and roof elements. The total preliminary picture is one of a complex used for both ritual and living functions. Readers may wish to pursue the arguments given here in the 1984 treatment of the city *Where Kings and Gods Meet.*

312. Fritz, John M and George Michell. "Interpreting the Plan Of A Medieval Hindu Capital, Vijayanagara," *World Archaeology* 19 (1) (June 1987): 105-129.

Observing that "before the period of the Muslim invasions (twelfth to thirteenth centuries) little material evidence of urbanization is available" (p. 105) for the medieval cities of India, this essay then focuses its attention on the ongoing study of the largest and most coherent site surviving from this era, Vijayanagara. The excellent state of preservation of a sizable portion of the city and the density of remaining structures has allowed for the retrieval of an overall city plan. Beginning with a consideration of the natural setting near the Tungabhadra River, several units are delineated and mapped: the sacred and royal centres, fortification walls, suburban settlements and a road system. An expanded treatment of this approach to Vijayanagara may be found in later articles and books by the authors, chiefly *Where Kings and Gods Meet.*

313. Fritz, John M. and George Michell. "Windows on the Past," *Archaeology* 42

(5) (September/October 1989): 40-47.

A discussion of the rediscovery of a set of photographic plates taken of Vijayanagara in 1856 by Alexander Greenlaw and their application to the interpretation of the standing structures of the site. Copies of several of the prints and modern views of the same public buildings are included.

314. Fritz, John M. and George Michell. *City of Victory: Vijayanagara, the Medieval Hindu Capital of Southern India*. New York: Aperture, 1991.

From the middle of the fourteenth century until its destruction by Muslim armies in the late sixteenth century, the "City of Victory" was the administrative center of Hindu rule over much of southern India. Its ruins are set within a striking landscape of granite hills two kilometers south of the Tungabadhra River valley and were in an unusually good state of preservation prior to their addition to UNESCO's World Heritage List. This lavishly illustrated volume discusses the ritual and social significance of all major structures, the political history of the regional Hindu dynasties, excerpts from accounts by visitors to Vijayanagara when it was a living city in 1520-1522 and full descriptions of every building and group of buildings. Recent work by an international team under UNESCO auspices is also reviewed.Appendices list the kings who ruled from Vijayanagara, a glossary of architectural terms and Hindu deities referred to in the text, and a bibliography of related literature.

315. Howell, J.R. et.al. *Excavations at Sannathi 1986-1989*. New Delhi: Director General, Archaeological Survey of India, 1995.

This ninety-third *Memoir* from the Archaeological Survey of India reports on three seasons of investigation of an early historic period city on the Bhima River. Work was centered on the second stupa mound and its associated platform and structures, with exploration of the fortifications system, the citadel, a bathing ghat, religious structures and the outer city carried out to expand general knowledge of the urban area. Separate chapters present an overview of the city and plan of excavation, the three main trenches and peripheral sampling conducted, and analyses of specific classes of artifacts found (pottery, coinage, sculptures and inscribed materials, and metal objects, chiefly copper and iron). The final chapter is unusually long and goes into detail as to procedures followed and conservation techniques applied to the Sannathi finds. Over fifty inscriptions dating to the Mauryan and Satavahana dynasties have been found, although the majority may be placed in the second century A.D. Forty photographs (some in color) depict the general features of the city site, major structures examined, details of remaining sculptures, coinage,beads and copper alloy artifacts.

Kerala

316. Poduval, R.V. "Travancore," in *Revealing India's Past: A Co-Operative Record of Archaeological Conservation and Exploration in India and Beyond.* London: The India Society, 1939: 297-305.

Travancore, a "Native State" with its capital at Trivandrum in southern Kerala, created its own Archaeological Department in 1896 "with a view to the collection and investigation of the available data relating to the political and economic history and ethnology of the country." (p. 297) In this essay, the Director of Archaeology reviews the progress of investigation during the previous forty years. Emphasis is laid upon the numerous ancient temples,megalithic monuments and burial urns which are the principal known prehistoric features. Fifteen hundred inscriptions provide ample data on Dravidian dynastic history, while the art of woodcarving is noted as a regional specialty. Special mention is made of the contacts enjoyed by this area in ancient times with the West, evidenced by finds of Roman coins dated betwwen 30 B.C. and 547 A.D. Direct excavation in Travancore had barely begun at the time this piece was written.

317. Thapar, B.K. "Porkalam 1948: Excavation of a Megalithic Urn-Burial," *Ancient India* 8 (1952): 3-16.

The urn-burial site selected at Porkalam was of a type common to both this region of central Kerala and Tamil Nadu, a circle of dresed stone blocks surrounding a pit with a pyriform vessel containing the actual burial, the whole sealed with a capstone. Finds included pottery types known from Brahmagiri and other sites in southern India with megalithic monuments and etched carnelian beads typical of the first century A.D. Detailed discussion and illustration of the artifacts recovered comprises the major part of this report.

318. Sharma, Y.D. "Rock-Cut Caves In Cochin," *Ancient India* 12 (1956): 93-115.

A discussion of data on five man-made caves in the laterite region of central Kerala originally surveyed in 1946. Following a discussion of the general features of their construction, the sites at Chovvannnur, Kandanisseri, Porkalam, Eyyal and Kattakampal are reviewed, with section plans and photographs provided. A possible sequence of development is suggested based upon details of construction. Artifacts from two of the caves (Kattakampal and Eyyal) recovered previously under controlled conditions link these excavations to the megalithic culture of the coast and identify them as burial sites.

319. Allchin, F.R. "A South Indian Copper Sword and Its Significance," in *South Asian Archaeology 1975* edited by J.E. Van Lohuizen-de Leeuw. Leiden: Brill, 1979: 106-118.

In 1928, a copper sword of the antenna style was discovered on a tea estate near Vandiperiyar in the Cardamom hills in southeastern Kerala. This paper discusses the find and sets it within a broader context of the Copper Age of southern India, proposing a common tradition of manufacture. Comparative dating assigns this sword and the possibly associated grave complexes of the local region to the second millennium B.C.

320. Rajendran, P. "Tenmalai Mesolithic Rockshelter- A Land Mark in the Prehistoric Research in Kerala," *Journal of Indian History* 62 (1-3) (April, August, December 1984): 7-9.

A note on excavations at the Mesolithic rockshelter habitation site of Tenmalai, located some one hundred kilometers inland on a spur of the Western Ghats in the Quilon district of southern Kerala, which has "laid a strong foundation in the case of the Mesolithic chronology of the region." (p. 7) Charcoal samples obtained along with the quartz flake tools yielded a date between 4000-3000 B.C. Researchers will find the lengthy bibliography reporting the series of excavations conducted by Rajendran at various sites across Kerala between 1974 and 1984 invaluable for tracing the development of archaeology within this state.

Madhya Pradesh

321. Cunningham, Sir Alexander. *The Stupa of Bharhut: A Buddhist Monument Ornamented With Numerous Sculptures Illustrated of Buddhist Legend and History in the Third Century B.C.* London, 1879: reprinted Varanasi, Indological Publishing House, 1962.

This edition of the primary site report on the field work done by Sir Alexander Cunningham at the ruins of the major Buddhist stupa at Bharhut was done as part of a planned series reissuing the entire corpus of his writings. The remains of the stupa and its surrounding railings and enclosure were first noted by him in November 1873 en route to Nagpur, with excavations occurring for a period of ten days in February 1874 and again in March, the entire circle of the railing being cleared. The bulk of the text is devoted to an identification and explication of the carvings recovered. Sixty-two high quality plates present Cunningham's original plan of Bharhut, sculptural elements of the inner and outer gateways (including illustrations of the Jataka tales) and copies of those inscriptions found. Of interest to the history of Indian archaeology are Cunningham' s comments in the introduction regarding the placement of the sculptures in the Indian Museum in Calcutta, a circumstance he preferred to their being "consigned to the still more oblivious vaults of the British Museum." (p. *vii*)

322. Chanda, Ramaprasad. *Dates of the Votive Inscriptions of the Stupas at Sanchi.* Calcutta: Superintendent Government Printing, India: 1919. Reprinted New Delhi: Indological Book Corporation, 1977.

This first volume of the *Memoirs of the Archaeological Survey of India* offers a detailed example of the application of epigraphical research techniques to the dating problems of a major ancient Indian structure, the stupa complex at Sanchi.

Topics involved center around the comparison of the varying forms of Brahmi letters with texts and inscriptions whose date is known. This particular research was instigated by Sir John Marshall, at the time Director of the Archaeological Survey, in an effort to reevaluate conflicting dates assigned to Sanchi by various scholars, beginning with Sir Alexander Cunningham's work in the late nineteenth century.

323. Garde, M.B. "Gwalior," in *Revealing India's Past: A Co-Operative Record of Archaeological Conservation and Exploration in India and Beyond* edited by Sir John Cumming. London: The India Society, 1939: 289-296.

Written by the Director of Archaeology for the then-independent State of Gwalior, this essay traces archaeological activity and conservation work in the region from the first surveys done by Alexander Cunningham between 1862 and 1885 to date. Following its creation in 1910, the local Archaeological Department first undertook a census of all architectural monuments, recording artistic features, inscriptions and actions necessary for preservation. Based on this data, a conservation program was initiated in 1920, with a museum opened in the Gujari Mahal in Gwalior city in 1922.

324. Chandra, Ramaprasad. "Bhopal: Sanchi Stupa," in *Revealing India's Past: A Co-Operative Record of Archaeological Conservation and Exploration in India and Beyond* edited by Sir John Cumming. London: The India Society, 1939: 313-317.

The now-famous Great Stupa at Sanchi in Bhopal State has been a center of antiquarian interest since its discovery in 1819. This article follows the excavation and restorations done at the site, noting the damage done by test shafts and the extensive work headed by Sir John Marshall between 1912 and 1919. Researchers will find the references to early publications and reports of particular value.

325. Chandra, Ramaprasad. "Nagod: Bharhut Stupa," in *Revealing India's Past: A Co-Operative Record of Archaeological Conservation and Exploration in India and Beyond* edited by Sir John Cumming. London: The India Society, 1939: 317-321.

A review of the principal features of the Mauryan era stupa at Bharhut, near Satna in northeastern Madhya Pradesh. Special attention is given to the artistic detail of the sculptured ground railing. The site was originally surveyed in 1873 by Alexander Cunningham.

326. Kala, Satish Chandra. *Bharhut Vedika: A Critical Study of Bharhut Scupltures in the Collection of the Municipal Museum, Allahabad.* The Museum, 1951.

This slim volume by the curator of the Allahabad Museum treats recovered sculptural elements from the *vedika* (carved railing) of the great stupa at Bharhut, first excavated by Alexander Cunningham in 1873-74. After summarizing in some detail the initial work at the site (including the excavation of an entire quadrant of the railing and the removal of various pieces to the Indian Museum in Calcutta), attention shifts to fifty-four stone carvings retrieved during the 1930's from villages in the Bharhut area, where they had been incorporated into existing structures. They include thirty-two pillars, cross-bars, coping-stones, and fragments of a stairway. Thirty-seven monochrome plates provide illustration. Readers unfamiliar with the site should consult Cunningham's original 1879 report, *The Stupa of Bharhut.*

327. Sankalia, H.D., B. Subbarao and S.B. Deo. "The Archaeological Sequence of Central India," *Southwestern Journal of Anthropology* 9 (4)) (Winter 1953): 343-356.

Between December 1952 and March 1953, two mound groups at Maheshwar and Navda Toli on the Narmada River in Madhya Pradesh were tested with a view toward establishing a cultural sequence for Central India bridging prehistory and historic times. This article summarizes the results of this initial season, emphasizing the discovery of a new phase marked by advanced microlithic technology and a wide range of painted and plain red wares. Microliths from both sites are illustrated in detailed line drawings. Given the subsequent importance of these sites for Central Indian archaeology, researchers will find it useful to begin with this original report.

328. Deva, Krishna. "The Temples of Khajuraho In Central India," *Ancient India* 15 (1959): 43-65.

Dating from the late ninth to the twelfth centuries A.D., the temple complex at Khajuraho has long been one of the most famous religious sites of all India. Each of the fifteen major structures at the site is profiled, followed by separate sections treating the sculptural art and iconography with accompanying photographs. A selected bibliography of related literature is provided. While not strictly archaeological in nature, this article provides readers with a useful summary of information on a frequently referenced site.

329. Joshi, R.V. "Stone-Age Industries of the Damoh Area, Madhya Pradesh," *Ancient India* 17 (1961): 5-36.

A detailed report on a survey of the Sonar, Kopra and Bearma Rivers in north central Madhya Pradesh carried out in November and December of 1958 which identified fifteen Stone Age sites. The area was chosen to permit comparison of occupation at this period between the Yamuna and Narmada drainages. Regional geologic structure and stratigraphy is set out, followed by an analysis of the one hundred Early Stone Age artifacts obtained from nine sites. Chief types of tools noted were handaxes, cleavers, scrapers, flakes and cores, each illustrated by both black and white photographs and line drawings. A second section analyses local finds of the microlithic flake tools and scrapers previously known from the Pravara River area of Maharashtra. Comparisons with the Narmada basin and the Palaeolithic of Europe and Africa are attempted.

330. Leshnik, Lorenz. *Sociological Interpretation in Archaeology: Some Examples From A Village Study in Central India*. Ph.D dissertation, University of Chicago, 1964.

The field work of this dissertation was done in the village of Navra Toli in the Nimar district of southwestern Madhya Pradesh between September, 1962 and August, 1963, and reflects the author's interest in the events and processes accompanying the rise of settled agricultural life in peninsular India. The theoretical focus centers on the relationship of specific material elements and social organization, using the village as an exploration of the idea that class (or caste) divisions can be retrieved from the archaeological record. Leshnik's approach emphasized "looking to the intra-cultural structure of an assemblage rather than to the inter-cultural significance." (p. 14) This study was also intended to create a body of data which could be used to clarify regional archaeological questions within Madhya Pradesh and test out the validity of then-current methods of sociological interpretation as applied to archaeology. Physical elements examined were agriculture and its associated tools and settlement patterns as a reflection of the caste system.

331. Joshi, R.V. "Acheulian Succession In Central India," *Asian Perspectives* 8 (1) (Summer 1964): 150-163.

The author defines the Central Indian region as "comprising the Narmada and the Tapti river basins and parts of the drainage area of the Son and the Godavari." (p. 150) This article begins by reviewing the status of knowledge on the region amassed by the prior thirty years of investigation, together with major physical geographic features. The majority of the work is devoted to the presentation and analysis of the two stone tool assemblages located on the hill of Adamgarh near Hoshangabad in Madhya Pradesh, first sampled in 1935. The role of pebble tools as a distinctive type in Indian palaeolithic archaeology is noted as requiring reevaluation on the basis of the Adamgarh data. Sample artifacts of both classes are illustrated.

332. Lal, Kanwar. *Immortal Khajuraho*. Delhi: Asia Press, 1965.

The grouping of some twenty-four temples near the village of Khajuraho in the Chhatarpur district of Madhya Pradesh is the focus of this lavishly illustrated volume. Concerning the condition of the site at the time of writing, the author notes that "more than fifty temples have totally disappeared." (p. 3) Maps offer an overall plan of the complex, with separate plans of the Lakshman and Kandariya Mahadev temples, and illustrate the development of the principal tower forms used over several centuries. A genealogy of the Chandel dynasty responsible for the creation of Khajuraho between the ninth and fourteenth centuries is included. Two hundred thirty-four plates present numerous sculptural elements, noting the world-famous erotic carvings. Researchers interested in obtaining a description of a specific structure should consult the eleventh chapter, "Among the Gods," which covers twenty-one buildings. While written more for the art historian than for the archaeologist, this volume offers a wealth of information on a frequently referenced site. A brief bibliography of related literature is provided.

333. Sankalia, Hasmukh Dhirajlal, Shantaram Bhalchandra Deo and Zainuddin Dawood Ansari. *Chalcolithic Navdatoli: The Excavations at Navdatoli, 1957-59.* Poona: Deccan College Postgraduate and Research Institute, 1971.

First sampled by a joint expedition mounted by the Universities of Bombay, Baroda and Poona in 1952-53, the site of Navdatoli (which lies on the Narbada River opposite Maheshwar in Madhya Pradesh) was revisited for three field seasons beginning in 1957. Taking as its goal the exploration of possible ancient cultural connections with Western Asia, the original investigators carried out "one of the first stratified horizontal excavations of a Chalcolithic site in India." (p. 8) This publication is the first formal report on this major excavation to be issued, albeit twelve years after completion of work. Beginning with discussion of the physical topography of the Narbada Valley, the overall stratigraphy, chronology of the four major phases of occupation, and analysis of material culture are presented. Individual sections are devoted to structures, pottery (illustrated by high quality line drawings and color plates), the stone blade industry, beads, terracotta objects, metals and items of bone, shell and ivory. Four appendixes discuss laboratory analysis of animal and plant remains. Readers will find the final summary chapter a useful framework relating Navdatoli to other similar sites elsewhere in India.

334. Ansari, Z.D. and M.K. Dhavalikar. "New Light on the Prehistoric Cultures of Central India," *World Archaeology* 2(3)(February 1971): 337-346.

A report on the discovery during 1968 test excavations at the site of Kayatha of a totally new Chalcolithic culture characterized by three distinct ceramic industries dated to 2000-1800 B.C. This article presents a detailed discussion of the Kayatha culture and its immediate successors, the Ahar and Malwa, as represented in the season's results. Subsequent exploration identified over forty sites with Kayatha pottery in northwestern Madhya Pradesh. Black and white photographs illustrate copper tools and ornaments, while type samples of Kayatha pottery are given in line drawings.

335. Wakankar, V.S. "Bhim-Betka Excavations," *Journal of Indian History* 51 (1)(April 1973): 23-32.

The author of this article discovered the rock paintings in the sandstone outcrop of the Vindhya Hills south of Bhopal known as Bhim-Betka in 1958 and has been exploring them since that time. The present article reports on test excavations carried out in 1972 in five of the more than five hundred shelters. Sample stratigraphy indicated five separate periods of occupation, with a microlithic tool industry uncovered dating to the Palaeolithic. For a fuller treatment of the site, readers should consult Yashodar Mathpal's 1984 work *Prehistoric Rock Paintings of Bhimbetka, Central India.*

336. Misra, V.N. "The Acheulian Industry of Rock Shelter III F23 at Bhimbetka, Central India: A Preliminary Study," *Puratattva* 8 (75/76): 13-36.

Between 1972 and 1975, three campaigns of excavation were carried out at the rock shelters on the hill of Bhimbetka in the northern margin of the Vindhya Hills. A deeply stratified deposit filled with the stone tools of the Acheulian industry was uncovered in F-23, one of the largest shelters. Misra's article is the first detailed typological analysis of the stone tools found in its eight layers, and is accompanied by statistical tables tracing the distribution of specific tool forms and illustrations of three types of scrapers. Results place the Bhimbetka assemblage in the late Acheulian period. Comparative data from seven other sites in Orissa, Uttar Pradesh and Karnataka where Acheulian tools have been found is presented in the final section. Sites noted include Kuliana, Hunsgi, Lalitpur, Adamgarh, Anagawadi, and Mahadeo Piparia.

337. Joshi, R.V., G.L. Badam and R.P. Pandey. "Fresh Data on the Quaternary Animal Fossils and Stone Age Cultures from the Central Narmada Valley,India," *Asian Perspectives* 21(2) 1981: 164-181.

Done as part of a five-year project initiated by one of the authors to re-examine the biostratigraphy and palaeoecology of the central Narmada River Valley in Madhya Pradesh, the survey reported in this article located five new sites in the region near Jabalpur. Their dates (based on the types of stone tool industries recovered) range from the the lower Palaeolithic to the Mesolithic. A section of the general Narmada stratigraphy is included for reference, along with three pages of drawings of cleavers, scrapers, points, microliths and burins from the region. Correlations of Narmada geology with other river valleys such as the Godavari and Pravara for which Carbon-14 dates have been assigned to specific strata place the Middle Palaeolithic at 40,000-150,000 years B.P.

338. Mathpal, Yashodar. *Prehistoric Rock Paintings of Bhimbetka, Central India.* New Delhi: Abhinav Publications, 1984.

The rock art site of Bhimbetka is composed of one hundred and thirty-three rock shelters on a hill in the Vindhyas near Bhopal. The author spent one year copying the more than six thousand drawings, which span over eight thousand years in sixteen superimposed layers. Rock art was first noticed in India in 1867 at the site of Sohagighat in Uttar Pradesh by Archibald Carlleyle, but his claim that such creations were the work of the Stone age peoples whose remains covered the floors of the rock shelters was not accepted. Subsequent research had uncovered some 150 rock art sites across India by the time of this publication, although none had been intensively studied as a unit. A chapter on the history of rock art research and the principal rock painting sites of India opens the work, followed by a presentation of the physical setting of Bhimbetka and its six groups of shelters. Subjects treated in the paintings are divided into individual figures, scenes, illustrations of mythology, material culture, nature (trees, bushes, grasses and flowers), decorations and a miscellaneous category. The range of styles and techniques used in the representation of the figures and the painting materials themselves are treated in separate chapters. Researchers will find the last chapter's review of the problems of dating Indian rock art instructive. Line drawings and color reproductions of selected Bhimbetka paintings are included, as is a map showing all major rock art sites then known in India.

339. Miller, Daniel. *Artefacts As Categories: A Study of Ceramic Variability in Central India*. Cambridge: University Press, 1985.

A study of the pottery forms produced in a village in Madhya Pradesh which is adjacent to a site where both Malwa and the later Jorwe Chalcolithic cultures were active. The aim of the work was to examine the viability of using a corpus of material cultural remains as it related to major known social dimensions, including networks of production and distribution affected by factors such as caste and class. The results of the Dangwara analysis indicate an absence of reflection of demonstrated artifactual varieties in culturally assigned categories. The author concludes that "the kind of translation in which archaeology is constantly engaged, between the material and the social, demands a conception of material culture which is not readily available in contemporary studies." (p. 198)

340. Sonaki, Arun. "Skull Cap of an Early Man from the Narmada Valley Alluvium (Pleistocene) of Central India," *American Anthropologist* 87 (3) (September 1985): 612-616.

The initial report of the finding of a fossil hominid skull (specifically, the complete right half of the skull cap) in alluvial deposits near Hoshangabad on December 5, 1982. Photographs of the specimen are provided and preliminary discussion of its affinities with *Homo erectus* reviewed.

341. Salahuddin, R.K. Ganjoo, G.L. Badam and S.N. Rajaguru. "On the Archaeological Association of the Fossil Hominid from Hathnora, Madhya Pradesh, India," *Asian Perspectives* 27 (2) (1986-1987): 193-203.

A fossil hominid skull cap of *Homo erectus* was discovered at the site of Hathnora on the northern bank of the Narmada River in Madhya Pradesh in the early 1980's. This article reports on a return season in February 1985, whose objectives were "to evaluate the association of a prehistoric stone tool assemblage found at the site and the assemblage's probable age." (p. 194) Late Acheulian cores, flakes and scrapers made from red Vindhyan sandstone were found in the same gravel layer which yielded the *erectus* specimen and fossil animals, permitting this culture to be assigned a more precise date than other occurrences of this type in India. Dating was assigned to the late Middle to Upper Early Pleistocene.

342. Kumar, Krishna. "The Silver Plates of the Gungeria Hoard: Their Monetary Significance," *Journal of the Economic and Social History of the Orient* 35 (1992-93): 72-94.

On January 21, 1870, a hoard of four hundred and twenty four copper implements and one hundred two silver plates was discovered in a field close to the village of Gungeria in Madhya Pradesh. The present article focuses on the latter, now dispersed to collections of the Indian Museum in Calcutta and the British Museum. The types of circular and horned plates are evaluated as representing a type of unstamped metallic currency wherein objects and ornaments of precious metal also functioned as units of value. Corroboration for this interpretation is drawn from terminology referring to units of exchange in the *Rigveda*. The history of silver use from Harappan times (mainly drawn from the mines of southern India) to the Copper Culture era is also summarized. A date of late second millennium B.C. is assigned to the silver pieces.

343. Kennedy, Kenneth A.R. "The Fossil Hominid Skull from the Narmada Valley: *Homo Erectus* or *Homo Sapiens*?" in *South Asian Archaeology 1989* edited by Catherine Jarrige. Madison, Wisconsin: Prehistory Press, 1992: 145-152.

On December 5, 1982, a fossil calvaria was found *in situ* on the northern bank of the Narmada River near the village of Hathnora in Madhya Pradesh, "the only preserved and authenticated discovery of a middle Pleistocene fossil hominid recovered from the Indian subcontinent." (p. 149) This article reviews the numerous publications issued about various aspects of the fossil and presents data from a re-evaluation of the actual specimen using multivariate statistical analysis. Comparison of the resulting measurements with established standards for *Homo erectus* and *Homo sapiens* favors the latter as the proper taxonomic category for this find. Readers will find the extensive bibliography useful for setting this find into the global context of human prehistory.

Madras

344. Soundara Rajan. K.V. "Stone Age Industries Near Giddalur, District Kurnool," *Ancient India* 8 (1952): 64-92.

In 1949, the Prehistoric Expedition sponsored by the Indian Department of Archaeology revisited six sites in northern Madras, identified in the 1920's by Cammiade and Burkitt during their primary surveys, where palaeolithic and microlithic tools had been noted. The present article sets out in detail the pebble choppers, handaxes, cleavers,end-scrapers, burins and blade tools collected. Illustrations are provided with line drawings and photographs. Researchers will find it useful to have read Cammiade and Burkitt's original 1930 article in *Antiquity*, "Fresh Light On the Stone Age of South India," as background.

345. Zeuner, Frederick E. and Bridget Allchin. "The Microlithic Sites of Tinnevelly District, Madras State," *Ancient India* 12 (1956):4-20.

The authors review the microlithic assemblages from eleven sites from the coastal region of Madras adjoining the Tambarparni River, all associated with the large sand dunes known locally as *teris*. A local stone tool industry characterized by equal use of chert and quartz as raw materials, flake and blade geometric forms, noted as being "at present,...the only ocurrence of the pressure-flaking technique in India," (p. 19) is outlined.

Maharashtra

346. Burgess, James. *Report on the Elura Cave Temples and the Brahmanical and Jaina Caves in Western India*. Varanasi: Indological Book House: 1970.

An exact reprint of a study issued in 1882 as the fifth volume of the Archaeological Survey of Western India, this tome's subtitle notes that it covers "the results of the Fifth, Sixth and Seventh Seasons' Operations" carried out between 1877 and 1880. It is one of two volumes originally issued as more detailed supplements to the 1880 publication *The Cave Temples of India*, which Burgess (the archaeological surveyor for western and southern India) co-authored with James Fergusson. Seven of the twelve sections of text deal with the various rockhewn temple complexes at Ellora in Maharashtra, most constructed between 200 B.C. and 700 A.D. Burgess divides them into three types, Buddhist, Jain and "Brahmanical" (Hindu). Detailed plans and sections are provided for each, with architectural elements and interior carvings highlighted as present. Other sites covered in the report are Badami, Aihole, Elephanta, Patna, Harischandragad, and Ankai.The drawings and photographs of the facades and other features are an invaluable record of the condition of these monuments as they were in the late nineteenth century. Researchers may wish to consult the companion work, *Report on the Buddhist Cave Temples and Their Inscriptions*, published in 1883.

347. Corvinus, G.K. "Excavations At An Acheulean Site At Chirki-on-Pravara in India," in *South Asian Archaeology* edited by Norman Hammond. London, Duckworth, 13-28.

Proudly remarking that "in wealth of Palaeolithic sites India can compete with Europe and Africa," (p. 12) the author first briefly reviews then-recent work before reporting on her own work at a site in the Pravara drainage of western Maharashtra. Over twenty four hundred artifacts were recovered, the majority shaped tools such as handaxes, cleavers and choppers. Both core manufacture and side-flaking techniques were employed. Distribution of the finds did not suggested redeposition but rather a working floor. There is no bibliography.

348. Todd, K.R.U. "The Microlithic Industries of Bombay," *Ancient India* 6 (January 1950): 4-16.

A review of microliths recovered from ten sites on Salsette Island, north of the city of Bombay. The data from this local industry will be better understood by consulting the lengthy study of Indian Holocene stone tools by D.H. Gordon in the same issue of *Ancient India*.

349. Sankalia, Hasmukh Dhirajlal and Moreshwar Gangadhar Dikshit. *Excavations*

at Brahmapuri (Kolhapur) 1945-46. Poona: Postgraduate and Research Institute, Deccan College, 1952.

A site report summarizing the results of four months field work at the mound of Brahmapuri on the right bank of the Panchaganga River in far southwestern Maharashtra.The campaign was initiated following the discovery in 1944 of a bronze figure of the god Poseidon, although the site had been known since 1877. The objective of this season was to place the Greek and Roman era finds into context and determine a general sequence of occupation. The presence of numerous coins in the areas chosen for sampling permitted the close dating of a detailed stratigraphic model from the Satavahana period of the first two centuries A.D. to the eighteenth century. Separate chapters review the coins, pottery, terracotta, beads, bangles, tools and weapons, and stone objects found, which are illustrated in thirty-five black and white plates.

350. Sankalia, Hasmukh Dhirajlal and Shantaram Bhalchandra Deo. *Report on the Excavations at Nasik and Jorwe, 1950-51.* Poona: Deccan College, 1955.

Although attested to in various histories and geographies over the centuries, the precise site of the ancient portion of the city of Nasik in Maharashtra was unknown until 1948, when the discovery of shards of polished black ware at a mound on the eastern edge of the modern town prompted test excavations. This publication opens with a discussion of the known history of the region (abandoned between 300 and 1300 A.D.) followed by a review of the excavation results and the five periods of occupation (from Palaeolithic to the Mughal and Maratha eras) revealed in the trenches' stratigraphy. Individual chapters present and analyse coinage, microliths, pottery, beads, glass objects and bangles, copper and iron artifacts, stone objects, terracotta, and fragile materials such as bone, steatite, shell and ivory. A separate chapter is devoted the Satavahana era bone points found at the site, "a huge number *in situ*- perhaps a million- lying buried over the layer of natural earth and covered by a thin layer of later deposits," (p. 130) comparing them to similar finds from Taxila.

The site of Jorwe on the Pravara River was discovered in 1947 following the collection of ancient pottery by villagers during a flood season. Excavations showed it to be a one-period site of a culture possessing a distinctive microlithic industry as well as painted pottery, documentation of the latter making up much of the Jorwe report text. The authors assign "the Jorwe culture...provisionally to a Copper or Early Bronze Age period." (p. 150)

351. Sankalia, H.D. "Animal-Fossils and Palaeolithic Industries From The Pravara Basin At Nevasa, District Ahmadnagar," *Ancient India* 12 (1956): 35-52.

A report on a series of stone tool industries from the basin of the Pravara River in the northern Deccan. Much of the argument here is devoted to climatic reconstruction of a succession of arid and wet cycles. The fossils referred to consist of five specimens recovered from river gravels, "the first time that lithic industries have been found in direct association with animal-fossils outside the Narmada basin." (p. 39) Available data indicate the use of both handaxes and flake/blade tool types in this region. Type specimens are illustrated.

352. Deshpande, M.N. "The Rock-Cut Caves of Pitalkhora In The Deccan," *Ancient India* 15 (1959): 66-93.

The complex of thirteen Buddhist cave temples at Pitalkhora, constructed between the second century B.C. and the seventh century A.D., were first noted in 1853, although they came under the care and management of the Department of Archaeology only in 1953. This article reviews the notable features of each cave and presents the sculptural elements, crystal reliquaries, pottery and copper objects retrieved during clearance of two temple forecourts in 1958.

353. Sankalia, Hasmukh Dhirajlal et.al. *From History To Pre-History At Nevasa (1954-56)*. Poona: Deccan College, 1960.

A lengthy and highly detailed report covering two seasons of archaeological field investigation done in and around the town of Nevasa on both banks of the Pravara River. Three mounds west of the southern section were the focus of scientific attention. The first chapter summarizes both the physical geography of the region together with known literary and traditional accounts of local history. Excavations revealed six distinct periods of occupation dating from the early Palaeolithic to the Muslim and Maratha eras ca.1700 A.D. The early and middle Palaeolithic are treated by the fourth and fifth chapters of this report. Of particular interest is the detailed presentation on the Chalcolithic blade industry given in chapter six. The remaining ten sections address specific classes of materials ranging from coins and seals through pottery and terracotta to glass, bone and shell. Comparisons of the Nevasa finds with similar sites in the Deccan and other regions of India complete the text. Eight appendixes report analyses of specific artifacts including plant and animal remains and urn burials. Readers should be aware that the text presupposes some familiarity with the regional archaeological literatures and geographies of India.

354. Sengupta, R. "Repairs to the Ellora Caves," *Ancient India* 17 (1961): 47-67.

Beginning in the second century B.C., the hill of Ellora was extensively sculpted into cave temples representing the Hindu, Buddhist and Jain faiths. Unlike the similar complex at Ajanta, these sites were never lost, remaining in use due to their proximity to a major road and numerous written accounts left by travelers such as the noted Arab geographer Al-Mas'udi in the tenth century. This article follows the history of one of the first priorities of the Archaeological Survey of India, conservation of monuments, as it was applied to this religious complex. Although noted in the nineteenth century by Major H.H.Cole, Curator of Ancient Monuments, direct preservation work at Ellora was not begun until 1910.Individual sections cover 1910-1914, 1914 to Partition in 1947, and activity under the independent government of India. Twenty-three individual caves and their curation under the comprehensive program of repair and restoration initiated at Ellora between 1956 and 1960 are reviewed. Numerous cross-section drawings and black and white photographs offer an unusually detailed look at a major Indian preservation project while underway.

355. Thapar, B.K. "Prakash 1955: A Chalcolithic Site in the Tapti Valley," *Ancient India* 20/21 (1964/65): 5-167.

This lengthy article reports on one season of fieldwork at the massive mound of Prakash at the confluence of the Tapti and Gomai Rivers in Maharashtra. Rising more than seventy feet above the surrounding country, the site was selected for investigation "to ascertain the succession of cultures at the sites and to produce a relative time-scale for the region." (p. 10) A fifty-seven-foot deep trench cut into a restricted area of the mound revealed four distinct periods of occupation, with a clear break between the first two. The relative lack of datable objects found during the testing forced the excavators to establish dating for the Prakash sequence through analogue with pottery forms from other regional sites such as Navdatoli and Nevasa, the presence of iron technology, tribal Ujjayini coins, and monochrome glass bangles. The result dates the earliest level of Prakash to ca. 1700-1300 B.C. (Period I), with an hiatus until the early Iron Age (ca. 600 B.C.) although occupation continued until the eleventh century A.D. The majority of this text is devoted to a detailed exposition of the types of pottery found, an assemblage including Malwa and Jorwe, Lustrous Red and Northern Black Polished wares as well as an early black and grey ware. Two analyses of metal objects (copper and iron) and seventeen charcoal samples of plant remains (the majority from Period I) complete the report. A lengthy appendix provides the series of radiocarbon dates from Navdatoli, Lothal, Nevasa, Chandoli, Ahar, Eran, Hastinapura, Rajgir, Atranjikera and Kausambi referenced in the text.

356. Deo, Shantaram Bhalchandra and Zainuddin Dawood Ansari. *Chalcolithic Chandoli.* Poona: Deccan College Postgraduate and Research Institute, 1965.

Discovered in 1957 through information provided by local people following the publicity surrounding earlier work at Nasik and Jorwe, surface collections at the site of Chandoli on the Ghod River indicated "cultural links both with the Deccan and Central India." (p. 1) This publication reports on the results of the 1960 field season, with substantial sections devoted to the polished stone tools, blade industry and pottery types found, as well as an overview of the twenty-four burials and their grave goods. Four appendixes provide data on the analysis of the human remains, copper objects found, items of shell and flax fibers retrieved. Radiocarbon dates obtained confirm occupation at Chandoli between 1645 and 1440 B.C. Most useful when read with other Maharashtran site reports such as Sankalia's coverage of the original discovery of Nasik.

357. Deo, Shantaram Bhalchandra and Ganesh Gangadhar Mujumdar. *Songaon Excavations 1965.* Poona: Deccan College, 1969.

A concise review of a three-week sampling excavation carried out at this site some sixty miles southeast of Pune. The site was chosen due to indications from ceramic surface collections that its two mounds "held out ...possibilities of linking up the Deccan Chalcolithic traditions with those of Rajasthan." (p. 1) Three periods of occupation were identified spanning several hundred years prior to the first millennium. The bulk of the publication is given over to detailed descriptions and good quality drawings of the ceramics recovered, along with lithic materials, house units and burials.

358. Dhavalikar,M.K. "A Prehistoric Deity of Western India," *Man* 5 n.1 (1970): 131-132.

A letter written by one of the excavators of Inamgaon discussing the male figurines made of coarse unbaked ceramics recovered from the site. Parallels are drawn with a practice still current in this region of Maharashtra, the making of a male deity figure out of wheat flour prior to the beginning of special occasions, said figure invoked for success in the celebration amd kept near the hearth. The recovery of two of the Inamgaon figurines from a courtyard containing an oven is noted as supporting this hypothesis.

359. Sankalia, H.D., Z.D. Ansari and M.K. Dhavalikar. "Inamgaon: A Chalcolithic Settlement in Western India," *Asian Perspectives* 14(1971): 139-146.

A review of the results of the first field season at Inamgaon, a site of the Jorwe culture consisting of five mounds spread over some sixty-five acres In the Ghod River drainage. A principal goal of the excavations was to gain further data about the beginning and end of the Jorwe, realized by analysis of the stratigraphic sequence. The final occupation level, Late Jorwe, is "a new feature...bridging the gap between the chalcolithic period and the Iron age in India." (p. 140) Researchers working on this era of Maharashtran archaeology should compare this article with the summary of the first five seasons published by the authors in 1975.

360. Sankalia, H.D. Z.D. Ansari and M.K. Dhavalikar. "An Early Farmers' Village in Central India," *Expedition* 17(2)(Winter 1975): 2-11.

"The first prehistoric farming communities excavated in central India were found at the sites of of Nasik, Jorwe and Nevasa" (p. 2) in Maharashtra. This article reports on the identification and first five years of excavation at the mound group at Inamgaon, a site where an extensive horizontal excavation could be conducted to obtain data on subsistence patterns, house plans and community structure of the Jorwe culture. Topics discussed include the field technique used for recovering house floors intact, the relative house plans, sizes and furnishings from both the Jorwe and preceding Malwa eras, and a separate comparison of ceramics and lithic materials of each stage. Religious images and types of inhumation thus far identified complete the report. Researchers will find the bibliographic references useful in tracking the progress of archaeology in Maharashtra.

361. Dhavalikar, M.K. "Settlement Archaeology of Inamgaon," *Puratattva* 8 (1975/76): 44-54.

A review of the results of six seasons field work at Inamgaon in the Krishna drainage from 1968 to 1975, which exposed the remains of an extensive Chalcolithic settlement extending over some five hectares and occupied from 1600-700 B.C. by the Malwa and Jorwe cultures. The goal of the Inamgaon project was to expose enough of the ancient village to establish a pattern of settlement and consistent features of domestic architecture. The semi-arid climate of this region of Maharashtra made possible the retrieval of cultural material in exceptional detail. The article opens with a summary of the local ecology then examines the shift from rectangular houses to circular closely spaced dwellings in the Jorwe eras. Specific structures have been tentatively identifed as a granary and a dwelling of an elite class, while craft specializations were restricted to houses on the western edge of the site, a pattern still to be seen in Maharashtra today. Crafts practiced at Inamgaon thus far known were ivory carving, lime-making, distilling, gold and copper working, and pottery making. Sample plans of the houses of the Early and Late Jorwe phases are included. Dhavalikar notes that Inamgaon is "one of the most extensive chalcolithic sites in Maharashtra…the only site of its kind where excavations have been carried out on such a large scale." (p. 46)

362. Mittre, Vishnu and R. Savithri. "Ancient Plant Economy at Inamgaon," *Puratattva* 8 ((75/76): 55-62.

During excavation of the extensive Chalcolithic village of Inamgaon on the Ghod River, numerous plant materials (chiefly carbonized cereals, fruit and seeds of edible plants, and charcoals) were recovered from both the Malwa and Jorwe layers of occupation deposits. This article reports on the archaeobotanical analysis of this material. Grains identified are rice, wheat, barley (found in all levels of the site) and sorghum, while other plants utilized include lentils and bamboo. Readers should be aware that most of the seventy-eight items in this sample are identified by genera and species rather than their more familiar vernacular names. The mixed economy visible at Inamgaon is compared with botanical data from other sites of the period such as Kayatha, Ahar and Navdatoli.

363. Burgess, James. *A Guide To The Elura Cave Temples*. Delhi: Neeraj Publishing House, 1981.

A reprint of the guide to the twenty-three cave temples constructed at Ellora in north-central Maharashtra, a publication in use at least since 1900. Each cave is described in meticulous detail, with special attention given to unusual architectural elements. Readers should note that the illustrations included in the original edition have been omitted.

364. Mate, M.S. "Daulatabad: Road To Islamic Archaeology In India," *World Archaeology* 14 (3) (February 1983): 335-341.

A discussion of the need to approach the archaeology of the Islamic era in India from a separate and unique perspective in the planning and evaluation of field work, using the site of Daulatabad (ancient Devgiri) in Maharashtra as an example. Although Islamic coinage, architecture and inscriptions have been a focus of Indian archaeology since its inception, "neither the official agency, the ASI, nor nonofficial ones...have crossed these narrow limits." (p. 335) The Daulatabad project is aimed at illustrating the value of excavations for cross-checking and expanding the copious written materials available from various Islamic court records. Mate also notes specific ways in which Islamic era sites differ sharply from Hindu or Buddhist settlements, notably in the lateral spread of occupation debris, centering of habitations around a major structure such as a mosque, and the presence of numerous fortifications. The need to re-establish the study of Persian and western Asian culture and literatures as a parallel to the historic emphasis on Sanskrit to bring balance to Islamic archaeology in India is also set forth.

365. Berkson, Carmel. *Elephanta: The Cave of Shiva*. Princeton University Press, 1983.

This volume contains three essays which explore in detail one of the major shrines on the island of Elephanta near Bombay. Topics addressed include the history and evolution of various art styles used in the carving in the cave of Shiva, a general treatment of the architecture of the island, and consideration of the myths depicted in the carved panels and lintels of the caves. Seventy-five high quality black and white photographs provide illustration. A brief bibliography is appended. Researchers dealing with the cave temple complexes of northern India will also wish to consult Berkson's later work, *The Caves At Aurangabad* (1986).

366. Sali, S.A. "Late Harappan Settlement At Daimabad," in *Frontiers of the Indus Civilization* edited by B.B.Lal and S.P. Gupta. New Delhi: Books and Books, 1984: 235-242.

This report on the cumulative results of excavations at the site of Daimabad on the Pravara River is set within the broader context of a several-decades-long debate over the relationship of the Harappan civilization with the ancient cultures of the Deccan plateau. Following a summary of known Mature Harappan influence from the Neolithic periods of Andhra Pradesh and Karnataka, the initial discovery and definition of the Savalda culture (suggested to be the oldest Chalcolithic assemblage so far known in Maharashtra) is noted. The five periods of occupation at Daimabad (2200-1000 B.C.) supported this placement of Savalda as contemporary with the Mature Harappan sites of Gujarat and the Indus Valley. Late Harappan settlements in the Godavari Valley indicate a regionalizing culture still retaining recognizable Indus traits such as stone seals and copper celts.

367. Dhavalikar, M.H. and Vasant Shinde. "Excavations at Kaothe in the Central Tapi Basin," in *South Asian Archaeology 1985* edited by Karen Frifelt and Per Sorensen. London: Curzon Press, 1989: 277-280.

The Tapi Valley has yielded evidence for "the earliest farming culture of Maharashtra," (p. 277) termed the Savalda culture after its type site and dated by stratigraphic evidence from Daimabad to 2000-1800 B.C. This brief report focuses on Kaothe, the most extensive early farming settlement then known (some 30 hectares) and one not overlain by successive occupations, although disrupted by cultivation. Pit dwellings used for storage, burials and residence, a distinctive assemblage of pottery (both regional black-on-red and painted ware known from Savalda) and the surprising absence of stone and metal tools are discussed. Skeletal remains from the five burials found are compared with those of Nevasa and Inamgaon.

368. Berkson, Carmel. *The Caves At Aurangabad: Early Buddhist Tantric Art In India*. New York: Mapin International, 1986.

A complex of nine cave temples located two miles west of the city of Aurangabad in the Sahyadri range of the Western Ghats is the focus of this work. Constructed during the fifth and sixth centuries, they represent some of the finest extant Buddhist carving of this era. Essays accompanying the wealth of photographs provide background on the various schools of Buddhism, the history and regional origins of the caves, detailed analyses of iconography and a highly useful glossary of technical Sanskrit terms used to identify themes and characters in Buddhist art. Useful as a reference source on this and other similar sites.

369. De Puma, Richard Daniel. "The Roman Bronzes from Kolhapur," in *Rome and India: The Ancient Sea Trade* edited by Vimala Begley and Richard Daniel. Madison: University of Wisconsin Press, 1991: 82-112.

On January 27, 1945, a group of 102 bronze objects was discovered during excavations in the Brahmapuri mound at Kolhapur in Maharashtra. This article examines ten of these items which have been ascribed to Roman manufacture as imports to India. They range from an exquisite statuette of Poseidon to bronze mirrors, vessels and their handles (some extremely elaborate) and a wine strainer. Evaluation supports a Western origin with dating ascribed to the first to third centuries A.D., with the exception of the Poseidon statue. Excellent quality photographs and cross sections of the pieces discussed are provided.

370. Spink, Walter M. "The Archaeology of Ajanta," *Ars Orientalis* 21 (1991): 67-94.

In contrast to previous investigators of the famed cave temple complex, this writer attempts to show that the "later phase of work at Ajanta represents a sudden burgeoning of activity…during a period of scarcely more than a decade and a half" (pp. 67,69) ending by 480 A.D. His analysis utilizes the principle of stratigraphy, applied to allow the grouping of architectural features into a developmental sequence. An excellent example of the interelated multidisciplinary nature of Indian art history and archaeology.

371. Dhavalikar, M.K. "Chalcolithic Architecture at Inamgaon and Walki: An Ethnoarchaeological Study," in *Living Traditions: Studies In the Ethnoarchaeology of South Asia* edited by Bridget Allchin. Columbia, Missouri: South Asia Publications, 1994: 31-52.

A report on excavations at the sites of Kaothe, Walki and Inamgaon in western Maharashtra whose dates range from 2000-1000 B.C. During the course of excavations ,the architectural remains of several types of structure were uncovered. The majority of this article is devoted to the presentation of plans of the Kaothe pit dwellings, the Inamgaon houses (one hundred and thirty of which were found) and the circular huts of Walki, and illustration of their possible appearance through analogies with styles of domestic architecture still practiced in Maharashtra.

372. Ray, Himanshu Prabha. "Kanheri: The Archaeology of An Early Buddhist Pilgrimage Centre In Western India," *World Archaeology* 26 (1) June, 1994: 35-46.

The three hundred and four caves of the Buddhist pilgrimage center of Kanheri near Bombay were originally excavated between the first and tenth centuries A.D. This article notes prior researches on the site as early as 1841 and places Kanheri within the known regional archaeology of Maharashtra and the development of various forms of Buddhist monastic architecture. Specific classes of artifacts from the site such as fragments of dedicated bowls, platters and miniature stupas and the spread of Buddhist pilgrimage forms into South East Asia are also discussed.

373. Bopardikar, B.P. *Excavations at Tuljapur Garhi 1984-85 (Vidarbha, Maharashtra)*. New Delhi: Director General, Archaeological Survey of India, 1996.

This ninety-fifth *Memoir* issued by the Archaeological Survey of India reports on a season's fieldwork at "the eastern most out-post of territorial expansion of Jorwe culture in the upper Deccan," (p. 2)the mound of Tuljapur Garhi on a tributary of the Tapi River.Seven chapters present the results of a preliminary excavation and section of the mound, ceramic finds, microliths, beads and metal artifacts. These data confirm the presence of the Malwa and Jorwe cultures as intrusive into this region of Maharashtra *ca.* 1000 B.C. Twenty-three black and white photographs covering a general view of the mound, burials, terracotta, plant remains and animal bones are included.

374. Smith, Monica Louise. *Strong Economies, Weak Polities: The Archaeology of Central India in the Early Centuries A.D.* Ph.D dissertation, University of Michigan, 1997.

The research upon which this dissertation is based was carried out in the Vidarbha region of eastern Maharashtra at the town site of Kaundinyapura, whose Early Historic occupation dates to between the third century B.C. and fourth century A.D. This investigation (done in 1994 and 1995) represents "the first time that an Early Historic period site in the subcontinent has been investigated in it entirety." (p. 5) The goal of the project was to analyse the role of durable goods as items of social exchange and communication in long-distance trading networks and the variety of trade activities engaged in by early complex societies. Ten chapters set the field work within anthropological studies of trade (including the motives for exchange and its essential elements), outline the political history of central India (noting that no one major governmental entity existed in the region during the Early Historic era) and report on both the methodology used in the surface collection and survey at Kaundinyapura and its results in the context of local climate and geology. Items present in the collection sample such as sandstone and pottery tempered with mica indicate widespread participation in trade, as both these materials are imports from outside the local basaltic area. An economic model involving the social value of goods as an impetus for trade and the variety of strategies required for a community like Kaudinyapura to create a surplus are analysed. Researchers concerned with Maharashtran archaeology will find the bibliography highly useful.

375. Behl, Benoy K. *The Ajanta Caves, Artistic Wonder of Ancient Buddhist India.* *New York: Harry N. Abrams, 1998.*

Writing in the sixth century A.D., the Chinese Buddhist pilgrim Hsuan Tsang spoke admiringly of "lofty halls and deep chambers...quarried in the cliff" at a monastery complex on a horseshoe bend of the Waghora River in what is now Maharashtra. This was the site of Ajanta, abandoned and not rediscovered until April 28, 1819. Its fame lies in both the detailed architecture of the twenty-eight cave temples and shrines and in the exquisitely detailed and preserved painted murals which adorn them. This volume (based on two extended visits by the author in 1991 and 1992) opens by discussing the physical structure of the cave complex and the various phases of Buddhism, ranging from the Hinayana (which allowed no representation of the figure of Buddha in any way) to the more familiar carved images of the Mahayana school. The scope and character of the murals is next analysed and factors affecting their state of preservation considered. The four principal painted caves (1, 2, 16 and 17) are then presented, with all murals illustrated in full-page color photographs. An appendix contains plans of each, along with reprints of travelers accounts of two visits in 1829 and 1843. A lengthy bibliography of previously published literature completes the work. Researchers unfamiliar with Ajanta and its place in the past of this region of India will find this volume a superb introduction to this important site. Those wishing a more detailed consideration within a framework borrowed from archaeology should consult Walter Spink's 1991 essay "The Archaeology of Ajanta."

Meghalaya

376. Sharma, A.K. "Excavation at Vadagokugiri (Meghalaya) 1991," *Puratattva* 22 (1991/92): 89-96.

A report on three months digging and survey at the city site of Vadagokugiri on the left bank of the Brahmaputra River in the Garo Hills of Meghalaya. Discoveries include the first stupa found in this state (now occupied by tribal peoples) and two groups of temples, with over twenty located thus far. A unique octagonal temple dedicated to Siva, a second temple of built of burnt brick, and the surrounding mudbrick fortification are presented in detail. Vadagokugiri is identified with the capital of the state of Kamarupa visited by Hsuan Tsang in 643 A.D.

Mysore

377. Wheeler, R.E.M. "Brahmagiri and Chandravalli 1947: Megalithic and Other Cultures in the Chitaldrug District, Mysore State," *Ancient India* 4 (July 1947-January 1948): 180-310.

Between March and May 1947, a series of excavations were carried out at two sites in northern Mysore, as part of an effort to establish "a fixed chronological point for a representative series of South Indian megalithic tombs and…the method of their use." (p. 183) This lengthy and detailed article begins with a discussion of the overall problems of fixing dates in the prehistory of southern India and cites the then-recent discoveries of Roman trade pottery of the first century A.D. at Arikamedu near Pondicherry as providing a point of departure. The approach taken was to select a site which had previously yielded first century Roman coinage and representative artifacts of the Andhra culture, Chandravalli, and attempt to establish a correlation with a site exhibiting both the Andhra culture and a group of megalithic tombs. The main body of this text outlines the season's work at the latter site of Brahmagiri, ancient Isila. Special attention is given to the circular megalithic cists (with several presented in photographs and plans), the types of pottery discovered in both the townsite and the tombs, stone objects (including polished stone axes), and the results of renewed excavations at Chandravalli. A provisional date of 200 B.C. is given to the construction of the megaliths. Readers unfamiliar with prior work in this part of India may wish to consult R.E.M. Wheeler's monograph on the 1945 season at Arikamedu, where the distinctive rouletted Andhra pottery found at Chandravalli was also noted.

North West Frontier Province

378. Marshall, J.H. and J.Ph.Vogel. "Excavations at Charsada in the Frontier Province," in *Archaeological Survey of India, Annual Report 1902-03*, reprinted Varanasi, Indological Publishing House, 1970: 141-184.

A report of the first trial excavations done at the site of Charsada near Peshawar between February 23 and April 15, 1902.Attention was devoted to the most prominent mound of the site, known locally as the Bala Hisar. After reviewing mentions made of the ancient city of Pushkalavati (with which Charsada had been identified)in historical accounts, Marshall describes the condition of the site in 1902 and his test trenching at various locations. The bulk of this report is devoted to an analysis of recovered artifacts. The methodology used by Marshall and his identifications of the fragmentary structural remains located would be severely criticized by later investigators such as Sir Mortimer Wheeler, whose 1962 volume *Charsada* should be read with this account. An excellent example of the early introduction of controlled excavation to Indian archaeology.

379. Marshall. John. *Excavations at Taxila: The Stupas and Monasteries at Jaulian*. Calcutta: Superintendent of Government Printing, 1921.

Between 1916 and 1918, the important group of Buddhist structures (a monastery and two stupa courts on different levels) near Taxila was excavated under the direction of Sir John Marshall, director of the Archaeological Survey. Notable for "their remarkable state of preservation" (p. 3), these edifices date to the third century A.D. and were destroyed approximately two hundred and fifty years later during the invasion of the White Huns. The text opens with a brief outline of the plans of the buildings and techniques of their construction, followed by sections treating the remains of the central and subsidiary stupas and chapels, the monastery and its assembly hall, and their associated artifacts. Among the most unusual of these were fragments of a birchbark manuscript, dated by its script to the fourth century A.D. A separate essay by A. Foucher, an expert on the Greco-Buddhist art of the Gandhara school, examines the fragments and full stucco figures found during the excavations, placing them within an expanded timeline of local artistic development in the Taxila valley. A catalog of the coinage as well as the clay, stone, stucco, copper and bronze, gold and iron objects found over the two year period is appended. Illustration is provided by a carefully drawn plan and section of the complex and twenty-eight dark and rather grainy photographs covering all classes of artifacts and all major structures cleared (the latter before and after excavation).

380. Childe, V.Gordon. "The Indus Civilization," in *The Most Ancient East*. London: Kegan Paul,1928: 201-219.

In his introduction to this general work interpreting the flood of new discoveries in archaeology for a (presumably) confused public, noted British prehistorian Childe notes "the disinterment of the forgotten Indus civilization" (p. 201) as one of the highlights. This chapter summarizes the facts about this new culture as then known, based upon the primary excavations at the type sites of Mohenjo-Daro and Harappa. A useful example of the manner in which Indian prehistory was conveyed to the reading public at large in the first decades of the twentieth century. No references or bibliography are provided.

381. Hargreaves, H. *Excavations in Baluchistan 1925, Sampur Mound, Mastung and Sohr Damb, Nal.* Calcutta: Government of India, Central Publication Branch, 1929.

The field excavations reported upon in this text were carried out in the immediate aftermath of the discovery of Harappa and Mohenjo-daro, when resemblances between this newly-found culture and early levels at Susa and other Mesopotamian sites shifted scientific attention to "Baluchistan, the country lying between these two important river basins and where connecting links between these two cultures might reasonably be expected to be recovered." (p.iii) The landscape of this sparsely settled region had been noted for years in travellers' accounts as possessing *dambs*, artificial mounds whose content and cultural context were unknown. This document (written by the superintendent of the Frontier Circle of the Archaeological Survey of India) reports in detail on the first two major archaeological excavations to be carried out in Baluchistan in the twentieth century. The first section outlines results of sampling work at the Sampur mound at Mastung, some thirty-three miles south of Quetta, which uncovered scant remains of a large structure of mud brick. The larger and more detailed second portion focuses on the massive mound of Sohr Damb at Nal, two hundred and fifty miles south of Quetta, which had yielded fifty-nine pieces of a unique type of pottery during field collection in 1904. Excavation began in May 1925, with four separate areas being tested. Results of this sampling revealed a substantial and varied amount of material(including burials) defining a previously unknown regional culture. Some 271 pottery vessels similar in form to the pieces collected earlier were found. Approximately half of this monograph is a section of twenty-four plates (black and white photographs interspersed with line drawings) covering site plans of both Sampur and Sohr Damb, views of all sections opened, styles of pottery decoration and vessel forms, copper implements, and human skeletal remains. Hargreaves concludes that "the hope that these excavations might yield evidence of connections between the early civilizations of Mesopotamia and the Indus valley has not been realized." (p. 38)

382. Stein, Aurel. *An Archaeological Tour in Waziristan and Northern Baluchistan*. Calcutta: Government of India Central Publication Branch, 1929.

Published as the thirty-seventh *Memoir* by the Archaeological Survey of India, this report presents the results of an extended field survey and investigation carried out by the author in 1927-28 of Waziristan (corresponding to the southeastern border area of contemporary Afghanistan) and three districts lying in the west-central portion of the Indus Valley. Stein's interest in this area was stimulated by the 1923-25 discoveries made by John Marshall at Harappa and Mohenjo-daro. He wished to explore the Zhob, Loralai and Quetta regions, where "investigations in 1898…had clearly proved the existence of prehistoric remains." (p. 2) Among the numerous ruins and mound groups visited and sampled were the sites of Periano-ghundai and Moghul-ghundai in Zhob, and Ranaghundai and Dabar Kot in the Loralai district. Eight pages of detailed site plans with topographic contours are appended.Twenty-one black and white photographic plates are devoted to illustrating the range of pottery samples collected during the expedition. Views of the sites as they existed at this time may be found in the twenty-seven figures scattered throughout the text.

383. Stein, Aurel. *On Alexander's Track To The Indus: Personal Narrative of Explorations On The North-West Frontier of India*. London: Macmillan, 1929.

The field work done by the author in 1926 in "the great transborder tract of Upper Swat and the adjacent valleys" (p. 1) and his explorations within the territory known in ancient times as Uddiyana are chronicled in this volume. His principal aim was the location of the site of Aornos, a major stronghold taken by Alexander the Great following his descent from the Hindu Kush en route to his final campaign in the Punjab. Stein observes that the fertile Swat valley "must have been crowded with Buddhist sanctuaries and religious establishments in the centuries immediately before and after Christ," (p. 13) and much of Stein's work in this area is based upon the accounts left by the Buddhist pilgrim chroniclers Fa Hsien, Sung Yun and Hsuan Tsang between 403 and 752 A.D. His detailed account of individual sites and the previous collecting work done at them includes numerous stupas, monasteries and fortresses. While not written as a strictly scientific monograph, Stein's investigations provide invaluable data on the condition of archaeological remains in this region as they existed in the early twentieth century and their administration by the British colonial regime.

384. Stein, Aurel. *An Archaeological Tour in Upper Swat and Adjacent Hill Tracts*. Calcutta: Government of India Central Publication Branch, 1930.

Between March and May of 1926, Aurel Stein achieved an ambition of some thirty years standing, being able (through what he refers to as "the recent development of tribal politics") (p. 1) to conduct a survey of the upper regions of the Swat River Valley, recording the number and condition of the ancient remains in the area, "the purely archaeological results of my tours." (p. 4) This volume, issued as the forty-second *Memoir* of the Archaeological Survey of India, shares the results of this long-deferred journey. Four chapters present and discuss the ruins of the lower Swat Valley, sites associated with the campaigns of Alexander the Great (including a survey which successfully identified the site of the fortress of Aornos) and the Buddhist stupas located across much of the upper valley. Many of the sixty-six black and white photographs used as illustrations of this trek are quite striking. Readers should consult Stein's five-volume Central Asian expedition report *Serindia (1921)* and *On Alexander's Trek to the Indus (1929)* for historical and geographical background on this section of southern Asia to supplement this text.

385. Stein, Aurel. *An Archaeological Tour in Gedrosia.* Calcutta: Government of India, Central Publications Branch, 1931.

This forty-third *Memoir* of the Archaeological Survey of India presents the account of Stein's 1927 field survey and exploration of ancient Gedrosia, the present Kalat state of southern Baluchistan, an area of approximately two hundred and seventy by three hundred miles. Ten chapters review the topography of the Makran coast and interior valleys, noting significant archaeological remains (including the site of Sutkagen-dor, known since 1875). A relief map of Kalat state with all sites mentioned in the text is provided at the end of the site plans, as are twenty-three black and white photographs. Readers will find this account invaluable both as background to later excavations and some of the areas surveyed, and reportage on the history of archaeology in this region of what would shortly become Pakistan. References are also made to the 1924 excavations by Hargreaves at a Chalcolithic burial ground at Nal, published as the thirty-fifth *Memoir* in 1929.

386. Majumdar, Nani G. *Explorations In Sind*. Delhi: Manager of Publications, 1934.

The subtitle of this text defines it as "being a report of the exploratory survey carried out during the years 1927-28, 1929-30 and 1930-31." The result covers three field seasons and begins with Majumdar's time of excavation at the site of Jhukar, then examines the results of site survey travel across the Indus delta, and concludes with a final trip begun in October 1930 near Mohenjo-Daro and extending west to Karachi. Thirty-two sites in all were noted, ranging from small mounds to more major locales such as Chanhu-daro and Lohumjo-daro. Useful as an overview of a region (at the time little explored) which was to become the focus of intensive archaeological activity over the next seven decades. Illustration is provided by forty-six plates covering site plans and assorted metal and pottery artifacts sorted by locale.

387. Vats, Madho Sarup. *Excavations At Harappa, Being An Account of Archaeological Excavations At Harappa Carried Out Between The Years 1920-21 and 1933-34*. Delhi: Bhartiya Publishing House, 1974. 2 volumes.

A reissue of the original two-volume set published in Delhi in 1940, this text was written by the director of excavation at Harappa between 1926 and 1934. These seasons concentrated on expanding work in areas of the city already opened up by the initial fieldwork from 1921 directed by Daya Ram Sahni, as well as beginning the investigation of the extensive cemetery. The text of the first volume begins with a review of the physiographic setting of Harappa, the extent and condition of the ruins (known since 1826 and heavily damaged by pillaging of its bricks for building material), and their importance "to Archaeologists as the find-place of a certain class of seals engraved for the most part with the effigy of a unicorn and bearing inscriptions in an unknown pictographic script" (p. 11) first documented by Sir Alexander Cunningham in 1875. The succeeding chapters summarize work done at Mound F (site of the first seasons' digging), and other new investigations (with a separate chapter devoted entirely to the finds from the cemetery), although most of the text is arranged by types of artifacts recovered. These include pottery (both plain and painted, parallels drawn with similar materials from Mohenjo-daro), human and animal figurines, stone and faience vessels, the now-famous seals and seal impressions, domestic objects, playthings and games, items of shell and ivory and the brick-lined furnaces from Mound F (possibly used for metalwork and glazing.) Guest analyses of ancient Indian copper technology and beads from the site preface Vats' own reportage of this type of artifact. The second volume of the report contains 139 black and white photographic plates (interspersed with folded maps) covering the results of all field seasons directed by Vats and the artifacts recovered. An unusual feature is the inclusion of a "sign manual" covering all items of the Indus script then known. This set was written as a complement to Sir John Marshall's three-volume set *Mohenjo-daro and the Indus Civilization* (1931) and

E.J.Mackay's *Further Excavations at Mohenjo-daro* (1938), entered separately in the present bibliography.

388. Prashad, Baini. *Animal Remains From Harappa*. Delhi: Manager of Publications, 1936.

The text of this fifty-first *Memoir* of the Archaeological Survey of India was written by the director of the Zoological Survey of India as a survey and analysis of the corpus of animal skeletal specimens collected between 1924 and 1931 at Harappa. Prashad notes that the size of the collection is notable, "almost four-to-five times the size of the animal remains from Mohenjo-daro." (p. 1) With a few exceptions (including the rhinoceros) all materials represent domesticated species. Emphasis is placed in this text on "tracing the probable ancestries and ...areas of domestication of the various animals." (p. 3) A systematic description of the collection is followed by seven high quality photographic plates illustrating type specimens.

389. Stein, Sir Mark Aurel. *Archaeological Reconnaisances In North-Western India and South-Eastern Iran*. London, Macmillan, 1937.

Intended as a volume recording the author's explorations (principally of the north coast of the Arabian Sea and the southern coast of Iran) in the years 1930-1931, this work is also connected to archaeological survey work in the northern reaches of the Indus Valley and the Salt Range. The first two chapters report on Stein's investigations of the site of Alexander the Great's battle with local Indian rulers, attempts to locate the altars he raised on the banks of the Hydaspes River (the modern Jhelum), and the surface collecting and site survey done at various points along the Salt Range. Locales visited include the fortress of Nandana, Ketas, and Murti. Researchers unfamiliar with the dissected topography of the region will find Stein's detailed maps an invaluable aid. References to related publications are provided in textual notes.

390. Barger, Evert. *Excavations in Swat and Explorations in the Oxus Territories of Afghanistan*. Delhi: Manager of Publications, 1941.

The subtitle of this sixty-fourth *Memoir* of the Archaeological Survey of India is "a detailed report of the 1938 expedition," which spent the summer of that year excavating a number of sites in the Swat Valley and making a survey reconnaissance in the Oxus River region of Afghanistan. The actual coverage of work at the sites of Kanjar Kote, Gumbar, Amluk and other locales occupies the first two-thirds of the text. The field survey of Afghanistan which closes the volume provides both a useful assessment of scientific investigations done in the region up to the 1940s and a graphic account of the difficulties of carrying out archaeology in such a remote environment. The Swat sculptures are described as "the first well-documented collection to reach museums from excavated sites in the hill tracts of the Indian Frontier." (p. 37) Twelve black and white plates illustrate sample carvings, plans of five of the sites, and selected views of Afghanistan.

391. Deva, Krishna and Donald E.McCown. "Further Exploration In Sind :1938," *Ancient India* 5 (January 1949): 12-30.

In the autumn of 1938, N.G. Majumdar resumed his survey of the Khirthar range on the western edge of the middle Indus Valley in Sind for prehistoric sites, a campaign cut short after three weeks due to his murder by robbers. This article is a report of the data gathered in that period, with one of the authors being a member of the field team. While surface collections and test excavations from several sites are included in this report, emphasis is given to the data from Pai-jo-kotiro, Rohel-jo-kund and Rajo-dero. The relationship of the Harappan, Amri and Nal cultures is explored, with data from Rohel-jo-kund "showing a large number and rich variety of motifs peculiar to Nal pottery." (p. 24) Eight black and white plates illustrate sample sherds from sites visited in this field season.

392. Vogel, J.Ph. "The Northwest Frontier and Hellenic Civilization: Taxila and Mathura," in *Revealing India's Past: A Co-Operative Record of Archaeological Conservation and Exploration in India and Beyond*. London: The India Society, 1939: 136-152.

The North West Frontier Province as an administrative unit of British India was not constituted until 1901, and was the site of some of the first scientifically conducted excavations done in the subcontinent. Sites examined in depth include the 1909 excavations of a famous Buddhist monastery and stupa outside modern Peshawar (where the relic casket of Kanishka was recovered), Sir John Marshall's twenty years of work at the city of Taxila (tracing the successive cultural developments) and the sculptural school of Mathura. The interplay of Greek and Buddhist elements in regional art is noted.

393. Beck, Horace C. *The Beads from Taxila*. Delhi: Manager of Publications, 1941.

This short publication was issued during World War II as the sixty-fifth *Memoir* of the Archaeological Survey of India and presents the results of study and analysis of a corpus of nine hundred and fifty selected beads, ranging in date from 700 B.C. to 500 A.D., found during excavations at Taxila between 1912 and 1934. Styles vary from beads modeled on animals and birds to purely geometric forms. The collection is notable for the wide variety of materials utilized, with over twenty-six individual substances represented. These range from familiar bone, shell, pottery and glass to the more exotic feldspar, iron pyrite, coral, beryl, malachite and lapis lazuli. Twelve plates (one a panel of colored drawings) depict the full range of the Taxila sample, with finds assigned to the sector of the excavations where they were found. Most useful when read in the context of the monographs on Taxila written by Sir John Marshall.

394. Mackay, Ernest J.H. *Chanhu-Daro Excavations 1935-36*. New Haven: American Oriental Society, 1943.

First discovered as part of a regional archaeological survey of Sind by N.G. Majumdar in February, 1931, the three mounds comprising the site of Chanhu-daro lie twelve miles from the modern course of the Indus. This report covers the results of the first field season carried out between October 1935 and March 1936 on the largest mound. The principal aim of this excavation was to seek the remains of any earlier cultures which might underlie the two strata of the Harappan civilization, whose remains were the chief components of the mound. Proof of no fewer than three floods was found. Individual chapters present and summarize data from the upper levels of Mound II (where pottery from the successor Jhukar culture was found overlying the Harappan city), pottery types distinctive to the Harappa and Jhukar cultures as then known, seals and seal impressions, figurines, copper and bronze utensils (ranging from fishhooks to razors, saws, axes and knives of varying shapes), and an unusual separate section on "toys and playthings." Ninety-six plates supply a variety of illustrations, beginning with plans and photographs of all site features and major cuttings from the season's work and including many photographs and line drawings of distinctive pottery designs. A bibliography of relevant archaeological literature is appended to the main text. Chanhu-daro would later be cited as one of the sites indicating the full territorial extent of the Indus Valley culture.

395. Wheeler, R.E.M. "Harappa 1946: The Defences and Cemetery R 37," *Ancient India* 3 (January 1947): 59-130.

This lengthy report contains the results of the 1946 field season at Harappa, when attention was focused on defining the nature and character of the defense works and "the only systematic cemetery of the true Harappa culture at present known to us" (p. 83), discovered in 1937. Cuttings made through the western mound AB (designated as "the citadel") revealed a substantial brick revetment and a massive mud-brick defense wall, which are presented in detailed cross-section. Most of the text is devoted to field work done in the cemetery, intended to link up both known areas used for interment stratigraphically and to attempt recovery of further burials from this culture under more controlled conditions. Of the ten graves identified in 1946, four were undisturbed, revealing a practice of extended placement of the body. The final forty pages analyse the pottery recovered from both work areas (including inscribed pottery, noted as being common at Harappa, while rare at Mohenjo-daro) and smaller finds, ranging from personal items such as beads, rings and a copper mirror to distinctive terracotta figurines depicting both humans and animals.High quality line drawings and black and white photographs illustrate all pottery types and selected artifacts. An appendix lists all sites then known from which identifiably Harappan pottery had been recovered, with references to publications available.

396. Piggott, Stuart. "A New Prehistoric Ceramic From Baluchistan," *Ancient India* 3 (January 1947): 131-142.

A paper reporting the results of surface collections carried out in 1944 at five sites in the immediate vicinity of Quetta. The primary focus of Piggott's work is to describe a new variant of "the prehistoric painted pottery which forms the most characteristic feature of the primitive village communities of Baluchistan in the second and probably the third millennium B.C." (p. 131) Following descriptions of the five sites visited (three of which were known from previous collecting done by Harold Hargreaves in 1925), the distinguishing features of "Quetta ware" are described and links with established pottery types in both India and Iran suggested. Six line figures showing variation in patterns of external and internal ornament are included. Context for this report may be obtained from the author's 1946 article "The Chronology of Prehistoric North-West India" in the present bibliography.

397. Ghosh, A. "Taxila (Sirkap), 1944-5," *Ancient India* 4 (July 1947- January 1948): 41-84.

In 1944, the Archaeological Survey of India conducted an extensive field training school for university students at the site of Taxila (on the border of the North West Frontier Province and the Punjab), chosen for the known richness of its several occupation areas. This account by the principal supervisor for that season reports on the work done at Sirkap, site of the second city of Taxila during the Indo-Greek era of the second century B.C. A trench 200 feet long was excavated in an attempt to establish the relationship of the stone fortifications to previously dated buildings within the city. A pentagonal bastion and system of drains were uncovered. The seventy-seven vessel types produced at Sirkap are described in detail, along with terracotta, metal, ivory and bone artifacts and coinage. Black and white photographs (including an aerial view of the excavations) and line drawings provide illustration.

398. Piggott, Stuart. "Sassanian Motifs On Painted Pottery From North West India," *Ancient India* 5 (January 1949): 31-34.

A vase from the Quetta region bearing the design of a mythical beast, the hippocamp, is related to the popularity of this image in the art of the later Sassanid era of Persia in the sixth and seventh centuries A.D. The possible spread of this design element eastward over caravan routes is set in the political and economic context of the time.

399. Chowdhury, K.A. and S.S. Ghosh. "Plant-Remains From Harappa 1946," *Ancient India* 7 (January 1951): 3-19.

During the 1946 field season at Harappa (which took the cemetery as one of its chief areas of investigation), the remains of four timbers were recovered, two from use in a coffin. This paper reports both on the process of their analysis and the results, identifying the trees used as deodar, ber, elm and rosewood. The authors (both wood technologists affiliated with the Forest Research Institute) discuss the implications of their findings as to long-distance trade networks and possible local climate at Harappa in the past. Wheeler's original report on the 1946 dig has been entered separately in the present bibliography.

400. Srivastava, H.L. *Excavation at Agroha,Punjab.* New Delhi: Manager of Publications, 1952.

Yet another scientific casualty of both World War II and Partition, the field work upon which this text reports was originally carried out at the series of mounds comprising the ruins of Agroha (between Hissar and Fatehabad) in 1938-39. Immediately thereafter, wartime restrictions on printing halted publication of the annual reports of the Archaeological Survey of India, delaying the appearance of the results of excavation. Upon Partition, the original records and many of the artifacts found became inaccessible due to their location in the former office of the Frontier Circle of the Survey, now in Pakistan. First investigated in 1888-89 by C.J. Rodgers of the Punjab Circle of the Archaeological Survey, the 1938-39 season at Agroha focused on sinking test trenches into one of the larger mounds, which exposed a planned settlement of brick structures apparently destroyed by fire. Notable finds included fragments of a birch bark manuscript and coins dating the site to the second century B.C. Thirteen black and white plates illustrate type finds and include a complete grid plan and section of the 1938 trench.

401.Childe, V.Gordon. "Indian Civilization in the Third Millennium B.C.," in *New Light On The Most Ancient East.* New York: Frederick A. Praeger, 1953: 172-188.

A second updated edition of Childe's 1928 popular work, this volume attempts to integrate new data from fieldwork done between 1938 and 1953. Note is made in the introduction of the excavations done by Sir Mortimer Wheeler, and numerous footnotes in this chapter reference the excavations at Chanhu-daro as well as the type cities of Harappa and Mohenjo-daro.

Orissa

402. Mitra, Rajendra Lala. *Antiquities of Orissa.* Calcutta: Indian Studies, Past and Present, 1961-63. 2 vols.

This two-volume set is the first reprint of the original 1875 and 1880 texts, which were published in Calcutta by the Baptist Mission Press "under the orders of the Government of India." Mitra's involvement with this subject began in 1868, when the Government of India, at the suggestion of the Royal Society of Arts, London, assigned a sum of money for the purpose of making casts of "some of the more important sculptures of ancient India." (p. i) He suggested to the Lieutenant-Governor of Bengal that the party should proceed first to Bhubaneshwar, and was deputed to accompany them so as to record historical and descriptive information about the structures to be copied. The results of the expedition in 1868-69 are reported in this text. The first volume covers the history of Indian architecture, general principles of Orissan temple architecture, sculpture and architectural ornamentation, the society which produced the Orissan temple and the religions active in the region. For the archaeologist, the second volume may be of greater value, as it focuses on specific localities within Orissa. The first chapter deals with the antiquities of the Khandagiri Hills, the second with the temples of Bhubaneshwar itself, the third and fourth with the structures of Konarak, Satyabadi and Puri, and the fifth a range of smaller sites. Both volumes are illustrated with reproductions of many of the plates in the original set, as some were too indistinct to be clearly duplicated, while others were photographic views of specific temples, better examples of which were in existence by the 1960s. These plates offer invaluable data on the condition of these Orissan monuments in the late nineteenth century.

403. Tripathy, K.C. "South Orissa Prehistory- The First Record of Stone Tools," *Asian Perspectives* 15 (1): (1972): 47-59.

While the first stone tools known from Orissa were identified by V. Ball in 1876, much of the field archaeological survey has been carried out in the northern districts of the state. This article reports on the early results of a project initiated by the author "of exploring river valleys and prehistoric sites in the vast area of South Orissa" (p. 47) lying below the Mahanadi River. Surface exploration had been completed in all districts of the region, with Koraput and Bolangir districts yielding prehistoric tools. The stratigraphy and typology of specimens thus far identified and their relationship to known materials from other parts of Orissa are presented.

404. Vasu, Nagendra Nath. *The Archaeological Survey of Mayurbhanja.*Delhi: Rare Reprints, 1981.

The result of archaeological investigations carried out by the author within the lands of the former state of Mayurbhanja during the years 1907-1909. The book opens with a summary of the presence and influences of various major Indian religions within the state,, chiefly Jainism, Hinduism and Buddhism. The body of the work is composed of reports ranging from one to eleven pages on forty-five sites, covering the presence of inscriptions, known associated historical events, structures extant at the time of survey and their physical condition, and sculptures when present. Sixty-five black and white plates illustrate sculpture, temple plans and sections, and reproductions of inscribed copper plates (these last also covered in an appendix). Indexed by geographic and personal names. Useful as an assessment of the condition of this group of sites at the beginning of the twentieth century.

405. Ganguly. Manomohan. *Orissa and Her Remains*. Patna: Eastern Book House, 1987.

This volume is a reprinted edition of the original 1912 survey of the state of Orissa done by a district engineer with a sharp interest in architecture. His attention to detail serves to make this work one of the pioneering studies of ancient construction within the modern boundaries of the state of Orissa, both by example and method. The first seven chapters discuss provincial history in general and the gradual coalescence and evolution of distinctive local forms (including cave temples), traces of Greco-Roman influence, medieval architecture, sculptural styles and building materials. Extensive analysis of the major sites at Puri, Konarak and Bhubaneswar completes the field work. Twenty-seven black and white photographic plates provide both interior and exterior illustrations and ground plans. Indexing is provided by site name, subject and author. Best used with Rajendralal Mitra's fundamental study *Antiquities of Orissa* for background to the archaeology of the province. Two appendixes provide a short unannotated bibliography and a glossary of Indian terms frequently used in the text.

406. Chanda, Ramaprasad. *Explorations in Orissa*. Calcutta: Government of India Central Publications Branch, 1930.

This forty-fourth *Memoir* of the Archaeological Survey of India by the superintendent of the Archaeological Section of Calcutta's Indian Museum was written "to give a short account of…sites and their monumental remains to serve as a background of the account of my acquisitions from Orissa in 1927-28." (p. 1)This last refers to Chanda's collecting tour, done with the object of procuring an adequate sample of Orissan sculpture for the Museum. Separate sections summarize the history and structures at the sites of Jajpur, Udayagiri, Ratnagiri, Nalatigiri, Kendrapatam and the Buddhist monuments of Orissa dating to the seventh century A.D., illustrated by nine black and white plates. Researchers wishing a more extensive treatment of this aspect of Orissa's past should consult the two-volume site report on Ratnagiri by Debala Mitra, published in 1981.

407. Chandra, Ramaprasad. "Mayurbhanj: Khiching Temples," in *Revealing India's Past: A Co-Operative Record of Archaeological Conservation and Exploration in India and Beyond* edited by Sir John Cumming. London: The India Society, 1939: 321-324.

Written by the director of the 1923-24 excavations at this former capital of the state of Mayurbhanj, this brief essay summarizes the history of the temple complex of Khiching, first noted by the Archaeological Survey in 1875. Emphasis is placed upon linking the style of ornamentation to such other centers as Bhubaneswar. Of particular value is the continuous usage of the site by successive generations of rulers, permitting the visitor "to follow the decline of North Indian architecture and sculpture from the eleventh to the sixteenth century." (p. 322) Prior to 1930, archaeological work in Mayurbhanj was directly administered by the Archaeological Survey of India.

408. Lal.B.B. "Sisupalgarh 1948: An Early Historic Fort In Eastern India," *Ancient India* 5 (January 1949): 62-105.

A report on the excavations carried out between April and June 1948 at the site of Shishupalgarh near Bhubaneswar in Orissa. The field objectives were the determination of the local cultural sequence, the nature and construction of the defensive system and the planning of one of the eight gateways. Occupation of the site (a major fortress roughly square in plan with some twenty-six feet of cultural deposits) was determined to have spanned the period from 300 B.C. to 350 A.D. The rouletted pottery already known from Arikamedu, Brahmagiri and Chandravalli was found at the site, extending the chronology of the eastern coast of India further north. A massive clay rampart was constructed in the second century A.D., the western gateway of which was excavated and structurally planned. Analysis of the types of the plain and decorated pottery wares, beads, ear-ornaments, iron objects and coins recovered from the various levels is presented in detail.Illustration of the stratigraphy of the defenses and general aspect of the site is provided by photographs and line drawings.

409. Panigrahi, Krishna Chandra. *Archaeological Remains at Bhubaneswar.*Bombay: Orient Longmans, 1961.

This volume is inaccurately titled, as no archaeological excavation is reported. One hundred and forty-three black and white plates offer highly detailed images of both free-standing structures and architectural elements of the Bhubaneswar complex. Topics covered by the ten chapters stress the individual features of Orissan architecture, shifts in iconography on those temples at Bhubaneswar which can be dated wth some accuracy, (and their chronologies) and a full discussion of the three most famed temples, the Lingaraja, Rajarani and Mukteshvara.Bibliographic notes are provided throughout the text.

410. Acharya, Paramananda. *Studies In Orissan History, Archaeology and Archives*. Cuttack: Cuttack Students Store, 1969.

This volume is a collection of studies in the fields of historical records, epigraphy, historical geography, literary history and related subjects written by the state archaeologist of Mayurbhanj between 1924 and 1948. In the preface, Acharya discusses his evolution in the profession, which has included the collection of stone tools (establishing the presence of this artifact type in Orissa) and his contributions to the clarification of the local historical record. Papers relating to the traditional work of archaeology will be found under the heading "Art and Architecture" and cover "Notes on the Archaeological Sites and Temples at Khiching" and a report on field survey done in the Talcher area,while a third paper reports on several hoards of ancient coins (including Roman and Kushan mints). An excellent example of the type of local investigation which laid the foundation for later research across much of the subcontinent.

411. Lal, Kanwar. *Temples and Sculptures of Bhubaneswar*. Delhi: Arts and Letters, 1970.

A concise and lavishly illustrated work dealing equally with the spiritual values embodied in the temples of the site and physical descriptions of their forms. An interesting feature noted is the origin of the city's name, which stems from the aspect of Shiva worshipped in the main temple, the Lingaraja, "in the form of Tribhuvneshwar, the Lord of Three Worlds." (p. 4) Researchers will find the third and fourth chapters most useful in their presentation of the principal structures, although a familiarity with the Hindu religion is presupposed in much of the text.

412. Dehejia, Vidhya. *Early Stone Temples of Orissa*. New Delhi: Vikas Publishing House, 1979.

The author states that "the foundations of the Orissan temple style were apparently laid around AD 600, and in this book I concentrate upon the birth of the Orissan temple, tracing its development up to the period of its early maturity around AD 950." (p. v) The heavily illustrated work opens with a discussion of the geographic and political context of ancient Orissa (useful as a reference for readers unfamiliar with tangled local dynastic history), and a separate chapter on the craft organizations responsible for temple planning and construction. Three phases of elaboration of the basic temple designs are traced over four centuries, with sculptural elements and themes considered as the fourth chapter. One of the most valuable sections of the work deals with the evolution of the local Orissan script and the numerous copper-plate inscriptions known from the state (a species of artifact avidly sought by pioneers of Indian archaeology such as Sir Alexander Cunningham) together with problems of dating structures via found texts.Major sites illustrated include Bhubaneswar, Ratnagiri, Khiching and Muktesvar. An essential reference for interpreting survey and excavation reports dealing with local Orissan archaeology. A brief unannotated bibliography is provided.

413. Mitra, Debala. *Ratnagiri (1958-61)*. New Delhi: Director General, Archaeological Survey of India, 1981. 2 vols.

This massive two-volume set was issued as the eightieth *Memoir* of the Archaeological Survey of India and reports on investigations in the area near the stupa and monastery atop the isolated hill of Ratnagiri in eastern Orissa. Four field seasons resulted in the discovery of a massive central stupa surrounded by two hundred and ninety satellite shrines, two quadrangular monasteries, remains of a single-winged monastery and the remains of eight temples, some with stupas of their own. These finds accord well with scattered textual references to Ratnagiri as an important philosophical and religious academy. The first volume presents the physiography, known history and previous investigation and collecting done at the complex in the first four brief chapters. The rest of the book is occupied by chapters five and six, which give in-depth reports on the excavations in the densely-built area of the central stupa and the larger of the two monastic residences. Each minor shrine is presented and grouped by cardinal direction, with all architectural features and individual separated sculptures found described in detail.

The second volume opens with the report of work at the second and smaller monastery and the area southeast of Monastery I. These are followed by analyses of the bronze, copper and brass objects (including images of the Buddha) sealings, plaques, moulds, inscribed slabs bearing Buddhist texts, and sculptures visible at ground level. Three hundred and fifty-one black and white photographs (evenly split between the two volumes) offer a detailed visual record of the excavation of all structures in various stages of clearance, associated sculptures and carvings, architectural details of the central and minor stupas, terracotta and metal artifacts, and inscriptions.

414. Yule, P., B.K. Rath and K. Hojgaard. "Sankarjang- A Metals Period Burial Site in the Dhenkanal Uplands of Orissa," in *South Asian Archaeology 1987* edited by Maurizio Taddei. Naples: Istituto Universitario Orientale, 1990: 581-584.

Discovered in 1971, the Orissan site of Sankarjang is composed of a cemetery containing some sixty-eight mounds, three of which were subsequently tested. Notable among the grave goods were basalt bars, which are interpreted as component elements of a musical instrument composed of individually cut stones. Parallels are noted with similar musical devices known from Vietnam. The authors note Sankarjang as a major source of data on the region, as "relative to the early cultures of Northwest India, prehistoric Orissa has received little attention." (p. 581)

415. Neumayer, Ernest. "Rock Pictures in Orissa," *Puratattva* 22 (1992/92): 13-24.

Much of this article is taken up with reproductions of rock art from the Sundargarh and Sambalpur districts of Orissa, a genre first noted in the 1930's at the Vikramkhole shelter. Observing that "today rock art from Orissa is generally unknown even among archaeologists and prehistorians," (p. 13) the author then reviews typical settings of the engravings and paintings (usually rock shelters in isolated sandstone formations) and dominant images and themes depicted in the characteristic polychrome red, white, black, yellow and beige images. The relationship of this regional style to other Central Indian rock art is explored. Reseachers wishing a broader context for the art of Orissa should consult Neumayer's comprehensive work on India's rock carving and paintings *Lines on Stone* (1993).

416. Mohanty, Pradeep. "Mesolithic Hunter-gatherers of Keonjhar District, Orissa, India," *Asian Perspectives* 32(1) 1993: 85-104.

The Mesolithic era in Indian prehistory has long been characterized by the appearance of an assemblage of highly varied small stone tool types, which are found widely across the subcontinent. This article reports on six seasons of survey carried out in the northern part of the state of Orissa between 1983 and 1989, yielding fifty-eight new Mesolithic sites. A notable find was the presence of both typical microliths and a heavy tool industry made of dolerite, principally core scrapers, picks, cleavers, knives and celts. The distribution pattern of these tools is viewed as reflecting varied activities within a climatic zone similar to the contemporary forest environment. The author calls for a reassessment of other Mesolithic sites from a functional perspective.

Punjab

417. Young, G.M. "A New Hoard From The Bhir Mound," *Ancient India* 1 (January 1946) 27-36.

In early 1945, a second hoard of eighteen bent-bar silver coins and jewellery was discovered at the site of Taxila, joining an earlier similar find from 1924. This article presents an analysis of the hoard by the Director of the British School at Athens, touching on their method of manufacture, mint imprints, and probable period of use, which Young ascribes to the fourth century B.C. The gold beads and chain, silver ornaments and carved gems from the 1945 find are illustrated along with the earlier finds for comparison.

418. Bala,Madhu. *Archaeology of Punjab*. Delhi: Agam Kala Prakashan, 1992.

An English translation of a Punjabi original, this concise work summarizes for the non-specialist the archaeology of the state of Punjab from prehistory to the historical period as known in the early 1990s. Beginning with a brief overview of the physical geography and the five river systems which give the region its name, each era is covered in some detail. The second chapter on "Prehistoric Punjab" notes the existence of seventy-six sites assignable to the early Stone age and traces fieldwork from the discovery of the Sohan tool assemblage to investigations carried out after Partition. Neolithic data is briefly presented in the third section. The most lengthy chapter is that on the protohistoric period, which reviews data from fourteen sites representing a complex "matrix of proto-historic cultures." (p. 24) Individual sites noted are Kotla-Nihang Khan, Dher Majra, Ropar, Bara, Sanghol, Sarangpur, Chandigarh, Salaura, Dadheri, Nagar, Katpalon, Rohira and Mahorana. Mentions made of the Punjab in ancient literature and available numismatic evidence are treated in chapters five and six. Historic era archaeology is represented by data from four selected sites including Ghuram and the three successive city sites of Taxila. A valuable feature for the reader unfamiliar with the available archaeological literature are the tables listing Stone Age, protohistoric and historic sites by district provided in chapters two, four,and seven. Twenty-seven line drawings (including maps showing the regional distribution of Harappan sites and building plans) and forty black and white photographs illustrate artifacts from most of the major sites referenced in the text.A bibliography covering Punjab archaeology from Alexander Cunningham's 1882 *Report of A Tour in the Punjab* to 1990 provides a useful beginning for the researcher unfamiliar with the region's archaeological history.

Rajasthan

419. Bhandarkar, Devadatta Ramkrishna. *The Archaeological Remains and Excavations at Nagari*. Calcutta: Superintendent, Government Printing of India, 1920.

The fourth in the series of *Memoirs* issued by the Archaeological Survey of India, this report summarizes the scientific investigations carried out since 1872 at the site of Nagari in Udaipur State, centering on Bhandarkar's two-month visit in 1919-1920. The initial section reviews five inscriptions (several in Sanskrit) found at or near the site, coinage, moulded bricks, and the two major ancient buildings known as Ubh-dival (a conical tower) and Hathi-bada (a rectangular enclosure possibly constructed to hold a site of religious worship). Excavations were carried out at the latter and "a mound in the southern half of the citadel surmounted by a modern shrine of Mahadeva." (p. 134) Terracotta artifacts, pottery, stone and metal objects found are listed, and twenty-four photographs and plans illustrate the ruins. Bibliographic references to related literature are interspersed throughout the text. A reprint appeared in 1977.

420. Sahni, Daya Ram. "Jaipur," in *Revealing India's Past: A Co-Operative Record of Archaeological Conservation and Exploration in India and Beyond*. London: The India Society, 1939: 305-312.

The territory of the state of Jaipur was among those areas visited by Sir Alexander Cunningham in his twenty-three years of surveying the ancient monuments of northern India. The present article is an account of the archaeological work done in this part of Rajasthan since the formation of the local Archaeological Department in 1935. Sites noted as worthy of further inspection include Bairat, Sambhar and Nagar. The author was the first director of the Jaipur department.

421. Misra, V.N. "Bagor- A Late Mesolithic Settlement in North-West India," *World Archaeology* 5(1) (June 1973): 92-110.

A report of three seasons of excavation carried out between 1968 and 1970 at Bagor, "the largest mesolithic habitation site discovered in India...the only one to have been horizontally excavated so as to expose extensive living floors." (p. 92) Three levels of deposits represent a span of occupation from 5000 B.C. to 200 A.D. A highly diverse microlithic stone tool kit is associated with copper and iron technologies, pottery and terracotta objects, a pattern corroborated at other sites such as Morhana Pahar and Langhnaj.

422. Allchin, Bridget and Andrew Goudie. "Pushkar: Prehistory and Climatic Change in Western India," *World Archaeology* 5(3) (February 1974): 358-368.

The Pushkar Basin lies northwest of Ajmer in Rajasthan, and consists of an enclosed valley with fossil dunes from past periods of extension of the Thar Desert. This article reports on the results of two field survey visits which yielded evidence of continuous usage by man beginning in Palaeolithic times. The Middle Palaeolithic tools from the Hokhra and Budha Pushkar basins are illustrated and discussed. Lower Palaeolithic tools found in January 1973 in a redeposited layer of debris washed from the hills are noted. The entire sequence "provides for the first time an indication of the nature and scale of climatic change during the Pleistocene in the Indian sub-continent outside the Himalayas." (p. 367) Readers interested in following up this field of research should consult the authors' 1978 work *The Prehistory and Palaeogeography of the Great Indian Desert.*

423. Thapar, B.K. "Kalibangan: A Harappan Metropolis Beyond the Indus Valley," *Expedition* 17 (2) (Winter 1975): 19-32.

Kalibangan (whose name means "black bangles," a reference to the weathered terracotta ornaments scattered across the site surface) lies on the left bank of the dry river Ghaggar in northern Rajasthan. First located during a survey in the early 1950's, its investigation began in 1961 and continued for nine seasons until 1969. This report summarizes in a readable fashion the distinctive pre-Harappan occupation termed Kalibangan I and the full Harappan city, presenting plans and analysis of the recovered materials (concentrating on pottery forms which can be aligned stylistically with Kot Diji and Amri, but including copper and stone objects as well). Unique features uncovered are "perhaps the earliest ploughfield excavated so far" (p. 22) from Kalibangan I and three distinctive burial patterns from the Harappan era cemetery. Occupation of Kalibangan is tentatively dated to 2300-1750 B.C., terminated by a diversion of the Ghaggar eastward to the Ganga drainage.

424. Kumar, Giri Raj. "Discovery of Microlithic Industry from Jaipur (Rajasthan)," *Journal of Indian History* 57: 31-39.

A note on the discovery of a series of crude microlithic tools in a group of fossilized sand dunes near Rajasthan University in Jaipur in December 1976 during a preliminary survey. Forms seen are scrapers, blades, burins and borers. Full measurements from all artifacts collected are presented and thirty samples illustrated in a line drawing.

425. Agrawala, R.C. "Aravalli, the Major Source of Copper for the Indus and Indus-related Cultures," in *Frontiers of the Indus Civilization* edited by B.B.Lal and S.P. Gupta. New Delhi: Books and Books, 1984: 157-162.

A summary of field work done between 1977 and 1981 in the Copper Belt regions of northern Rajasthan. Data are presented on the occurrence of copper tools and the sources for their metal during the protohistoric Ahar culture of the area, at the major Harappan site of Kalibangan, and at the newly-discovered site of Ganeshwar. The possible interrelation of these groups is discussed.

426. Misra, V.N. and N. Rajaguru. "Palaeoenvironment and Prehistory of the Thar Desert, Rajasthan, India," in *South Asian Archaeology 1985* edited by Karen Frifelt and Per Sorensen. London: Curzon Press, 1989: 296-320.

A synthesis of the findings made in the period 1978 to 1985 by an ongoing palaeoenvironmental and archaeological project centered in the western Thar desert of Rajasthan. This region was selected as "in no other part of India are such drastic hydrological and climatic changes...documented as in the Thar." (p. 314) Four major programs of investigation are profiled: field survey in eleven local districts (resulting in the discovery of over fifty Palaeolithic, Mesolithic and historic era archaeological sites), the taking of core samples from several salt-lakes to permit climatic reconstuction during the Pleistocene and Holocene, collection of ethnoarchaeological data on contemporary nomadic and semi-nomadic peoples of the Thar, and excavation of selected sites. Data from these last (Jayal, Singi Talav, Indola-ki-Dhani and a dune site designated as 16R) is presented and analysed. The project has verified human occupancy of the Thar beginning with an Acheulean stone tool industry in the Late to Middle Pleistocene followed by a break due to increased aridity before the return of man during the Mesolithic ca. 6000-4000 B.C. The accompanying detailed charts present maps of known Mesolithic and Palaeolithic archaeological sites, the Thar stratigraphic sequence as then known,and sample stone tools from the excavations at 16R and Singi Talav. Excellent background on this region may be found in the 1978 volume by Allchin, Goudie and Hegde, *The Prehistory and Palaeogeography of the Great Indian Desert.*

427. Deitmer, Stephen. "The Observatories Of Jai Singh," *Astronomy* 13 (January, 1985): 18-22.

This article presents each of the structures erected as part as part of the mammoth open-air *jantar mantars (*computing devices) at Jaipur from an astronomical point of view, emphasizing their construction and intended functioning. Researchers wishing to gain a clearer idea of these buildings should consult the 1993 article by Peter Engel in *Natural History,* "Stairways to Heaven," as this essay is not well-illustrated.

428. Hooja, Rima. *The Ahar Culture and Beyond: Settlements and Frontiers of Mesolithic and Early Agricultural Sites in South-Eastern Rajasthan c.3rd-2 nd Millennium B.C.* Oxford: B.A.R., 1988.

Following the partition of India and Pakistan in 1947, archaeologists within the newly-drawn borders began intensive field survey and programs of excavation in an effort to expand the relatively limited information available on the prehistoric eras for much of the subcontinent. Among the discoveries was the site of Ahar in southeastern Rajasthan, where a copper-using agricultural culture was revealed dating to 2000 B.C. Subsequent investigations in Rajasthan and adjacent sections of Madhya Pradesh eventually raised the number of sites of what became known as the Ahar Culture to more than eighty. In the same region, a culture marked by an extensive microlithic tool industry was noted at Bagor and other locations. Radiocarbon dating indicated that some levels of these sites were occupied at the same time periods, leading to questions regarding possible interactions locally and with the later stages of the Harappan civilization. This study focuses on the latter question and offers a model based on the historic interaction of settled village communities with the Bhil tribal peoples. The opening chapters collate and summarize the available data on the Ahar culture (known principally from the original excavations and later work at the site of Gilund), the methodology used in the sample, and Rajasthan history and physical geography. The range of Ahar sites is traced and the distribution of microlithic sites assessed. Local history of hunting and gathering populations and the Rajput villages is then outlined, with the idea of the frontier zone in archaeology suggested as an interpretive model.A gazetteer of known Ahar sites and a lengthy bibliography complete the work.

429. Engel, Peter "Stairways To Heaven," *Natural History* 102 (June, 1993): 48-57.

A detailed discussion intended for a general audience of the history and construction of the five stone observatories of Jai Singh, all of which were completed between 1719 and 1737 in Jaipur, Agra, Mathura, Delhi and Ujjain. The goal was to permit correction of the official astronomical tables used to reconcile the Hindu and Muslim calendric systems. Striking color photographs of the major structures at Jaipur accompany the text.

430. Kramer, Carol. *Pottery In Rajasthan: Ethnoarchaeology in Two Indian Cities.* Washington, D.C.: Smithsonian Institution Press, 1997.

The two cities of the title are Jodhpur and Udaipur, where the fieldwork reported here was carried out in the early 1980s, Rajasthan being chosen for its continuing tradition of pottery manufacture and the absence of prior ethnographic studies. Three types of questions were explored in this study: the number, diversity and sources of utilitarian pottery found in modern settlements of varying sizes, factors affecting their predictable variation, sociological relationships between the producers of the vessels and those who distribute them, and effective sampling methods for large-scale sites. Kramer notes that "archaeologists need empirical information about the scales at which pottery moves across a landscape." (p. 3)The six chapters present theoretical cosiderations of the project, profiles of the cities and their potters' communities,actual processes of vessel manufacture,decoration and distribution, patterns of sales and marketing, and external sources of pottery. Results of the Rajasthani seasons indicate several implications for archaeological recovery of diverse sources, craft specializations, and transfer of technologies. Researchers unfamiliar with Rajasthan will find the excellently detailed illustrations and the lengthy bibliography helpful.

Tamil Nadu

431. Srinivasan, K.R. "The Megalithic Burials and Urn-Fields Of South India In The Light of Tamil Literature and Tradition." *Ancient India* 2 (July, 1946): 9-16.

A review of linguistic,literary and epigraphical references to the numerous megalithic monuments of southern India in the Tamil language of the region. Full translation of all cited texts accompanies the originals. A range of dates for the construction and use of urn burials and megaliths is set at between 300 B.C.-500

A.D. The author, a former museum curator from the region, notes in his introduction that "their correct interpretation still awaits the spade of the scientific archaeologist." (p. 9)

432. Wheeler, R.E.M. "Arikamedu: An Indo-Roman Trading Station on the East Coast of India," *Ancient India* 2 (July 1946): 17-123.

A report on the fieldwork done in 1945 on two sectors of the site of Arikamedu, previously noted by French investigators near Pondicherry and identified by this season's work as one of the "Yavana," trading stations mentioned by classical writers, and dated by internal evidence to the first century A.D. The extremely detailed text opens with an exploration of the historical background of Indian trade as represented in both Roman and Tamil literature. This is followed by discussion of the stratigraphy found in the 1945 season, the two structures located and their possible uses as warehouse and textile manufacturing center respectively. Over half of the report is devoted to an examination of both the domestic and imported pottery, as "upon the ... Mediterranean wares the whole chronology of the site and its special importance therefore to Indian archaeology, depend." (p. 34) Three categories are noted; red to red-orange Arretine ware, a widespread product of Italy with a terminal date of 50 A.D., amphorae used in wine or oil shipments (corroborated by classical Tamil texts) and rouletted black ware. These known forms and styles are used by Wheeler to give an approximate chronology to the locally made pottery, which comprised the bulk of the materials recovered. Medieval Chinese celadon ware is also noted and considered as marking the later despoiling of the site through robbery for bricks. Other small objects indicating contact with the Graeco-Roman world are lamps, glass bowls, and engraved intaglio gems. Inscriptions are limited to potsherds bearing proper names in early Tamil. Appendixes summarize data on the distribution of Roman coins dating between the first century B.C. and fourth century A.D. known from India and Ceylon, the distribution of semi-precious stones and the ancient name of Arikamedu. The text of this article is lavishly illustrated with full-page line drawings and black and white photographs covering all pottery forms, the physical location of the site, and sections of the structures uncovered during the 1945 excavations. The author notes in the preface that "by establishing at last the precise chronological position of an extensive South Indian culture, the archaeologist has provided a new starting-point for the study of the pre-medieval civilizations of the Indian peninsula." (p. 17) Researchers working in the area of southern Indian prehistory should also consult the 1949 volume by J.M. Casal, *Fouilles de Virampatnam-Arikamedu*, for data on subsequent work at the site.

433. Casal, J.M. *Fouilles de Virampatnam-Arikamedu. Rapport del'Inde et de l'Occident aux environs de l'ere chretienne.* Paris: Librairie C. Klincksieck, 1949.

Discovered in 1937 through surface collections made by a faculty member of the College of Pondicherry, Arikamedu lies south of that city on the north bank of the Ariancoupom River.This report presents data from the first three seasons of excavations. Beginning with the September, 1941 work by Fr.Facheux, the 1945 work done by the Archaeological Survey of India under the direction of Sir Mortimer Wheeler and the 1947 and 1948 field sessions (the latter directed by Casal himself), are reviewed. Much of the main text of the report deals with analysing the stratigraphic sequences from two sample areas and presents a summary plan of the sections worked. Appendixes supply data on the Roman Arretine trade pottery found at the site, a unified stratigraphic profile, and twenty black and white plates illustrating structural features (chiefly foundation elements), pottery types found (both Indian and imported) and specialized artifacts in ivory. A short bibliography of reports done on the site prior to 1949 in both French and English is provided. Readers wishing to familiarize themselves with Arikamedu should be aware that the 1945 season is covered in Sir Mortimer Wheeler's memoir *My Archaeological Mission To India and Pakistan* (1976) and a lengthy report in the July, 1946 issue of *Ancient India*.

434. Banerjee, N.R. "The Megalithic Problem of Chingleput In The Light of Recent Exploration," *Ancient India* 12 (1956): 21-34.

A report and analysis of the results of excavations carried out between 1950 and 1955 at two megalithic sites, Sanur and Amirthamangalam, in the Madras area. The area had been comprehensively mapped for remains, permitting analysis of locale, building materials and construction, method of inhumation and associated artifacts. Readers should also consult the 1959 article by Banerjee and Soundara Rajan on the 1950 and 1952 seasons at Sanur.

435. Banerjee, N.R. and K.V. Soundara Rajan. "Sanur 1950 and 1952: A Megalithic Site In District Chingleput," *Ancient India* 15 (1959): 4-42.

A report on the excavation of five tombs at Sanur, whose object was "to obtain a picture of the varieties of megalithic tombs in the area, together with dating evidence, if possible." (p. 5) The site contains more than three hundred structures, chiefly of the cairn circle and dolmenoid cist types. All five of the tested tombs yielded sarcophagi and pottery and ranged in diameter from eighteen to fifty feet. Correlation with similar materials from Brahmagiri suggests a date betwwen 200 B.C and 50 A.D.

436. Banerjee, N.R. "Amirthamangalam 1955: A Megalithic Urn-burial Site in District Chingleput, Tamilnadu," *Ancient India* 22 (1966): 3-36.

The initial survey of the megalithic sites in the Chingleput district done by the Archaeological Survey of India from 1944 to 1948 resulted in the discovery of over two hundred sites. Excavations at the largest of the typical sites in the southern zone, Sanur, were carried out from 1950 to 1955. In addition to the megalithic sites, the northern zone of the District contained barrows without accompanying megaliths. Amirthamangalam was selected for excavation by the Southern Circle of the Survey "to expose the burial-urns (without megalithic appendage) and establish their role and chronology in megalithism in general" (p. 4) Some two hundred and fifty damaged urns containing skeletal remains and placed in pits cut into the laterite rock constituted the bulk of the finds. A provisional date of before the third century B.C. is assigned to the site on the basis of similarity of the urns to those found at Amaravati. The bulk of this article is taken up by a set of black and white plates depicting the general aspect of the urn field and a detailed presentation of the stratigraphy from the four cuttings made during the 1955 field season. A report on the cranial and skeletal remains by H.K. Bose is appended, accompanied by a full *List of Urn-Burial Sites Explored* (sixty-two in all) giving a complete description and remarks on the character of each. This data permits Amirthamangalam to be placed effectively in the local context of regional Tamil Nadu archaeology.

437. Sarma, Akkaraju V.N. "Upper Pleistocene and Holocene Ecology of East Central South India," in *Ecological Backgrounds of South Asian Prehistory* edited by Kenneth Kennedy and Gregory Possehl. Ithaca, New York: Cornell South Asia Program, 1974: 179-190.

This paper offers a fresh approach to the question of why the active ports of the kingdoms of southeastern India declined and their international trade ceased. In the summer of 1972, an intensive palaeoecological and archaeological survey was undertaken along the southeast coast from Cape Comorin north to Pondicherry. Four distinct terraces indicating past fluctuations in sea level were delineated. The author combines both Tamil historical references and contemporary geological data to suggest that a reconsideration of regional uplift should be factored into local archaeological research.

438. Nagaswamy, R. "Roman Sites in Tamil Nadu: Recent Discoveries," in *Madhu: Recent Researches in Indian Archaeology and Art History* Atlantic Highlands, New Jersey: Humanities Press, 1984: 337-339.

Notes on three sites whose newly-found remains expand the evidence of Roman occupation in Tamil Nadu. Vasavasamudram, Karur, and Kodumanal are placed in local archaeological and historical context.

439. Kennedy, Kenneth A.R. "Hauntings At Adittanalur: An Archaeological Ghost Story," in *Studies in the Archaeology of India and Pakistan* edited by Jerome Jacobson. Warminster: Aris and Phillips, 1987: 257-295.

In 1876, a field of urn burials was discovered at the village of Adittanalur in southern Tamil Nadu by German archaeologist Dr. Fedor Jagor, who collected a number of specimens and sent them back to Berlin, "the first time prehistoric human skeletal remains from India were brought to Europe for scientific study." (p. 260) His work was followed in 1903 by that of Louis Lapicque, who, like Jagor, subscribed to the theories of racial paleontology, a typology which assigned human skeletons to a particular racial group on the basis of morphological features. The fact that the Adittanalur specimens seemed to represent a pre-Dravidian Negroid race was taken as fulfillment of a hypothesis which saw a band of such races encircling the globe in the tropics.

This article both reviews the importance and varied interpretations (the "hauntings" of the title) which have been assigned to the Adittanalur skeletons since their discovery, and presents the diverse results of morphometric analyses done between 1924 and 1972 as well as a recent study done between 1975 and 1980 of both the German and Indian specimens taken from the site. The latter attempted an evaluation without utilizing either racial preconceptions or using cultural and linguistic data from contemporary populations. Kennedy notes that a "comparative study of the Adittanalur skeletal series with those of modern populations of southern India has yet to be undetaken...the definitive study is still to be done." (p. 281) Researchers will find the lengthy bibliography of publications relating to Adittanalur useful for their own examination of this tangled question.

440. Raman, K.V. "Further Evidence of Roman Trade from Coastal Sites in Tamil Nadu," in *Rome and India, The Ancient Sea Trade* edited by Vimala Begley and Richard Daniel. Madison, University of Wisconsin Press, 1991: 125-133.

A report on the identification of two new sites, Karaikadu and Alagankulam, on the Coromandel Coast, each of which has yielded artifacts related to trade with the West. Of particular value is the section of text which discusses the ancient political structure of this region of Tamil Nadu and the state of archaeological knowledge pertaining to the cities and industries cited by ancient sources. Speculation is also advanced as to the borrowing of Roman ornaments and forms (such as rouletting and the amphora) by local potters.

441. Comfort, Howard. "Terra Sigillata at Arikamedu," in *Rome and India, The Ancient Sea Trade* edited by Vimala Begley and Richard Daniel. Madison, University of Wisconsin Press, 1991: 134-150.

A highly technical evaluation of the Western red trade ware termed *terra sigillata* found during excavation at the site of Arikamedu near Pondicherry in context of known Mediterranean potters, manufacturers stamps, and graffiti. The suggestion is made that the wares were produced and used by and for local resident communities of Roman merchant and freedmen as well as for trading purposes. Use of the term "Arretine" is also challenged pending further research.

442. Will, Elizabeth Lyding. "The Mediterranean Shipping Amphoras from Arikamedu," in *Rome and India, The Ancient Sea Trade* edited by Vimala Begley and Richard Daniel. Madison, University of Wisconsin Press, 1991: 151-156.

A stylistic analysis of the corpus of amphorae accumulated through several successive field campaigns at Arikamedu. Shape and form indicate that the principal items of trade shipped in them were olive oil, garum and wine, the latter both from the Greek vineyards of the islands of Kos, Knidos and Rhodes and later Roman presses.

443. McConkey, David K. *A Survey of a Number of Megalithic Grave Complexes in Tamil Nadu, South India*. M.A. thesis,Western Michigan University, 1992.

The research project summarized in this thesis centered upon exploring the degree of relationship between two areas of Megalithic culture in the Western Ghats of Tamil Nadu, the lower Moyar shelf and the isolated plateau of the Nilgiri Hills. Seven cemeteries from the Moyar area numbering eight hundred and forty graves were mapped during a surface survey, with grave types (ranging from dolmens, slabbed cists and menhirs through a variety of stone circles) and pottery forms (Black, Black Polished and Red Ware) collected compared to Megalithic graves known from the Nilgiri complexes. Results indicate the use of similar physical forms of graves but different pottery styles, cemetery size and grave orientation. The author proposes colonization of the Nilgiri area by a displaced population from the lower plains,, where the Megalithic culture ends about 100 A.D.

444. Soundara Rajan, K. V. *Kaveripattinam Excavations 1963-73 (A Port City on the Tamilnadu Coast)*. New Delhi: Director General, Archaeological Survey of India, 1994.

The ninetieth *Memoir* issued by the Archaeological Survey of India, this text reports on a decade of survey and excavation at "one of the most outstanding port-cities…on the Coromandal coast" (p. 15) of Tamil Nadu. The contents refect a series of separate excavations,begun with a survey conducted by the Southern Circle of the Archaeological Survey of India in 1962. The aim of the overall project was to establish an historical framework of the Kaveri River basin, which was documented in numerous Tamil texts and chronicles as having been an active center of political, economic and religious activity. Kaveripattinam, as the best known port of the Chola rulers, was selected for test excavations and sampling, as were six outlying villages representing different sections of the city. Taken together, the results of this effort traced the general development of the city from the third century B.C. to the tenth century A.D. The first three chapters provide the reader with historical background on this region of southern India and local geomorphology, while the fourth profiles three specific digs at a wharf site, a Buddhist temple and a section of an irrigation system. The highly varied pottery assemblage is discussed and illustrated at length in the fifth chapter, followed by analysis of material culture remains. These later include bangles, beads (a possible local industry), stone, terracotta, copper, bronze and iron objects, as well as coins ranging from Roman to twelfth-century Chola issues. Eight technical appendixes list sites explored in the Kaveri delta, radiocarbon dates obtained from the site, the distribution of rouletted pottery in Tamil Nadu, and architectural features noted in the buildings cleared. Forty-four black and white photographic plates are appended, covering both individual classes of artifacts and selected views of all sites worked.

445. Rajan, K. "Early Maritime Activities of the Tamils," in *Tradition and Archaeology: Early Maritime Contacts in the Indian Ocean* edited by Himanshu Prabha Ray and Jean-Francois Salles. New Delhi: Manohar, 1996: 97-108.

The plains of the present states of Tamil Nadu and Kerala were during the first several centuries A.D. home to early kingdoms, part of whose economic base lay in external trade. The text portion of this paper interweaves known historical texts with evidence obtained through excavations at Kaveripattinam and Kodumanal.Maps of the principal sites in the Coimbatore region of Tamil Nadu and in the state as a whole dated to between 500 B.C. and 500 A.D. are included. The bibliography is more lengthy than expected for an article of this size and will serve as a useful introduction to the archaeology of this era in south India.

Uttar Pradesh

446. Prinsep, James. "The Discovery of An Ancient Town Near Behat, in the Doab of the Jamna and the Ganges," in *Essays on Indian Antiquities*, Historic, Numismatic and Palaeographic, Varanasi: Indological Book House, 1971: 73-79.

This article is a reproduction of the original piece which opens with an extract from a letter read at the meeting of the Asiatic Society of Bengal on January 30, 1834 from Captain P.T.Cautley, then assigned to the clearing of the Doab Canal. He notes the finding of "the site of an ancient (apparently Hindu) town, which…is now seventeen feet below the general surface of the country," (p. 73) during the process of clearing out the canal bed near Saharanpur in extreme northwest Uttar Pradesh. This report (accompanied by an analysis of the coinage done by James Prinsep, matching them with known types from the Society's collection) gives a clear idea of the approach to antiquarian reseach taken at this time and the beginnings of scientific archaeology in this region of India. A more lengthy text following Prinsep's report provides details of specific types of artifacts located.

447. Law, Bimala Churn. *Sravasti in Indian Literature*. Delhi: Manager of Publications, 1935.

This fiftieth *Memoir* of the Archaeological Survey of India focuses on one of the eight great places connected with the life of the Buddha, the ancient city of Sravasti and its Jetavana monastery where the Buddha delivered many of his sermons. In contrast to the majority of publications issued by the Survey, this volume deals not with the actual ruins of Sravasti in the northeastern area of Uttar Pradesh, but rather on references to it in ancient Indian literature. The introduction describes the site (then known as Saheth-Maheth) as it existed at the time of publication, and archaeological attention to the site since the first excavations by Alexander Cunningham in January 1863. Literary sources mentioning Sravasti ranging from Jain, Hindu and Buddhist texts and commentaries to the travel accounts of Fa Hsien and Hsuan Tsang are combined into a discussion of the kingdom of Kosala, the Jetavana garden where the Buddha preached, the place of Sravasti in various religious traditions and its eventual decline until its abandonment in the twelfth century A.D. The compiler takes as his purpose the gathering of scattered texts "so as to render them useful to the archaeologist and the student of history." (p. 1)

448. Law, Bimala Churn. *Kausambi in Ancient Literature*. Delhi: Manager of

Publications, 1939.

Based chiefly on "literary sources and the itineraries of Chinese pilgrims," (p. 1) (most notably the chronicles of Hsuan Tsang and Fa Hsien), this study follows the pattern of Law's previous textual analyses for Sravasti (1935) and Rajagriha (1938). Topics addressed in the concise volume are the antiquity and origin of the city's name, general descriptions and topography (with a valuable section reviewing the dispute within Indian archaeology over the identification of the site's location by Alexander Cunningham) the Vasa dynasty and their political links ,and the life of Udayana, the final ruler. Researchers tracing the historical archaeology of Uttar Pradesh may wish to consult Law's earlier volume *Sravasti in Ancient Literature* (1935). This was the sixtieth *Memoir* of the Archaeological Survey of India.

449. Vats, M.S. "Repairs To The Taj Mahal," *Ancient India* 1 (January 1946): 4-7.

A report by the Superintendent of the Northern Circle of the Archaeological Survey of India on historic and recent structural repairs to Agra's famous Taj Mahal. Beginning with the report of Prince Aurangzeb in 1652, the physical condition of the tomb is assessed, being found not to have substantially altered in the three centuries since its construction. An excellent illustration of the emphasis on preservation characteristic of the Survey from its inception.

450. Ghosh, A. and K.C. Panigrahi. "The Pottery of Ahichchhatra, District Bareilly, U.P.," *Ancient India* 1 (January 1946): 37-59.

Research at the city of Ahichchhatra in northern Uttar Pradesh is offered as an example of the type of analysis of local pottery industries badly needed in Indian archaeology at this time. The introduction by Ghosh (at the time Superintendent of the Excavations Branch of the Archaeological Survey) covers the results of past field work at the site, yielding nine separate periods of occupation dated by coin types. The bulk of this essay is a survey of the major pottery styles and vessel shapes created over fourteen centuries. Full-page line drawings of each of the seventy-seven types are included, as is an appendix by Krishna Deva and Sir Mortimer Wheeler covering the distribution of "Northern black polished ware," a distinctive type known from at least seventeen sites on the Ganges plain but whose provenience had not been identified. Comment is also provided on the painted gray ware found at Ahichchhatra.

451. Agrawala, V.S. "Terracotta Figurines of Ahichchhatra, District Bareilly, U.P," *Ancient India* 4 (July 1947-January 1948) :104-179.

Between 1940 and 1944, excavations were conducted at the site of Ahichchhatra, yielding among other finds a large number of figurines of molded terracotta and a rough stratigraphic occupation sequence reaching from before 300 B.C. to 1100 A.D. This article continues the site analysis by grouping these sculptures into eleven categories by subject, including representations of the Mother Goddess, molded plaques, dwarfs, votive tanks, gods and goddesses (ranging from Vishnu and Siva to Maitreya, the Buddha of the future), Gupta molded plaques, riders (of both horse and elephant), foreign ethnic types and images from the Siva temple.Full descriptions of the terracottas found comprise the bulk of this text, with high quality black and white photographs provided as illustration. The typology from the 1940-44 work was taken as referent for dating other pieces found out of context elsewhere in the city.

452. Kala, Satish Chandra. *Terracotta Figurines From Kausambi, Mainly In the Collection of the Municipal Museum, Allahabad.* Allahabad, The Museum, 1950.

Lying on the left bank of the Yamuna River some forty miles southwest of Allahabad, the ruined city of Kausambi has been a focus of archaeological interest since Sir Alexander Cunningham's pioneering surveys of the nineteenth century.This publication reports on surface finds of terracotta artifacts made at the site between 1931 and 1950 (a collection numbering some four thousand items) with fifty-five black and white plates as illustration. Researchers unfamiliar with the varieties of Indian terracotta art will find the analysis of types found useful.

453. Krishnaswami, V.D. and K.V. Soundararajan. "The Lithic Tool-Industries of the Singrauli Basin, District Mirzapur," *Ancient India* 7 (January 1951): 40-65.

The district of Mirzapur in extreme southeastern Uttar Pradesh was noted as early as 1883 as possessing evidence of prehistoric stone tool manufacture. Investigation of this region was seen as useful in determining the intersection of two major assemblages, the Sohan and Madras industries. This article reports on the results of a re-examination of the river terraces of the Singrauli Basin done in 1949. The original find site was identified and a microlithic quartz industry delineated. The hand axes, cleavers, cores and scrapers of the older palaeolithic industry, as well as the later microlithic implements, are thoroughly described and presented in both line drawings and photographs. Much of the article presupposes a familiarity with the stone age archaeology of India which the general reader may not possess. The authors note that the palaeolithic site on the Balia Nadi was scheduled to be drowned by completion of a planned dam.

454. Dikshit, Moreshwar G. "Beads From Ahichchhatra, U.P," *Ancient India* 8 (1952): 33-63.

An unusual analytic report, this article takes as its subject the numerous small beads recovered at Ahichchhatra in the excavations of 1940-1944, comparing them with known material from other sites. Substances used include agate, carnelian, chalcedony, crystal, garnet, amethyst, jasper,several varieties of quartz,and copper. Separate sections are devoted to glass and terracotta beads. While the use of such artifacts as a technique for assigning age to a specific site was well developed in the archaeology of Egypt and the Near East, the editor notes that "the value of beads as a dating factor has not yet been extensively tested in the historical archaeology of India, a chief reason being the limited amount of stratified material." (p. 33)

455. Lal, B.B. "Excavations At Hastinapura and Other Explorations in the Upper Ganga and Sutlej Basins 1950-52: New Light On the Dark Age Between The End of the Harappa Culture and the Early Historical Period," *Ancient India* 10/11 (1954/1955): 5-151.

As the subtitle indicates, the primary goal of this excavation was to attempt to begin "to bridge this vast gap of nearly twelve centuries" (p. 5) separating the field data from Mohenjo-daro and the records associated with the arrival of Alexander the Great. Site selection used the *Mahabharata* as a guide, with Hastinapura chosen to test the viability of this approach. The present text summarizes the results of the first two seasons' work, emphasizing the ceramic sequence of Painted Gray Ware and Northern Polished Black Ware as a common feature of at least three sites mentioned in the epics. The bulk of the report is devoted to presentation and analysis of the five periods delineated at Hastinapura, with animal, plant and pollen remains also noted. Cross-correlation of this data with other sites yielding pottery of the Hastinapura types as well as Harappan is made in a very useful listing of data then available. Illustrations of each type of ware (through both line drawings and photographs) and details of the stratigraphic sections of the mound are also included.

456. Allchin, Bridget. "Morhana Pahar: A Rediscovery," *Man* 58 (1958): 153-155.

In the early 1880's, A.C. Carlleyle of the Archaeological Survey of India noted several sites yielding microliths in the Mirzapur area of Uttar Pradesh but did not specify their precise location. This article reports on recent analysis of Carlleyle's material in the British Museum and the re-discovery in 1957 of the caves of Morhana Pahar. Notable among the paintings in red, purple, orange and white which adorn the caves are two unusual depictions of chariots.

457. Sharma, Govardhan Raj. *Excavations at Kausambi 1949-50.* Delhi: Manager of Publications, 1969.

Issued as the seventy-fourth *Memoir* of the Archaeological Survey of India (and some eighteen years after the completion of the field season under review), this volume offers an instructive look into the factors involved in selecting a site for excavation in the initial post-Partition years. Prior to this campaign, the Archaeological Survey had excavated at Kausambi in 1937-38 and collected antiquities, but no written report of the activity was ever issued. The present fieldwork was initiated by the University of Allahabad, as part of the effort by Sir Mortimer Wheeler to move archaeology from its position as an exclusively government-sponsored science to one with a solid place in the academic life of Indian universities. This site was chosen both due to its prior exploration (which had laid bare a horizontal section of the city), and indications of long-term occupation, promising to yield a controlled stratigraphic sequence of cultures spanning the pre-Mauryan period. An area near the pillar of Asoka and adjacent to the section opened in the earlier season was worked during the two field seasons.

In three trenches, sections were cut revealing some thirty feet of cultural materials over natural soil. The thirteen chapters of the report begin with a summary of scientific interest in Kausambi, which was first identified by Sir Alexander Cunningham in 1861. The stratigraphy, chronology (based chiefly on the over six hundred copper and silver coins found, which are treated in the ninth chapter), layout of the excavated area (including a road and by-lanes,, houses and a drainage system) and artifacts of stone, terracotta and iron are presented in individual chapters. Over seventy pages are devoted to a detailed discussion and depiction of the pottery types found. Sixty-nine black and white photographic plates cover the general aspects of the site as it existed at this time, an overview and detail of specific sections of the dig, numerous terracotta figurines (both human and animals) coins, stone sculptures, beads and styles of pottery decoration. A detailed plan of the digs is also provided.

458. Hartel, H. "The Apsidal Temple at Sonkh," in *South Asian Archaeology 1973* edited by J.M. Van Lohuizen-De Leeuw. Leiden: Brill, 1974: 103-110.

During the seventh season of field work at the mound of Sonkh in the Mathura district of Uttar Pradesh, completed in March,1973, one of the few remaining areas of uncultivated ground surrounding a local shrine was cleared. A trial trench set in place in 1971 stimulated work in 1972-73. This article reports on the discovery of a second apsidal temple at this location and analyses the sculptural fragments associated with it.

459. Bhardwaj, H.C. *Aspects of Ancient Indian Technology*. Delhi: Motilal Banarsidass, 1979.

An expanded version of the author's thesis from Banaras Hindu University, this monograph is one of the few available works to attempt to assess the levels of technological expertise attained at a specific period of Indian prehistory. The artifacts studied come from excavations being conducted at the mound of Rajghat within the boundaries of Varanasi, and dating to 800-200 B.C. After a brief review of the state of writing on archaeological chemistry and its applications (both within India and overseas), separate chapters examine glass technology, copper metallurgy, silver and gold working and iron production. Forty-two ancient copper mines known from India are listed in an appendix.

460. Lal, B.B. and K.N. Dikshit. "Sringaverapura: A Key-site for the Protohistory and Early History of the Central Ganga Valley," *Purattava* 10 (1978/79): 1-7.

The results of three field seasons work at the ten-meter-high mound of Sringaverapura near Allahabad, begun in December 1977, are summarized in this essay. A stratigraphic cross-section of the mound revealed a detailed sequence of occupation from ca. 1050-1000 B.C. to the eighteenth century A.D. The earliest levels yielded a previously unknown variety of red ware pottery, while the fourth level (200 B.C. to 200 A.D.) contained a massive tank, whose presence pushed back this type of construction in known early historic Indian archaeology. Readers should be aware that the authors assume an awareness of the standard types of ceramics already known from both Uttar Pradesh and the Ganga Valley in their readers. A plan of the tank is included.

461. Soundararajan, K.V. "Mesolithic-Megalithic Links- New Thoughts for Study in India," *Puratattva* 10 (1978/79): 62-65.

A challenge to the accepted model of the development of megalithic architecture in India, based upon recent discoveries in Ireland which forced the conclusion that local barrows and passage tombs were created by "a pre-existing mesolithic population." (p. 63) The author reviews available data from sites in Karnataka and Kerala in detail, focusing on questions of local economic adaptation and possible links to the stone tool industries found in the passage graves.

462. Irwin, J. "The Prayaga Bull-Pillar: Another Pre-Asokan Monument," in *South Asian Archaeology 1979* edited by Herbert Hartel. Berlin: Dietrich Riemer Verlag, 1981: 313-340.

In 1837, epigraphist James Prinsep used the inscriptions on a carved stone pillar standing in the fort at Allahabad (ancient Prayaga) to unlock the Brahmi script and initiate the explosion of recording and translation which marked the activitives of late Victorian antiquarians in India. This study re-examines the various observations of the pillar and concludes that, in light of new data, that the monument was already in existence (although not at Prayaga) when the edict of Asoka was carved upon it. Original drawings and copper-plate tracings are reproduced, adding to the quality of the work. Pillar worship is set within its religious context, "the sacred pillar...rising nakedly out of the Waters that lay below the earth, after penetrating our...sphere at the earth's Navel, is extended to the heavens, uniting with the sun at its daily zenith." (p. 334)

463. Kennedy, Kenneth A.R., Nancy C. Lovell and Christopher B. Burrow. *Mesolithic Human Remains from the Gangetic Plain: Sarai Nahar Rai*. Ithaca, New York: South Asia Program, Cornell University, 1986.

Discovered in 1968 but not excavated until 1972, the site of Sarai Nahar Rai in the central Ganga Valley of Uttar Pradesh lies within a region heavily occupied by man in Mesolithic times. Its importance for regional prehistory stems from both its archaeological record of artifacts and faunal remains, and "its mortuary series of fifteen human skeletons...one of the largest skeletal series of Mesolithic hominids from India discovered to date."(p. 1) Their heavily mineralized condition resulted in extraordinary states of preservation, permitting the recovery of complete skulls and postcranial bones. This concise volume presents the results of analyses conducted on ten specimens removed from the site done at the University of Allahabad in 1980. The opening section provides background on the history of research into ancient human morphology in South Asia, the problems of establishing a chronology for the Indian Mesolithic, and a brief summary of the archaeology of the site. The bulk of the monograph is devoted to detailed morphological presentation of each specimen and consideration of their meaning relative to questions of biological adaptation and affinity with other South Asian skeletal assemblages from the same period. A bibliography of references cited gathers a widely scattered literature for further reading. Black and white photographs of the site and selected specimens are included.

464. Hartel, Herbert. *Excavations At Sonkh: 2500 Years of a Town In Mathura District.* Berlin: Dietrich Reimer Verlag, 1993.

This well-written and beautifully illustrated site report covers eight seasons of work (1966-1974) carried out in the Mathura district of Uttar Pradesh by a team from the Museum of Indian Art in Berlin. Sonkh itself consists of a large plateau mound fourteen miles from Mathura city bearing the remains of a significant citadel. The relatively undisturbed nature of the site made it the best choice for the excavations, whose object was "a reassessment of the antiquity of Mathura and the nature of early historical settlements in its environments." (p. 12) Initial digging centered on the northeastern corner of the citadel, with the resulting discovery of eight distinct periods of occupation in forty separate levels beginning at 800 B.C. and extending to the destruction of the fort in 1775 A.D. Given the disturbed nature of the upper fourteen strata (covering roughly the Gupta, post-Gupta, Medieval and Fortress eras of activity at Sonkh), "the richer lower levels with all their wealth of remains and finds occupy much more space in this report." (p. 9) The fourth chapter presents finds from the site in materials ranging from terracotta (figurines both human and animal) through bone, shell, ivory and glass to gold and silver items, seals, molds for coins and jewelry, and potter's stamps. The discovery of an apsidal temple dating to the Kushan era is separately reported. A brief bibliography covering works in both English and German is provided. Researchers unfamiliar with the archaeological history of this region of India will find the chronological chapters invaluable.

West Bengal

465. Dikshit, K.N. *Excavations at Paharpur, Bengal.* Delhi: Manager of Publications, 1938.

First noted in a survey of eastern India commissioned by the East India Company in 1807-1812, scientific attention to the the mound of Paharpur began in 1879, when the ruins were visited by Sir Alexander Cunningham as part of his exploration of ancient Buddhist sites. Paharpur came under official government protection by the Archaeological Survey of India following passage of the Ancient Monuments Preservation Act in 1919. The first chapter of this report summarizes the results of prior digging between February 1923 and 1934, the bulk of under the direction of the author. Paharpur has been identified with the Buddhist *vihara* of Somapura, active under the Pala dynasty at the end of the eighth century A.D. Chapters two and three profile and discuss the massive main temple and associated monastery complex, while the fourth through sixth focus on the stone sculptures, reliefs, terracotta plaques and "minor antiquities." These last include inscriptions on both stone panels and copper dedication plates, the earliest dating to 479 A.D. A separate excavation at the adjacent mound of Satyapir Bhita, east of the central Paharpur complex, is reported in the final chapter. A ground plan of the central temple showing the position of surviving relief panels is supplemented by a section of the mound and sixty-four black and white photographs. Particularly striking are views of various sections of the temple before and after conservation. Researchers involved with study of this site should also consult the later paper by Johanna Van Lohuizen-De Leeuw published in *South Asian Archaeology 1983* and entered in the present bibliography under *Bangladesh*.

466. Lal, B.B. "Birbhanpur, A Microlithic Site in the Damodar Valley, West Bengal," *Ancient India* 14 (1958): 4-48.

The site designated Birbhanpur was investigated in 1954 and 1957 through both surface collection and the cutting of a small trench to establish local stratigraphic referents for the stone tools if possible. Analysis of the geologic context of the river terrace yielding the microliths indicated an early Holocene date. Comparisons are drawn with other microlithic finds likewise associated with an absence of pottery.

467. Lal, B.B. and S.B. "The Microlithic Site of Birbhanpur: A Geochronological Study," *Ancient India* 17 (1961): 37-45.

Originally excavated in 1954 and 1957, Birbhanpur yielded a non-geometric microlithic industry marked by an absence of pottery. In an effort to better fix a date for the site, a new test trench was opened for the purpose of obtaining further geological data which could be used to reconstruct past environmental conditions.

468. Mitra, Debala. *Telkupi, A Submerged Temple-Site in West Bengal*. Delhi: Manager of Publications, 1969.

As a consequence of the construction of a dam across the Damodar River in West Bengal in 1957, a complex of temples dating from the ninth to the fifteenth centuries was drowned before they could be salvaged. This monograph, written by the Superintendent of the Eastern Circle of the Archaeological Survey of India, begins by summarizing the community's history as a seat of a regional dynasty and previous descriptions of the temples, beginning with the first by J.D. Beglar in 1872 (reproduced in full in the Appendix). Twenty-six temples are individually profiled and their sculptures and ground plans discussed when possible. Individual sculptures and sacred sites associated with the Telkupi temples are also presented. An excellent example of historical salvage archaeology occasioned by India's postindependence development.Forty-three black and white photographs of the complex taken in 1872, 1903, 1929,and during the salvage visit of the Survey in 1960 are included.

469. Chakrabarti, Dilip K. "Some Ethnographic Dimensions of the Archaeology of the Chhotanagpur Plateau and the Adjoining Areas in West Bengal in Eastern

India," in *Living Traditions: Studies in the Ethnoarchaeology of South Asia* edited by Bridget Allchin. Columbia, Missouri: South Asia Publications, 1994: 219-234.

Noting that "there has been no attempt to systematically investigate the archaeological character of the region as a whole," (p. 219) the author explores the available data on past occupations of the Chhotanagpur Plateau. A preliminary survey done between 1981 and 1987 yielded information on linkages with adjacent regions as a site of ancient copper and tin mining. Emphasis is placed on the continuous occupation of the plateau by tribal groups whose distribution, metallurgy (particularly iron-smelting) and interaction with plains populations are set out as an ethnographic source of interpretation for the overall archaeological record.

470. Sengupta, Gautama. "Archaeology of Coastal Bengal," in *Tradition and Archaeology: Early Maritime Contacts in the Indian Ocean* edited by Himanshu Prabha Ray and Jean-Francois Salles. New Delhi: Manohar, 1996: 115-127.

An overview article presenting the archaeological picture of coastal West Bengal as known at the time of publication. Beginning with a summary of the physical geography of the region, the two major periods represented in the archaeological record, the early medieval and early historic eras, are summarized. Emphasis is placed upon both the extensive character of textual documentation available for the region and the relative lack (until recently) of controlled field excavation. Major sites noted are in clusters around Chandraketugarh and Tamluk. Information is also provided on the shifting of river channels in the Ganges delta and its impact on occupation. A map showing the distribution of archaeological sites within coastal West Bengal is included.

Bangladesh

471. Morrison, Barrie. M. *Lalmai, A Cultural Center of Early Bengal: An Archaeological Report and Historical Analysis*. Seattle: University of Washington Press, 1974.

The Lalmai Hills in the Comilla district of Bangladesh and their extensive architectural remains are the focus of this work, which represents a summary of the results of the author's investigations and surveys during April and May, 1966. First noted in 1929, this assemblage of ruined temples and stupas was further surveyed in 1946 and again in 1955, with a total of fifty sites located. The 1966 survey focused on forty-seven sites of the post-Gupta and pre-Muslim eras, ranging from Buddhist monasteries, Hindu shrines, a palace (Mainamati Mandir) and monastic cells to unidentifiable building remains. The first chapter reviews the size, configuration and location of each site in detail, with plans and dating information included when available. Spatial clusters of sites associated by common dates derived from inscriptions are then noted and analyzed in the context of regional urbanization and political history. Pottery types and the distribution and interpretation of extant inscriptions are considered in the second and third chapters. The Lalmai sites are seen as a distinctive combination of palace centers and religious complexes. Readers unfamiliar with the ancient political history of this portion of the subcontinent will find Morrison's final analysis useful as an introduction. An appendix examines technological data on local pottery manufacture.

472. Shamsul Alam, A.K.N. *Mainamati*. Dacca: Department of Archaeology and Museums, 1975.

The extensive ruin complex of Mainamati on the Lalmai Hills near Comilla in south eastern Bangladesh was brought to light during World War II, when the Lalmai Hills were made the headquarters of the 14th division of the British Army. Controlled excavations were conducted from 1955 to 1963 at three sites: Salbanpur (renamed Salban Vihara due to the determination of its use as a Buddhist monastery), the Triratna Stupas at Kotila Mura, and Charpatra Mura, this last a rectangular Buddhist shrine of unknown purpose. Upon the claiming of independence by Bangladesh, all original materials from the site were left in Karachi. The present work is based upon duplicate copies of field reports, and provides background on the physical geography and known history of this region between the eighth and thirteenth centuries A.D. Eighteen archaeological sites so far located in the Mainamati area are then profiled, with work at the three major sites discussed in detail and illustrated by plans. Samples of the chief types of artifacts recovered (copper dedication plates, votive stupas, sculptures in bronze and stone, coins, terracotta plaques, and pottery) are then presented and illustrated with black and white photographs. Readers will find the maps showing all ancient monuments of Bangladesh and the general plan of the Mainamati complex useful as references.

473. Van Lohuizen-De Leeuw, Johanna. "The Recent Excavations at Paharpur," in *South Asian Archaeology 1983* edited by Janice Schotsmans and Maurizio Taddei. Naples: Istituto Universitario Orientale, 1985: 741-750.

First discovered between 1807 and 1812, the site of Parharpur in northeastern Bangladesh is the location of the former Buddhist *vihara* of Somapura and "one of the largest Buddhist monasteries in South Asia." (p. 743) Background historical information and the results of excavations between 1923 and 1933-34 by K.N. Dikshit are presented. This article focuses on the 1981-82 season whose aim was the establishment of the three phases of monastic cell construction mentioned in the prior reports. The overall ground plan of Paharpur, problems of drainage and preservation, and arguments proposing the first structure on site belonged to the Jains are also reviewed, the last hypothesis discredited in favor of two successive phases of Buddhist occupation.

474. Chakrabarti, Dilip K. *Ancient Bangladesh: A Study of the Archaeological Sources*. Delhi: Oxford University Press, 1992.

The only available treatment of the prehistory of Bangladesh as known in the early 1990's in one volume, this work "offers a systematic review of the pre-Islamic archaeological data...with reference to the excavated and explored sites." (p. 1.) The book opens with an introduction detailing the political and physiographic divisions of the country (including information on climate, soil types, and ancient political units known from literary sources). The second chapter considers known artifacts from the Palaeolithic and centers on a discussion of the Lalmai Hills fossilwood industry. The early historical period's archaeology is next examined, the author noting that currently the data "are unevenly spread and imperfectly understood." (p. 44) The only site at which an early historic level has been explored, Mahasthangarh, is discussed at length, with a brief overview of ten other sites in North Bengal included. A separate chapter is given over to the excavated data on Buddhist monasteries, stupas and temples, with ten sites known at the time of publication summarized. Miscellaneous information on a variety of subjects ranging from sixteen settlement sites identified but not excavated to questions relating to regional coinage and inscriptions is explored. Researchers unfamiliar with this region of South Asia will find the bibliography useful.

Pakistan

Researchers should note that the archaeological survey and excavation work done in the area defined by the political boundaries of Pakistan prior to Partition in 1949 will be found under the region's older administrative name, the North West Frontier Province of India.

475. Wheeler, Robert Eric Mortimer. *Five Thousand Years of Pakistan: An Archaeological Outline*. London, 1950.

The preface to this volume (written by Pakistan's Minister of Education) characterizes it as "presenting...a brief sketch of the material heritage of Pakistan in the form of ancient buildings, sites and cultures prior to the death of the Emperor Aurangzeb in A.D. 1707." (p. 5) The author was then serving as archaeological adviser to the new government. The text is written for a general audience, successive chapters covering known stone tool occurrences, the prehistoric village cultures of Baluchistan and Sind, the Indus Valley civilzation, megaliths, the results of excavations at Taxila in the Punjab and Charsada, Hindu temples and monuments and the Islamic heritage of both East and West Pakistan, the latter occupying the bulk of the text. A selected bibliography and listing of works protected under the Ancient Monuments Preservation Act complete the work.Illustration is provided by thirty-two black and white plates.

476. Wheeler, Sir Robert Eric Mortimer. *The Indus Civilization*.Cambridge: The University Press,1953.

Even as the first volume of the *Cambridge History of India* was appearing in print in 1922, its assertion that little or nothing remained of the most ancient cities of the subcontinent had been vitiated through the discoveries of the sites of Harappa in the Punjab and Mohenjo-daro in Sind. The early 1920's saw the beginning of an intense period of activity in Indus archaeology, much of it focused on excavation at the type sites to ascertain the nature of this entirely new culture. By 1950, several dozen sites yielding material remains of this civilization had been identified and some aspects of its nature made clear. The present volume is the first discussion of this unique body of fieldwork and analysis for a general audience, and is authored by the then-retired Director of the Archaeological Survey of india.

477. Wheeler, Sir Robert Eric Mortimer. *The Indus Civilization.* Cambridge: The University Press, 1960.

The second edition of Mortimer Wheeler's essay on Indus Valley archaeology, originally written as a new chapter for the first volume of the *Cambridge History of India* in 1953. The author observes in a prefatory note that, while substantial field work has been carried out on Indus sites since 1953 "the results of this recent work are still largely unpublished and unanalysed." The bibliography found in the third edition in 1968 is not present, and the author does not indicate which specific sections of text have been expanded to reflect new information.

478. Paterson, T.T. and H.J.H. Drummond. *Soan, The Palaeolithic of Pakistan.* Karachi: Department of Archaeology, Government of Pakistan, 1962.

The foreword to this volume notes that "though a preliminary report of the joint Yale-Cambridge Expedition was published in 1939, this is the first publication of its complete work in the Soan Valley." (p. 5) The work begins with a review of the Pleistocene geology of the Potwar Plains, then presents the stratigraphy of the twenty-five sites at which stone tools were found. Soan type tools, notable for the extensive use of pebbles as basic raw material, are discussed in the fifth chapter, being divided into flat-based, nucleate and oblate forms. The occurrence of the Soan culture in the Middle ,Upper and closing eras of the Pleistocene is presented in separate chapters, with extensive detail on individual tool types and their distribution. The presence of artifacts at some sites which resemble stone tools known from Europe and South Africa is also noted. A set of fifty-nine figures illustrates Soan pebble-tools of all phases then known as well as petroglyphs in the region and tools found at the site of Kotah sugesting a survival of some aspects of Soan technology. Literary references are limited to individual page notes.

479. Wheeler, Robert Eric Mortimer. *Charsada, A Metropolis of the North-West Frontier, Being A Report On The Excavations of 1958.* Oxford: Oxford University Press, 1962.

In November and December of 1958, Sir Mortimer Wheeler was invited by the government of Pakistan to resume the plan of excavations originally set for the site of Charsada near Peshawar in 1947 but delayed by Partition. Correctly identified in 1863 by Sir Alexander Cunningham as Pushkalavati, the "City of Lotuses," it had been the site of desultory and inconclusive testing work by John Marshall in 1903 but had not been studied since that time. Wheeler's project focused on the most prominent mound group, locally known as the *Bala Hisar,* the "High Fort." In seven weeks, a step trench was cut from the top of the mound down to natural undisturbed soils, providing a provisional occupation chronology from the sixth to first centuries B.C. A line of ditches and ramparts was located east of the Bala

Hisar and attributed to the siege of the city by troops of Alexander the Great in 327 B.C. The majority of this report summarizes the four areas investigated during the 1958 campaign, these being the old river bed dividing the Bala Hisar from the outlying mound groups of Shaikhan and a partly exposed house as well as the stratigraphic control trench and the defensive wall. Pottery types, terracotta figurines and small finds (including carvings in the Gandhara style) are presented in some detail.Forty-five photographic plates (some in color) illustrate both the geography of the site and various stages of the 1958 campaign. The account given by John Marshall of the initial work at Charsada, originally published in the first *Annual Report* of the Archaeological Survey of India (covering the years 1902-1903) under the title "Excavations At Charsada in the Frontier Province" should be evaluated within the context offered by this field season. Aerial photography by the Pakistan Air Force also revealed the outlines of a substantial structure (much damaged by mining for bricks) on the crest of the Bala Hisar.

480. Hasan Dani, Ahmad. "Prehistoric Pakistan," *Asian Perspectives* v.7, nos.1-2 (Summer-Winter 1963): 183-188.

An examination of the history of investigation of Pakistan's prehistory, with prehistoric here referring to the Stone Age. Following a description of the basic geology of the country, the discovery of the palaeolithic tool complex termed "Soan" by the Yale-Cambridge Expedition in 1935 is recounted and its defining features summarized. Later Stone Age materials, chiefly microliths, are noted as having been only sparsely found to date.The latter half of the article consists of a report from the current seasons fieldwork in a well-stratified cave site near Sanghao, where were found "for the first time in...Pakistan neolithic tools of an advanced character." (p. 186)

481. Casal, Jean-Marie. *Fouilles d'Amri*. Paris: Librairie C. Klincksieck, 1964. 2 volumes.

Almost as soon as it was discovered at Harappa and Mohenjo-daro, the Indus civilization presented a problem to archaeologists, as it was clearly fully developed. The question then became one of seeking its antecedents in the archaeological record. The December, 1929 excavations at two mounds near the village of Amri, one hundred miles downstream from Mohenjo-daro, by N.G. Majumdar, provided the first evidence for what would subsequently be termed "the Amri culture." The first volume of the present report summarizes both the earlier excavations and those carried out between 1959 and 1962. Following a chart showing the stratigraphic sequence of occupation at the site, the text of the report reviews known data on the four stages of the Amri culture, the presence of Harappan civilization at Amri (as evidenced by diverse ceramic finds and Indus script graffiti) and its relationship to Amri materials, and fragmentary finds from a sixteenth-century Muslim occupation. Emphasis is placed on discerning the evolution of pottery types and attempting to establish the relationship of Amri to the Indus civilization, with which it appears to overlap. A catalogue of the ceramic specimens recovered (keyed to the illustrations which comprise the second volume of the report) and twelve appendixes presenting analysis of faunal remains,architectural elements, figurines, and items of bone,metal,stone and terracotta complete the text. The second volume contains one hundred and thirty-one drawings of pottery forms and designs (as well as site plans and comparative stratigraphy) and thirty-one photographs. The latter show the physical setting of the two mounds excavated, views of sections representing each period of occupation, and ceramics. A brief English summary follows the French text of the first volume. A bibliography of referenced publications is also included. Researchers should be aware that much of Casal's speculation assumes a familiarity with regional archaeology and may wish to consult more general works prior to reading this report.

482. Dani, A.H. and F.A. Durrani. "A New Grave Complex From West Pakistan," *Asian Perspectives* v.8, n.1 (Summer,1964): 164-165.

Observing that "very little has been found in...Pakistan to bridge the gulf between the Bronze Age Indus Civilization and the early Buddhist cultures of the historic period," (p. 164) this note reports on the preliminary results of test excavations at three Bronze and Iron Age cemeteries in the Gandhara region. Associated pottery and burial forms are discussed. An interesting feature is that some of these sites remain in use as burying grounds for the contemporary population.

483. Graziosi, Paolo. "Prehistoric Research in Northwestern Punjab," in *Italian Expeditions to the Karakorum and Hindu Kush, Scientific Reports V: Prehistory-Anthropology,* volume 1. Leiden: E.J. Brill, 1964: 7-54.

This report is part of a larger series of studies done in the summer of 1954 as part of a general exploration of the Karakorum range. The prehistoric researches centered on the Jhelum, Soan,and Indus river regions (the same areas visited in 1932 and 1935 by the Yale North India Expedition and the De Terra-Paterson-de Chardin party respectively). This text presents a mixture of information, covering the typology of stone tool industries from the Punjab as then known, and survey reports from nine sites, the largest collection from Morgah. A bibliography and a series of ninety-five high quality line drawings of artifacts from the visited sites are appended.

484. Dales, George F. "New Investigations of Mohenjo-Daro," *Archaeology* 18 (2) (June, 1965): 145-150.

A report on the results of the first phase of a joint project being carried out by the University Museum of Philadelphia and the Pakistan Department of Archaeology "to study and re-evaluate the ancient geography and ecology of the lower Indus Valley." (p. 145) Three test boreholes have revealed a depth of occupational debris at the site beginning thirty-nine feet below present ground level, while details of a possible wall around the lower city are noted. Photographs illustrate a section of the wall, one of the test pits and terracotta masks. A site plan and regional distribution of referenced excavations are included.

485. Casal, Jean-Marie. "Nindowari- A Chalcolithic Site in South Baluchistan," *Pakistan Archaeology* 3 (1966): 10-21.

A report on the first three field seasons of excavation carried out at the mound of Nindowari one hundred and fifty miles from Karachi on a tributary of the Porali river from 1962 to 1965. The goal of this program was to choose a site in southern Baluchistan which would provide a stratigraphic sequence of cultural development similar to that established at Amri in the north. Sampling was done in the central area of the mound, in buildings bordering the eastern side of the quadrangular platform, and in one of the isolated rectangular masonry blocks, Results indicated occupation by the Kulli culture and possible use of the site as a place of ritual significance. Full details of the excavations are presented for each area, along with excellent overall plans of the site and each section cleared, together with black and white photographs and line drawings illustrating both bichrome and monochrome pottery and a possible script.

486. Buchanan, Briggs. "A Dated Seal Impression Connecting Babylonia and Ancient India," *Archaeology* 20(2) (April,1967): 104-107.

A detailed examination of the design on a seal from Failaka Island in the Persian Gulf held in the Yale Babylonian Collection. Parallels with similar finds from Ur and other Mesopotamian sites and the port of Lothal are offered as evidence for establishing the end of the mature phase of the Indus Valley culture at ca.2000 B.C. Full illustration of the design elements and seal types is included, as are references to other published data on this topic.

487. Mughal, Muhammad Rafique. "Excavations at Tulamba,West Pakistan," *Pakistan Archaeology* 4 (1967):11-152.

The site of Tulamba consists of a massive mound some seventy-five feet high (near the modern town of the same name in Multan district) and formerly fortified. Geographic and historical evidence identify it as one of the cities conquered in 326 B.C. by Peithon, one of the generals of Alexander the Great. This extensive and highly detailed report covers the field season from November 6, 1963 to January 25,1964. Investigations centered upon verifying the existence of a moat and earthen ramparts (neither of which were substantiated), with the most lengthy analysis and discussion reserved for the pottery types from each of the eight periods of occupation. A virtually unbroken cultural sequence spanning some two thousand years (a first for the lower Punjab) was uncovered by a stratigraphic section taken in an undisturbed sector of the mound. Thirty-three black and white photographs illustrate general views of the site, the deep cross-section taken to natural soil, structural remains as then known, and pottery types from all levels. The author has the happy diffculty of reporting that "the bulk of the material recovered from Tulamba presented difficulties in working out a chronological sequence...most of it was new to our knowledge." (p. 24)

488. Wheeler, Sir Robert Eric Mortimer. *The Indus Civilization*. Cambridge: The

University Press, 1968.

The third edition of Wheeler's comprehensive survey of data on the Indus culture as it was known by the mid-1960s. The preface notes that "new sites and new research continue to fill out the picture of the Indus civilization and are here summarily indicated down to 1967."

489. Dani, Ahmad Hasan. "Gandhara Grave Complex in West Pakistan," *Asian Perspectives* 11 (1968): 99-110.

Continuing the analysis of an group of sites dating to the Bronze and Iron Ages first noted in a prior article in 1964, this highly detailed article reports results from the first season of excavation at the site of Timurgarha, adding data from the Italian campaign at Mingora. A clear sequence of three cultural periods based on pottery typologies and grave forms is outlined, each featuring both red and grey wares. Correlations with similar forms known from Charsada is made in the drawings which illustrate the report. The author presents a tentative chronology of this culture from the middle of the second millennium B.C. to historic times, while acknowledging that radiocarbon dates have not yet been obtained.

490. Sharif, Mohammad. "Excavations at Bhir Mound,Taxila," *Pakistan Archaeology* 6 (1969): 6-99.

The site profiled in this report is one of the successive sites of the ancient city of Taxila. Between 1913 and 1934, large scale excavations were conducted but their results (chiefly a somewhat haphazard city plan) were not placed in a secure stratigraphic context. The present report covers a campaign of field study begun in 1967 emphasizing stratigraphical digging. Four separate periods of occupation were revealed, verifying the Bhir as the earliest city of Taxila while not yet substantiating local traditions. The text briefly reviews the scope of the project and results as of the time of publication, then presents in heavily illustrated detail structural remains from all four levels, minor antiquities, terracotta, bone, stone, metal and ivory objects, pottery and coins. Site chronology was based upon a variety of traits including the presence of Northern Black Polished Ware, punch marked and uninscribed coins, and terracotta figurines. Comparison of this new data with previously published information on Taxila (including the later city of Sirkap, which succeeded the Bhir community), and Charsada published by Sir John Marshall and Sir Mortimer Wheeler respectively indicates a time span for the four periods from the fourth through the first centuries B.C.

491. Rahman Dar, Saifur. "Excavation at Manikyala-1968," *Pakistan Archaeology* 7 (1970-71): 6-22.

A report on the June 1968 campaign of digging at the village of Manikyala sixteen miles southeast of Rawalpindi and famed for its gigantic Buddhist stupa. The aim of this season was to obtain a cross-section of the high mound northwest of the stupa and gather data regarding its possible contents. Two distinct periods of occupation were clearly marked in the stratigraphy, with evidence of a heavily ornamented building (possibly a shrine) in the first layers, destroyed by fire. Earlier surface finds of coinage date the primary activity at Manikyala to between the first and eight centuries A.D. Local masonry types appear to be variants of previously known forms from Taxila. Full-scale excavation of the site is recommended.

492. Halim, Muhammad Abdul. "Excavations at Sarai Khola, Part I," *Pakistan Archaeology* 7 (1970-71): 23-89.

The deeply stratified mound of Sarai Khola lies in the Taxila Valley on the Potwar Plateau east of the Indus River in northeastern Pakistan, and close to the Bhir mound, site of the first city of Taxila. This report reviews the results of investigations carried out at the site from 1968 to 1971 whose goal was to establish as complete a chronology as possible and explore the relationship of the Kot Diji culture with that of the later Neolithic period. Four separate eras of occupation were marked, beginning with an assemblage marked by stone blades and celts, bone points and red burnished pottery, datable by analogy to similar finds at Kili Ghul Mohammed to approximately 3100-3000 B.C. Period two dates to 2800-2400 B.C. and contains wheel-made globular vessels typical of the Kot Diji ceramics, although here this phase overlaps with the previous culture and may represent an earlier stage of development. The third occupation level to be explored in this field season revealed two superimposed cemeteries, dated ca.1000 B.C. and characterized by the introduction of iron. Fifty graves from the first and sixty-five of the second are profiled individually in the last section of this text.Following a lengthy abandonment, the final settlement at Sarai Khola was founded in early medieval times and flourished in the period 700 to 800 A.D. Topics addressed in this first section of the field report are the layout of the five trenches and test sections, a detailed illustrated discussion of the twenty stratigraphic layers thus far identified, and the burial forms and graves of the two cemeteries. Twenty-nine black and white photographs are included covering the general physical aspect of Sarai Khola, all major sections and trenches, and selected burials. Analysis of the items of material culture found during the excavations is presented by Halim in Part II of the report, published in the 1972 number of *Pakistan Archaeology*. Researchers working on this era of Pakistani archaeology should consult both sections.

493. Johnson, Elden. "Notes on a Palaeolithic Site Survey in Pakistan," *Asian Perspectives* 15 (1972): 60-65.

A resurvey of the Potwar Plateau region of Pakistan, first noted in 1939 as possessing a palaeolithic stone tool industry given the name Soan after the river on whose terraces the type specimens were collected. The goal of this re-examination was "the location of sites of the 3rd interglacial and 4th glacial age which could be excavated at a later date." (p. 60) The final stage of the Soan, a developed chopper industry, also exhibits a flake industry. Four sites spanning the time period in question were sampled and the results summarized: Mohra Battan, Ghila Kalan,

Adiala and two caves near Khanpur.

494. Halim, Muhammad Abdul. "Excavations at Sarai Khola, Part II," *Pakistan Archaeology* 8 (1972): 1-112.

Continuing the presentation of results of the 1968-71 field seasons at the mound of Sarai Khola begun by the author in the 1970-71 number of *Pakistan Archaeology*, the two chapters of this report focus on the six hundred and seventy-six artifacts of stone, bone, metal, shell, faience, steatite and terracotta retrieved, and the pottery assemblage. The largest classes of stone objects were microliths, chisels and celts, maceheads, household objects and beads. Metallic finds were limited to copper and iron, the former appearing first in level II of the site (2800-2400 B.C.) while iron is restricted to the periods after 1000 B.C. The second (and heavily illustrated) section of this text is composed of six articles discussing vessel forms and decoration in all four periods of the site, some authored by Halim,others by M. Rafique Mughal. Researchers should read both sections together to achieve a better understanding of the total results of excavation.

495. Brunswig, Robert H. "A Comprehensive Bibliography of the Indus Civilization and Related Subjects and Areas," *Asian Perspectives* 16 (1) (1973): 75-111.

An unannotated listing of books, articles, site reports and bibliographies in English, French, Dutch, Spanish, Swedish, and German published between 1834 and 1972 dealing in some fashion with the Indus culture. Thirteen subdivisions are provided, ranging from general materials and the relationship of the Harappan culture to ancient Western Asia to specific sites, artifacts of daily life, flora and fauna, architectural techniques, religion, and the Indus script. Researchers unfamiliar with the vast literature generated on the Indus civilization will find this listing an essential starting point.

496. Khan, Gulzar Mohammed. "Excavations at Zarif Karuna," *Pakistan Archaeology* 9 (1973); 1-94.

The site of Zarif Karuna, discovered in September 1971 sixteen miles north of Peshawar, was identified as an extensive (and badly churned) cemetery of the Gandhara Grave Culture(thirteenth to tenth centuries B.C.), thus expanding the known range of occupation of this cultural complex into the plains of the Kabul river. This report covers the results of the salvage investigations carried out in November 1971. A stratigraphic sequence was retrieved from an undisturbed sector. Topics explored are the varied types of grave construction, modes of burial (urn burials and inhumations), three separate periods of use and a detailed presentation of vessel forms seen in the red and grey ware. Personal objects of gold, bone and stone are treated in detail and include terracotta bulls and a goddess figurine. Burial rituals and cult objects are analysed and the three eras represented at Zarif Karuna linked to other post-Harappan cultures known in the region. A survey of the surrounding area revealed no sign of a habitation site. Black and white photographs illustrating the site, individual graves of each class, and type artifacts are included.

497. Fairservis, Walter. "Preliminary Report on Excavations at Allahdino (First Season- 1973)," *Pakistan Archaeology* 9 (1973): 95-102.

The aim of the initial fieldwork at the mound of Allahdino was both to complete a survey of the geomorphology of the local environment and to clear the latest identifiable coherent settlement. This latter included obtaining "a coherent plan of an Harappan village" (p. 98) and defining an occupation sequence, which revealed five separate phases. Evidence of techniques of water management was uncovered with more detailed clearance of the village planned for the next season.

498. Hoffman, Michael A. "The Harappan Settlement at Allahdino: Analyzing the Sociology of an Archaeological Site," in *Ecological Backgrounds of South Asian Prehistory* edited by Kenneth Kennedy and Gregory Possehl. Ithaca, New York York: Cornell South Asia Program, 1974: 94-117.

The analysis referred to in the article's title reflects the overall goal of the 1973 and 1974 excavations at Allahdino, which eventually resulted in the clearance of one-third of the site, "one of the largest percentages of any Bronze Age site in the Middle East or South Asia ever excavated." (p. 96) The substantial body of artifacts permitted division of the site into usage areas. Architectural styles, ceramics, and lithic materials are reviewed.

499. Van Lohuizen-De Leeuw, J.E. "Mohenjo Daro- A Cause of Common Concern," in *South Asian Archaeology 1973*. Leiden: E.J. Brill, 1974: 1-11.

A report on the physical status of the ruins of Mohenjo Daro as they existed in the early 1970's. At this time the remains were in a severely threatened condition due to a variety of factors, most centrally the rise in the level of groundwater, erosion by the Indus itself, increased irrigation, and the destruction of ancient brickwork by salt crystals deposited by capillary action. A salvage plan approved in 1962 by the government of Pakistan is reviewed and the potentials for success assessed.

500. Van Lohuizen-De Leeuw, J.E. "The Pre-Muslim Antiquities of Sind," in *South Asian Archaeology 1975* edited by J.E. Van Lohiuzen-De Leeuw. Leiden: Brill, 1979: 151-174.

This essay by a noted art historian and archaeologist centers attention on the structural remains in the archaeological record of Sind dating from after the Muslim conquest in 711-712 A.D. The myth of wholesale destruction of all Hindu and Buddhist sites by this conquest is demonstrated to be inaccurate, although some specific sites were in fact demolished as consequences of individual sieges and battles. Noting that (due to the furor caused by the discovery of Mohenjo-daro and other Indus sites in the 1920's) "archaeologists have paid insufficient attention to the early historical period," (p. 154) the author then illustrates the benefits of a re-examination of all work done in Sind on this period through a re-analysis of selected examples. Sites noted are the stupa at Thul Mir Rukan and the now destroyed Buddhist shrine of Kahujo-daro near Mirpur Khas, while correlations with Sindhi history are drawn from the stupa at Devnimori in Gujarat as well as numismatics.

501. Hasan Dani, Ahmad. "Origins of Bronze Age Cultures in the Indus Basin: A Geographic Perspective," *Expedition* 17 (2) (Winter 1975): 12-18.

An in-depth interpretation of the patterns of known Bronze Age cultures within the Indus Basin (here taken to include the now-dried tributary rivers such as the Sarasvati) in light of the physical geography of northwestern India, Pakistan and Afghanistan. The influence of landforms on possible routes of trade and travel as well as their limiting force in such regions as the northern plateaus and deserts offers a perspective useful for readers unfamiliar with the geography and geology of the subcontinent.

502. Mukherjee, S.K. "The Beginnings of Terracotta Art in India," *Journal of Indian History* 54(3) (December 1976): 477-484.

The "beginnings" of the title are the ancient terracotta figurines of Baluchistan and the Quetta Valley in Pakistan, which first appear in the third millennium B.C. Opening with a summary of the earliest terracottas then known (from the site of Mundigak near Kandahar in Afghanistan), this article then presents and analyses three distinct groupings of terracotta figurines from the Pakistan region, the female and animal images from the Zhob culture sites of northern Baluchistan, full-body figurines from Damb Sadaat in the Quetta Valley, and the Kulli figures of southern Baluchistan.

503. Lechevallier, M. and G. Quivron. "The Neolithic In Baluchistan: New Evidence From Mehrgarh," in *South Asian Archaeology 1979* edited by Herbert Hartel. Berlin: Dietrich Riemer Verlag, 1981: 71-92.

This article reports on three seasons of fieldwork at the site of Mehrgarh, where a preceramic village site had been located. This was a significant find, as "no early stratified site has been excavated on a large scale" (p. 71) anywhere in Pakistan. Illustrations of the stratigraphy of the site accompany the discussion of the types of structures located in four separate levels. The contents of twenty-nine burials and evaluation of the abundant lithic industries (chiefly of flint), dominated by borers and geometric microliths, completes the work.

504. Jarrige, J.F. "Economy and Society in the Early Chalcolithic/Bronze Age of Baluchistan: New Perspectives from Recent Excavations at Mehrgarh," in *South Asian Archaeology 1979* edited by Herbert Hartel. Berlin: Dietrich Riemer Verlag, 1981: 93-114.

A reassessment of the models traditionally used to interpret the past of this westernmost section of Pakistan. Data used come from eleven years of excavation in the Kachi plain by the French Archaeological Mission. Time span covered is the fifth to the third millennium B.C. The picture shown is one of regional complexity to a greater degree than previously thought, so that "the emergence of the Indus civilization must be seen in the context of regional developments linked to a local neolithic tradition going back at least to the 6th millennium B.C." (p. 113)

505. Meadow, R. "Early Animal Domestication in South Asia; A First Report of the Faunal Remains from Mehrgarh, Pakistan," in *South Asian Archaeology 1979* edited by Herbert Hartel. Berlin: Dietrich Riemer Verlag, 1981: 143-180.

During the field seasons of 1978 and 1979 at Mehrgarh, the author undertook an analysis of the faunal remains found, a problematic type of material for retrieval due to the highly destructive level of salt in the soil. This report begins by noting the placement of Mehrgarh at the intersection of three ecosystems-hill, plain, and river-and reviews modern domesticated animals present in the region as well. Three trends are noted:an increase in the presence of cattle, decreasing numbers of wild species, and variation in the proportion of sheep and goats. Researchers should bear in mind that most of the Mehrgarh data comes in the form of bones and teeth and that only approximately one-fifth to one-third of the bone fragments found could be assigned to a particular genus. Selected specimens are illustrated by line drawings.

506. Allchin, F.R. "Preliminary Report On the Bannu Basin Project (1977-1979): Introduction," in *South Asian Archaeology 1979* edited by Herbert Hartel. Berlin: Dietrich Riemer Verlag, 1981: 217-218.

An overview of the purposes of the Bannu Basin project, which by the time of publication (the end of two seasons of fieldwork) had examined some thirty sites in this area of northern Pakistan ranging in time from the modern era to the fourth millennium B.C. The aims of the project were to record the Pleistocene geology of the Bannu Basin, then select one or more settlement sites for intensive excavation, followed by a regional site survey. Sites chosen were Lewan and Tarakai Qila, materials from which are analysed by other members of the field team elsewhere in the same volume. The absence of any sites in the area from the mature phase of the Harappan culture and the lack of Muslim-era glazed wares are noted.

507. Rendell, Helen. "A Preliminary Investigation of the Sedimentary History of the Bannu Basin in the Late Holocene," in *South Asian Archaeology 1979* edited by Herber Hartel. Berlin: Dietrich Riemer Verlag, 1981: 219-225.

A concise presentation of the local soil types within the Bannu Basin and their deposition as it relates to the then-known archaeological occupation of the area. The sites of Lewan, Tarakai Qila and Lak Largai are reviewed and placed in context of their natural settings.

508. Thomas, K.D. "Palaeoecological Studies in the Bannu Basin: The Sources of Evidence," in *South Asian Archaeology 1979* edited by Herbert Hartel. Berlin: Dietrich Riemer Verlag, 1981: 227-232.

The aim of the palaeoecological portion of the Bannu Basin field work was to locate evidence for ancient environments with a view to relating them to specific local archaeological sequences of occupation. The essay reviews all local microenvironments delineated, noting the presence of pollen in paleosols as a useful marker of climatic change. Archaeological remains of relevance are charred seeds and animal bones from Tarakai Qila and Lewan, with barley, lentils and wheat identified to date.

509. Allchin, B. "Stone Industries of Lewan, Tarakai Qila and Lak Largai in the Bannu Basin," in *South Asian Archaeology 1979* edited by Herbert Hartel. Berlin: Dietrich Riemer Verlag, 1981: 233-239.

A review of the stone tool manufacturing tradition of the Bannu Basin as represented by materials recovered during excavations at the above-named sites. Lewan's function as a primary workshop is examined in depth. Types of artifacts known are flake and blade tools (the latter including an extensive microlithic assemblage), ringstones, palettes and tools for bead making.

510. Allchin, F.R and J Robert Knox. "Preliminary Report on the Excavations at Lewan (1977-78)," in *South Asian Archaeology 1979* edited by Herbert Hartel. Berlin: Dietrich Riemer Verlag, 1981: 241-244.

A brief note on the findings from the first season of survey and testing at the site of Lewan, located west of Bannu. While undated as yet, the excavations yielded evidence of structures similar to those constructed by historic nomads and pottery figurines of mother goddesses with affiliations to other pre-Harappan sites in Pakistan.

511. Stacul, G. "Painted Pottery from the Swat Valley, Pakistan (c.1700-1400 B.C.)," in *South Asian Archaeology 1979* edited by Herbert Hartel. Berlin: Dietrich Riemer Verlag, 1981: 305-311.

A well-illustrated analysis of red painted pottery found at the site of Bir-kot-ghundhai in the central Swat Valley in an assemblage of the black-grey burnished ware dated to the third millennium B.C. The painted pottery is interpreted as a local stylistic evolution rather than as a derivation from the Harappan culture of the adjacent Indus region.

512. *The Soviet Decipherment of the Indus Valley Script: Translation and Critique.* edited by Arlene R.K. Zide and Kamil V. Zvelebil. The Hague: Mouton, 1976.

In 1964, scholars from the Institute of Ethnography of the Academy of Sciences of the Soviet Union and a team of philologists headed by Yuri Knorozov began the task of attempting to decipher the unidentified language found on numerous artifacts and seals recovered from sites of the Indus Valley civilization. Utilizing computer technology to permit the amassing of a database of approximately 6,300 known signs and their contexts, various linguistic analyses were performed. This volume is a translation and publication of both the 1965 preliminary papers reporting the groups' conclusion (that the Indus tongue possessed a structure similar to known Dravidian or Altaic languages) and a secondary report done in 1968. Readers should be aware that much of the text presupposes familiarity with the technical terminology of linguistics. Prospects for the eventual complete decipherment of the language are seen to be limited by the absence of lengthy texts. The later works by Rao (1982) and Parpola (1994) will be far more accessible to the general reader.

513. Jarrige, Jean-Francois and Richard H. Meadow. "The Antecedents of Civilization in the Indus Valley," *Scientific American* 243, n.2 (August, 1980): 122-133.

A highly detailed report on the six seasons of excavation conducted at the site of Mehrgarh on the Bolan River in Baluchistan since December 1974, where remains of settled communities representing both the transition to agriculture and animal husbandry dating between the sixth millennium and 2600 B.C. have been located. Data on burial customs, lithic technologies (chiefly flint blades, but including soapstone as well) agriculture,pottery forms and housing construction are provided for the seven periods of occupation so far delineated. Among the artifacts found are three exceptional pottery depictions of humans, at this time "the earliest figurines yet discovered in southern Asia." (p. 128) Each era is set into regional context with available data, although the authors emphasize that, due to this new information, "the theoretical models used to interpret the prehistory of southern Asia must be completely reappraised." (p. 133)

514. Ratnagar, Shereen. *Encounters: The Westerly Trade of the Harappa Civilization*. Delhi: Oxford University Press, 1981.

Originally a doctoral thesis at Jawaharlal Nehru University, this volume examines one of the more elusive aspects of the Indus Valley civilization, its highly varied trade connections with Mesopotamia and the Persian Gulf. The opening chapter places the major participants of the trade network within a geographic and environmental context, using textual materials as applicable to delineate specific products imported. Areas covered are the Tigris and Euphrates Valleys, Elam, the shallow sea that is the Persian Gulf, the Zagros mountains, the Helmand River system in modern Afghanistan, ancient Magan, Meluhha and Dilmun (whose locations are noted as somewhat speculative), the sites of the Makran coast of Pakistan, and the Harappan region of western India. Individual commodities cited in ancient sources or known from excavation at sites in the regions noted are next considered, ranging from copper, bronze and tin to textiles, food, wood, certain types of precious stones (diorite and carnelian, among others) gold, ivory, lapis lazuli, pearls, silver, lead, shell and turquoise.The third chapter, "Trade

Mechanisms" examines the actual technology of both the ships used, climatic factors affecting sailing patterns (the monsoons most importantly) land and river transport, and types of packaging, weights and measures and seals used. Chronology of the trade systems is noted as being problematic for several reasons, chiefly the difficulty of accurately correlating textual references with the archaeological record, inconsistencies of available carbon-14 dates with stratigraphic sequences, and the possibility of parallel innovation. Speculation is offered in the conclusion as to the influence of trade in Harappan culture. Given the diversity of sites discussed within the trading net, this volume will be valuable background reading for any researcher dealing with Indian archaeology and its overseas connections. A lengthy bibliography is included.

515. *Harappan Civilization: A Contemporary Perspective* edited by Gregory Possehl. New Delhi: Oxford, 1982.

This massive volume contains the full texts of forty papers given at the conference on Harappan culture as then known held in Srinagar, Kashmir June 22-24, 1979 by scholars from India, Pakistan, the United States, France and Great Britain. Seven topical sections addressed the nature of Harappan urbanization; the results of then-recent field excavation (which include reports on the sites of Mehrgarh, Daimabad, Manda, Allahdino and Banawali with survey data from the Ganges Valley, the Cholistan Desert and Gujarat); ecology, technology and trade (covering food production as well); biological anthropology (based chiefly on the cemeteries at Harappa, Mohenjo-daro and Kalibangan); the Indus script; late Harappan civilization and its possible evolution, and the history of researches on the Harappan era. A lengthy section of black and white photographs illustrates both sites named and classes of artifacts discussed. Researchers should use this collection for background to the explosion of Indus-related field research which took place during the 1980s and 1990s.

516. McKean, Margaret Bernard. *The Palynology of Balakot, A Pre-Harappan and Harappan Age Site In Las Bela, Pakistan.* Ph.D Dissertation, Southern Methodist University, 1983.

The research upon which this dissertation reports was "the first palynological study of a proto-historic site in Pakistan," (p. 2) and as such addressed questions on the possible involvement of climate with the termination of the Indus culture and the role of internal agriculture and trade within this ancient culture region. The opening chapter explores the hypothesized links between the classical civilizations of Mesopotamia and India, then focuses on the Makran coastal site of Balakot, presenting results of botanical, faunal and marine remains obtained from the excavations carried out between 1973 and 1977. Succeeding chapters set out previous theories about the interrelation of climate, agriculture and environment during the Harappan era and the contemporary climate of the Las Bela region where Balakot is situated. The fourth chapter is especially valuable for researchers, as it summarizes all major palynological studies done in the subcontinent. Chapters five and six discuss the field methods used to retrieve pollen during the seasons of work at Balakot and the results of the analysis, which indicated no significant climatic changes between the Indus era and the present. Comparison with the pollen samples from Kalibangan, the only other Indus site to have yielded such materials as of the time of publication, is included. Scanning electron microscopy was also used as part of the analysis, the results presented in chapter seven. Conclusions regarding the place of Balakot in coastal trade (both internal and overseas) complete the work. Lengthy appendixes of plant and pollen data and a bibliography are provided.

517. Jettmar, Karl. "Non-Buddhist Traditions in the Petroglyphs of the Indus Valley," in *South Asian Archaeology 1983* edited by Janice Schotsmans and Maurizio Taddei. Naples: Istituto Universitario Orientale, 1985: 751-777.

This paper reports on the then-current state of knowledge regarding the array of petroglyphs discovered in the northern mountains of Pakistan, numbering some twenty thousand drawings and over fifteen hundred inscriptions in a variety of languages. Jettmar's specific focus is the formulation of "conclusions...in respect to the interethnic system, and...the indigenous religious heritage of the area," (p. 751) based on the carvings near Chilas in the Indus Valley. This massive grouping occupies both banks of the river and reaches for a distance of sixty kilometers. Correlations with other Inner Asian art styles are used as the basis for a hypothetical reconstruction of a mixed population similar to that of contemporary Nepal. Dates for the carvings range from 1000 B.C to the advent of Islam.

518. Thewalt, Volker. "Rockcarvings and Inscriptions Along the Indus: the Buddhist Tradition," in *South Asian Archaeology 1983* edited by Janice Schotsmans and Maurizio Taddei. Naples: Istituto Universitario Orientale, 1985: 779-800.

Part of the continuing analysis of data obtained in a survey of the petroglyphs of northern Pakistan between 1979 and 1983, the concentration of Buddhist inscriptions and iconography near Chilas on the upper Indus is examined. Subjects discussed include several variant forms in the development of the *stupa* shrine form (the oldest resembling the Indian sites of Sanchi and Bharhut), figures of the Buddha and *bodhisattvas*, horses, floral ornaments and Buddhist folklore.

519. Thapar, B.K. "Six Decades of Indus Studies," in *Frontiers of the Indus Civilization* edited by B.B. Lal and S.P. Gupta. New Delhi: Books and Books, 1984: 1-25.

Perhaps the most readable assessment of the tangled history of Indus archaeology to date, this essay by one of the veteran excavators of postwar India opens with a detailed summary of the familiar initial discoveries at Harappa and Mohenjo-Daro. This is followed by a virtual year-by-year chronology of the major sites investigated up to Partition and their significance for the growth in understanding of regional archaeology. The era 1947-1981 is next examined, stressing various surveys done within the redrawn boundaries of India to locate further Harappan culture sites and delineate insofar as possible the area of Indus influence. The final section reviews "some of the aspects and traditional paradigms which need revision," (p. 11) updating both data and debate on the Indus culture's distribution and settlement patterns, cultural homogeneity (an early hypothesis largely discredited by this time), climate, origins, trade and external contacts, chronology, the question of decline (seen to vary between regions due to local environmental factors) and the changes in field methods used. The bibliography is lengthy and very valuable for the novice.

520. Possehl, Gregory L. "Archaeological Terminology and the Harappan Civilization," in *Frontiers of the Indus Civilization* edited by B.B.Lal and S.P.Gupta. New Delhi: Books & Books, 1984: 27-36.

This essay calls for a re-examination of the terms being used in the study of India's "Harappan" culture, noting that "there is a close relationship between terminology and theory in archaeology." (p. 27) The history of the terms "Harappan" and "Indus Civilization" is presented, followed by a detailed exploration of the accepted definitions of civilization, urbanization, complex society and state as formulated in Western archaeology. Assessing the archaeological record of the Indus culture, the author sees little direct evidence for many of the broader institutional configurations of the Indus cultural system, emphasizing the regional variations visible in the later eras as then known. A sequence of "Pre-Urban, Urban and Post-Urban" (p. 34) phases is seen as depicting more accurately the known evolution of such centers as Mohenjo-Daro from a generalized pattern of village cultures. One distinguishing feature of this ancient culture is "that until excavation took place there was never a hint that this great human achievement was buried beneath the plains of the greater Indus Valley" (p. 33), a sharp contrast to its contemporaries in Mesopotamia and Egypt which were known from recorded fragments of history.

521. Kesarwani, Arun. "Harappan Gateways: A Functional Reassessment," in *Frontiers of the Indus Civilization* edited by B.B.Lal and S.B. Gupta. New Delhi: Books and Books, 1984: 63-73.

Beginning from the observed pattern of construction that "most large Harappan towns were encompassed by elaborately designed walls with gateways," (p. 63) attention is then focused on the gateways themselves and their structure as a clue to their possible functions. The plans of these structures from Harappa, Kalibangan, Mohenjo-Daro, Lothal, Desalpur, Sutkagen-dor and Surkotada are reviewed and compared with illustrated plans from Western Asian fortified sites such as Troy, Kish, Tell el Farah, Tel Brak and Schechem. The author concludes that the simpler plans of the Indus gates indicates a differing purpose from the clearly defensive multiple chambers and guardrooms seen in the Western examples, with the Indian fortifications serving as both protections against floods and visible symbols of social authority.

522. Fairservis, Walter A. "Archaeology in Baluchistan and the Harappan Problem," in *Frontiers of the Indus Civilization* edited by B.B.Lal and S P. Gupta. New Delhi: Books and Books, 1984: 277-287.

A detailed profile of the border region of Baluchistan, lying between India and Iran, and its known archaeology to date. Following a review of the physical geography, fauna and range of settlement types known from the ethnographic record, a history of field archaeology in the valleys and basins of the region is given, providing a highly useful concise summary of a complex body of research beginning with the pre-Partition surveys of Sir Aurel Stein and N.G. Majumdar. The rise of the Indus civilization and larger settlements in Baluchistan is seen as due to common developmental factors yet to be defined. Fairservis observes that "what is desperately needed in the archaeology of Baluchistan are less surveys and sondages and more extensive, sensitive and skillful excavations of key sites on a horizontal basis." (p. 286)

523. Gupta, S.P. "Internal Trade of the Harappans," in *Frontiers of The Indus Civilization* edited by B.B. Lal and S.P. Gupta. New Delhi: Books and Books, 1984: 417-424.

Beginning with the premise that "without a strong internal trade network, ...external trade was not possible," (p. 417) this article examines the questions of trade routes and exchange among the known sites of the Harappan era. Manufacturing centers are noted at Lothal, Chanhu-daro and Harappa itself. Available data are compared with the traditional industrial pattern of Indian trade, which was based on specialized crafts and their products, with Delhi serving as a central market for all. Gupta reviews the research done to date on Indus trading systems (all focusing on long-distance transport) and suggests that a system of guilds may have existed in Harappan times. The summary included of specific products and raw materials (ranging from seashells to copper and chert) manufactured and used at this era is a useful reference for readers examining individual site reports.

524. Raikes, R.L. "Mohenjo-Daro Environment," in *Frontiers of the Indus Civilization* edited by B.B. Lal and S.P. Gupta. New Delhi: Books and Books, 1984: 455-460.

A review of the major factors necessary for an exploration of past tectonic and sedimentary activity in the Indus basin and their relationship to the site of Mohenjo-Daro, where evidence of substantial flooding has been uncovered. Said evidence is the presence of silt beds which could only have been deposited under still water conditions. The author assumes the stability of all major climatic factors and notes the historic 1819 creation of the Allah bund by subsurface tectonic activity. While many of the assumptions are admitted by the author to be unproven, the research necessary to do so is laid out. Given the often tangled discussions about Indus geology and the Harappan culture, this article will serve as a valuable summary of the chief points.

525. Dennell. R.W. "The Importance of the Potwar Plateau, Pakistan, To Studies of Early Man," in *South Asian Archaeology 1981* edited by Bridget Allchin. Cambridge University, Press, 1984: 10-19.

In 1939, a lengthy climatic and archaeological sequence was presented by de Terra and Paterson for the Potwar Plateau of what is now northern Pakistan. Said chronology has since been shown to be defective due to seafloor core studies indicating seventeen eras of glaciation instead of the four which they posited and tied to established fluctuations known from European prehistory. This paper reviews potential contributions the South Asian region may make to both the investigation of hominid species and the archaeology of stone tool production. Two seasons of excavation at the site of Riwat are noted.

526. Jarrige, Jean-Francois. "Chronology of the Earlier Periods of the Greater Indus as seen from Mehrgarh, Pakistan," in *South Asian Archaeology 1981* edited by Bridget Allchin. Cambridge University Press, 1984: 21-28.

Utilizing the cultural materials recovered from Periods I-III of the Mehrgarh site, this article calls for a reassessment of the complexity of civilization's development in the Indus Valley and Baluchistan, challenging the more accepted diffusionist model.Particular attention is given to the two overlapping aceramic mounds at Mehrgarh, the finds of compartmented buildings and the rise of mass-produced pottery in Period II, dating to the sixth and fifth millennia B.C.

527. Costantini, Lorenzo. "The Beginning of Agriculture in the Kachi Plain: The Evidence of Mehrgarh," in *South Asian Archaeology 1981* edited by Bridget Allchin. Cambridge University Press, 1984: 29-33.

Due to local environmental conditions at the Neolithic site of Mehrgarh, a large number of mudbricks bearing the impressions of straw and grain were preserved. This article reports on the sieving technique used to recover them from occupation levels and details of the individual species of wheat, barley, grapes, dates and cotton identified.

528. Lechevallier, Monique. "The Flint Industry of Mehrgarh," in *South Asian Archaeology 1981* edited by Bridget Allchin. Cambridge University Press, 1984: 41-51.

A review of the types of flint artifacts recovered from the levels of the Mehrgarh site dating to the sixth to third millennia B.C. Some thirty-two thousand pieces had been collected over seven years of field work, including microliths, sickle elements, scrapers and burins,borers, axes and adzes. Each class is illustrated by high quality pen drawings. The Mehrgarh assemblage is placed into a more general context with the Indus Valley and Iran.

529. Rao, S.R. *The Decipherment of the Indus Script.* Bombay: Asia, 1982.

In this work, the author offers his hypothesis that "the Indus script was gradually evolved into an alphabetic system of writing and...the language...is Indo-European." (p. vii) He notes that other approaches to decipherment have avoided tackling the compound signs, and accepts the identity of signs in both the Harappan and Semitic writing systems. A work requiring background in Indian linguistics to be comprehended fully, and one illustrating the complexity of issues surrounding the Indus script.

530. Pal, Yash, et.al. "Remote Sensing of the 'Lost' Sarasvati River," in *Frontiers of the Indus Civilization* edited by B.B. Lal and S.P. Gupta, 1984: 491-497.

A report of analyis of LANDSAT images of the region lying between the Yamuna and Satluj rivers taken in the period 1972-1977. The goal was the delineation of the vanished course of the Sarasvati River, cited in the *Rigveda* as a major waterway. The photo mosaic allowed for the reconstruction of past river channels, revealing that several of the contemporary river systems had in fact fed the Sarasvati in past times. Correlations with regional archaeology lie in the pre-Harappan, Harappan and Painted Grey Ware eras.

531. Dennell, R.W., H. M. Rendell and M.A.Halim. "New Perspectives on the Palaeolithic of Northern Pakistan," in *South Asian Archaeology 1983* edited by Janine Schotsmans and Maurizio Taddei. Naples: Istituto Universitario Orientale, 1985: 9-20.

A brief discussion of the results of field research conducted since 1980 by the authors as part of the British Archaeological Mission to Pakistan.Their aim was "locating artefacts and archaeological sites in datable contexts, and placing these contexts in a palaeoenvironmental framework." (p. 11) The Jhelum and Soan regions of northern Pakistan yielded artifacts dating to circa 400,000 B.P. and a blade industry of at least 30,000 years B.P. respectively. Readers wishing a fuller exposition of the eventual six year span of the project should consult the 1989 report by the authors entitled *Pleistocene and Palaeolithic Investigations in the Soan Valley, Northern Pakistan.*

532. Cucarzi, Mauro. "A Methodology for Geophysical Prospecting in Archaeology. An Example: Mohenjo-daro," in *South Asian Archaeology 1983* edited by Janine Schotsmans and Maurizio Taddei. Naples: Istituto Universitario Orientale, 1985: 279-295.

This report opens by reviewing the theoretical approaches taken in the planning and execution of the application of geophysical survey techniques to any archaeological context, then focuses on the site of Mohenjo-daro in Sind. In March, 1982, soil and burnt brick samples were taken from the site for laboratory analysis, resulting in the decision to utilize "the intensity of magnetic field and electrical resistivity" (p. 285) as parameters to augment knowledge of the city. The magnetic field survey revealed a long anomaly, which test borings indicate is the boundary of a brick building platform from one phase of Mohenjo-daro's history.

533. Shendge, Malati J. "The Inscribed Calculi and the Invention of Writing: The Indus View," *Journal of the Economic and Social History of the Orient* 28 (1985): 50-80.

An unusual piece of scholarship relating to the invention and use of writing in the Indian subcontinent, this detailed article takes as its subject a very specific class of artifact, small inscribed objects of steatite, faience and terracotta. The author advances the hypothesis that they are comparable to a reckoning system using clay pebbles as counters known from the Iranian site of Susa. The paper discusses and illustrates the types of these small carved "seals" known from Harappa (where a greater portion of the early levels of the site have been reached than at Mohenjo-daro), their stratification and evolution, and possible relationship to the later seals and the development of the Indus script. Analogies with data from Susa and Uruk on the evolution of cuneiform signs are invoked to buttress the argument.

534. Hassan, Mohammed Usman. "Ras-Koh: A Crossroads of Ancient Civilizations," in *South Asian Archaeology 1985* edited by Karen Frifelt and Per Sorensen. London: Curzon Books, 1989: 189-195.

When considering the prehistory of Baluchistan, in addition to mounds located by field survey, "there is another group of antiquities to which little atttention has...been paid... the rock carvings found in several areas" (p. 189) along the old trade routes between the Indus Valley and Iran. This note (lavishly illustrated with full-page black and white photographs) focuses on the Jallawar Pass through the Ras Koh range and its associated ruins and petroglyphs. Historical background on the Zoroastrian and Muslim occupations of the site is outlined.

535. Cucarzi, Mauro. "Cemeteries, Huge Structures, Working Areas Through Geophysical Investigation," in *South Asian Archaeology 1985* edited by Karen Frifelt and Per Sorensen. London: Curzon Press, 1989: 211-215.

The application of geophysical technology to field archaeology in India and adjacent regions has been underway for ten years. This brief paper summarizes the major findings made thus far using geomagnetic and geoelectric measuring techniques. They include the delimitation of two boundaries of the central region of Mohenjo-daro, surveying cemeteries at Harappa and the protohistoric site of Aligrama in northern Pakistan, and testing for pit graves at the Iranian site of Shahr-i Sokhta.

536. Dayton, John E. "The Faience of the Indus Civilization," in *South Asian Archaeology 1985* edited by Karen Frifelt and Per Sorensen. London: Curzon Press, 1989: 216-226.

A highly detailed comparison of the faience objects and technology known from the Indus sites of Mohenjo-Daro and Harappa with those of Minoan Crete and Mycenean Greece. Classes of objects found include segmented beads, spindle whorls, inlaid faience, seals (five hundred and fifty from Mohenjo-daro alone) pots and fragments of statuary. The relationship of the Indian trade network to the Mediterranean is used to suggest a date for the Indus cities of 1650-1400 B.C., correlating with observed stratigraphy.

537. Flam, Louis "Recent Explorations in Sind: Palaegeography, Regional Ecology, and Prehistoric Settlement Patterns (ca.4000-2000 B.C.)," in *Studies in the Archaeology of India and Pakistan* edited by Jerome Jacobson. Warminster: Aris and Phillips, 1987: 65-89.

A report covering the 1976-77 field reconnaissance carried out in Sind by the author, re-examining the series of sites noted by N.G. Majumdar prior to his death at the hands of bandits while in the field in November, 1938. Given the extensive research done in both Pakistan and India folllowing Partition, "the prehistoric significance of Sind needed to be reconsidered." (p. 65) Three ecological regions were defined for analysis: the lower Indus basin, the Kirthar Mountains and their adjacent plains, and Kohistan. The first section presents the paleogeography of Sind as then known, tracing the variant course of major rivers between 4000 and 2000 B.C. Regional ecosystems of each area are next outlined, with emphasis placed on local resources capable of supporting subsistence strategies. A comparison of this data with Sind's archaeological succession of settlement patterns of the Amri-Kot Diji, Kulli (Transitional) and Harappan eras suggests a shift from upland to valley sites and the increasing use of rivers as a major means of communication. A distinctive arrangement of urban centers into upper and lower towns is also noted.

538. Dennell, R.W. et.al. "Preliminary Results of the Palaeolithic Programme of the British Archaeological Mission to Pakistan, 1983-1987," in *South Asian Archaeology 1987* edited by Maurizio Taddei. Naple: Istituto Universitario Orientale, 1990: 17-30.

Updating an earlier paper published in *South Asian Archaeology 1983*, this essay reports on the four continuing priorities of the project for the years 1983-1987. These centered on finding artifacts *in situ* which could be reliably dated by either thermoluminescence or paleomagnetism, locating animal fossils sufficient to permit the reconstruction of local environmental sequences, and tracing climatic evolution through the study of sediments and paleosols. Of greatest significance in these seasons was the conclusive dating of a stone tool found in 1983 at Riwat to 2 million years of age, indicating a comparable time depth of manufacture to that known from Africa. The data presented here are explicated more fully in the 1989 work *Pleistocene and Palaeolithic Investigations in the Soan Valley, Northern Pakistan.*

539. Biagi, Paolo and Mauro Cremaschi. "The Early Palaeolithic Sites of the Rohri Hills (Sind, Pakistan) and Their Environmental Significance," *World Archaeology* 19 (3) (February 1988): 421-433.

A report on the use of scanning electron microscopy in the study of artifact patinas as a method of retrieving ancient environmental data. Objects chosen for this experiment come from seven palaeolithic and early palaeolithic period sites in the Rohri Hills of southern Pakistan, first located in 1986. Comparison of the results with known regional geological features is also presented.

540. Khan, Farid, J.R. Knox and K.D. Thomas. "Sheri Khan Tarakai: A Neolithic Village in Bannu District, NWFP," in *South Asian Archaeology 1987* edited by Maurizio Taddei. Naples: Istituto Universitario Orientale, 1990: 11-127.

A report on work carried out since 1985 at the occupation site of Sheri Khan Tarakai in the North West Frontier Province, dating to the fourth millennium B.C., where at least two meters of cultural deposits have been verified. Much of the text is devoted to the presentation and comparative discussion of the unique pottery types and terracotta figurines depicting both human beings and and animals found at the site. Line drawings illustrate sample artifacts of each class.

541. Mughal, M. Rafique. "The Protohistoric Settlement Patterns In the Cholistan Desert," in *South Asian Archaeology 1987* edited by Maurizio Taddei. Naples: Istituto Universitario Orientale, 1990: 143-156.

With the help of LANDSAT imagery, it has been possible to identify various palaeo-channels in the Sutlej-Yamuna Divide and in Cholistan, (p. 143) an extension of the Thar desert in the east-central Indus Valley. Site survey along the old course of the now-dry Hakra River revealed 377 protohistoric sites ranging in date from the fourth millenium to 500 B.C. This paper presents the distribution of these sites and links them to the various shifting courses of the Hakra over time.

542. Vidale, Massimo. "On the Structure and the Relative Chronology of a Harappan Industrial Site," in *South Asian Archaeology 1987* edited by Maurizio Taddei. Naples: Istituto Universitario Orientale, 1990: 203-244.

The industrial site of the title is the Moneer Southeast Area of Mohenjo-daro. This paper focuses on the results of sampling done during the 1984 and 1986 fieldwork seasons, aimed at establishing a possible interpretation for successive stratigraphic layers of waste deposits from the manufacture of steatite and chert stone objects. Existing models of analysis for the remains of specialized craft areas of settlements are seen to require expansion to include the dump sites, which may reflect key aspects of technology and various stages of production.

543. During Caspers, Elisabeth C.L. "Harappan Temples-Fact or Fallacy?" in *South Asian Archaeology 1987* edited by Maurizio Taddei. Naples: Istituto Universitario Orientale, 1990: 245-261.

Beginning with established specific artistic parallels between the Indus Valley culture and the civilizations of Mesopotamia and Elam,the author then raises the question of whether recognizable images of sacred structures may also be present in Harappan art. Noting that, for the Harappan sites known, "the archaeological records ...do not show any structural remains which can readily be recognized as sanctuaries or…as having once fulfilled a religious function, despite the wish of the excavators," (p. 249), the question of enclosed areas as sanctuaries for sacred trees or groves is explored. Evidence from Mohenjo-daro suggesting that the pipal tree was regarded as the abode of a divinity and possibly planted in courtyards for veneration is offered to support this hypothesis.

544. Tusa, Sebastiano. "Ancient Ploughing in Northern Pakistan," in *South Asian Archaeology 1987* edited by Maurizio Taddei. Naples: Istituto Universitario Orientale, 1990: 349-376.

During the 1981 season of excavations at the Neolithic site of Aligrama in the Swat Valley, a flood deposit was uncovered dating to 1100-800 B.C., beneath which was a well-preserved area of soil showing clear evidence of plough furrows. This discovery is placed in context both of its implications for regional post-Harappan archaeology of this region (termed the Northwestern or Gandhara Grave Culture) and of similar finds from Europe and India (Kalibangan). Researchers unfamiliar with this aspect of historical archaeology will find the discussion of ploughing technology instructive.

545. Rendell. H.M., R.W. Dennell and M.A. Halim. *Pleistocene and Palaeolithic Investigations in the Soan Valley, Northern Pakistan.* Oxford: B.A.R., 1989.

The second publication of the British Archaeological Mission to Pakistan and monograph 544 of the *British Archaeological Reports International Series*, this report contains the results of a re-examination of the Soan Valley's prehistory and geology. The work opens with a presentation of the original research by de Terra and Paterson in the area in 1939, subsequently published as *Studies of the Ice Age of India and Associated Human Cultures.* The scientific mindset of Palaeolithic archaeology at that time is noted as contributing to conclusions about the Soan Valley archaeological and geologic sequences (and their correlations with European glaciations) which the authors reject as untenable. The construction of a new framework of analysis for the Soan is seen to be required. Over a period of six years, beginning with a field survey in 1979, the Riwat area was chosen as a sample area for intensive study to begin this task. Individual chapters cover the Soan and the Palaeolithic in the northern Indian subcontinent, the stratigraphy and tectonic history of the Potwar Plateau and the Soan Valley, the Upper Siwalik deposits at Riwat and the artifacts they contained, and the excavation of a specific locality dated by thermoluminescence to ca. 45,000 years B.P. Emphasis was placed on both the processes of site formation and functional analysis of the lithic assemblages found, providing an updated perspective of the problems of Palaeolithic archaeology in the region. A site plan of Riwat, detailed illustrations of artifacts found, and a bibliography of cited references are appended.

546. During Caspers, Elisabeth C.L. "The 'Calendar Stones' from Moenjo-daro Reconsidered," in *South Asian Archaeology 1989* edited by Catherine Jarrige. Madison, Wisconsin: Prehistory Press, 1992: 83-95.

In the course of excavations at Mohenjo-daro, a group of large bored stone objects was uncovered, four in a row on the floor of a room. This paper challenges and successfully refutes their interpretation as calendrical measuring devices, offering instead a possible association with a cult of veneration of the pipal tree.

547. Mughal, M. Rafique. "Jhukar and the Late Harappan Cultural Mosaic of the Greater Indus Valley," in *South Asian Archaeology 1989* edited by Catherine Jarrige. Madison, Wisconsin: Prehistory Press, 1992: 213-221.

The site of Jhukar, northwest of Mohenjo-daro in Sind, was re-excavated for two seasons in 1973 and 1974, with the goal of defining more precisely its distinctive cultural remains dating to the Late Harappan period. Four clear layers of occupation were marked, yielding some fifty types and sub-types of pottery. This article notes that Jhukar is best considered as a new style of pottery shape and decoration distinctive to a local region within the Late Harappan period, similar to other such complexes known from Gujarat, the Punjab and Baluchistan. Available data on all three areas is summarized to provide a context for the Jhukar materials.

548. Callieri, Pierfrancesco. "Bir-Kot-Ghwandai: An Early Historic Town in Swat (Pakistan)," in *South Asian Archaeology 1989* edited by Catherine Jarrige. Madison, Wisconsin: Prehistory Press, 1992: 339-346.

During excavation at the site of Bir-kot-ghwandai in the central Swat Valley in the autumn of 1987, a stretch of the massive fortification wall of the town was exposed. This paper discusses the stages of construction visible and attempts to place this wall within known traditions of defensive architecture from the region, both the Macedonian heritage of Alexander the Great and the Mauryan.

549. *Forgotten Cities on the Indus: Early Civilization in Pakistan from the 8th to the 2nd Millennium BC* edited by Michael Jansen, Maire Mulloy and Gunter Urban. Mainz: Philipp von Zabern, 1991.

An English translation of a group of twenty-one articles originally written to accompany the international exhibition of Indus Valley materials which opened in Aachen ,Germany on June 27,1987. Born out of the international project to conserve and study Mohenjo-daro, this lavishly illustrated volume presents a range of papers covering not only the city itself but specific aspects of its life from craftwork and art to burial practices, as well as plant domestication and discussion of the Neolithic era in the region as represented by the site of Mehrgarh. Two bibliographies are included. Selected papers from this catalogue have been entered separately in the current work.

550. Urban, Gunter. "The Indus Civilization: the Story of a Discovery," in *Forgotten Cities on the Indus: Early Civilization in Pakistan from the 8th to the 2nd Millennium BC* edited by Michael Jansen, Maire Mulloy and Gunter Urban. Mainz: Philipp von Zabern, 1991: 18-26.

A highly readable general history of archaeological involvement with the site of Mohenjo-Daro, which means "Mound of the Dead" in Sindhi. Although artifacts were noted from the mound by Sir Alexander Cunningham (including a seal depicting a zebu ox, the first known example of what would later be recognized as a cognate writing form of this culture), actual excavation and discovery followed the 1921 work by Daya Ram Sahni at Harappa. Beginning in 1922, some eight hectares of Mohenjo-Daro had been unearthed by the 1925/1926 season, revealing the now-familiar street plans, house features, and brick walls. Urban notes that the confusing division of the site into sections which do not follow proper alphabetic order is based on the fact that each area was tagged with the initials of the investigating archaeologist. The first wave of excavation tailed off after 1928, resuming in the era 1944-1965 under Sir Mortimer Wheeler and G.F. Dales respectively. Results of the German project begun in 1979 include verification of the existence of an massive brick platform underlying the "Citadel" area. Readers will find the selected photographs illustrating the 1925-27 field seasons useful as a chronicle of changing excavation methods.

551. Ardeleanu, Janse, Alexandra. "The Sculptural Art of the Harappa Culture," in *Forgotten Cities On The Indus: Early Civilization In Pakistan From the 8th to the 2nd Millennium B.C.* edited by Michael Jansen, Maire Mulloy and Gunter Urban. Mainz: Philipp von Zabern, 1991: 167-178.

While much of the scientific literature on Indus Valley civilization discusses various art forms as finds from specific sites, these objects are not usually considered in an art historical context. The present article focuses on all sculptural forms known from the Harappan period at the time of this exhibition, beginning with sixteen large pieces in stone from Mohenjo-Daro depicting both animals and human beings, the latter including the famous fragmentary "Priest King" bust discovered in 1924. Stylistic links with Mesopotamia are used to illustrate both common features of clothing and depiction of human figures. Sculpted animal figurines (preponderantly cattle, suggesting a religious cult similar to that of the Sumerian "Bull of Heaven," two bronze figures of young women apparently dancing, terracotta figurines (a type widely found, depicting a large number of species as well as men and women, the latter represented as well by cast masks) and faience objects are reviewed. The presence of composite objects is also noted. Readers will find this article's color illustrations a welcome change from the standard monochromatic photographs of Indus Valley art.

552. Franke-Vogt, Ute. "The Glyptic Art of the Harappa Culture," in *Forgotten Cities On The Indus: Early Civilization In Pakistan From The 8th to the 2nd Millennium B.C.* edited by Michael Jansen, Maire Mulloy and Gunter Urban. Mainz: Philipp von Zabern, 1991: 179-187.

A discussion of the seals and seal impressions produced by the Indus Valley culture within the context of Near Eastern "glyptic art," more familiar as the craft of gem cutting. Beginning with the publication of a square stamp seal bearing an ox and script characters found at Harappa by Sir Alexander Cunningham in 1875, the various types and forms of seals are reviewed, along with the animal, human, and hybrid figures which decorate them. Although jar seals from Lothal indicate usage as part of commercial trade, lack of mythological context and the undeciphered script pose major obstacles to in-depth analysis.

553. Fairservis, Walter A. *The Harappan Civilization and Its Writing: A Model for the Decipherment of the Indus Script.* Leiden: Brill, 1992.

The preface to this work notes that "the following account represents some ten years of work…it began out of frustration with our inability to more than record the seal-tablets and tablets…from our excavations at the …site of Allahdino near Karachi." (p. ii) The opening section reviews the types of materials bearing the script and the variety of the 419 known signs used, then moves to a consideration of the possible language families which the script might represent. The result of this is seen to be that "the Harappan language was basically an early Dravidian language and …the script was a logo-syllabic system using that language with the formal boundaries created by the utilitarian needs of the Harappan Civilization." (p. 23) The main section of the text sets forth identifications of signs and numerical symbols based on this approach, followed by a derived vocabulary and attempted translations. An illustrated list of symbols and main motifs found on Harappan seals is included.

554. Franke-Vogt, Ute. "The 'Early Period' At Mohenjo-Daro," in *From Sumer To Meluhha: Contributions to the Archaeology of South and West Asia in Memory of George F. Dales, Jr.* edited by Jonathan Mark Kenoyer. Madison, Wisconsin: University of Wisconsin Department of Anthropology, 1994: 27-49.

A re-examination of the proposed "Early Harappan" materials retrieved at Mohenjo-Daro since the late 1930's by the excavations of Mackay, Sir Mortimer Wheeler and George Dales. Detailed information on the depth of the soundings made, stratigraphic profiles, artifacts found, and their relationship to later work at Nausharo and Harappa itself is presented. Available data indicate that "convincing evidence for a horizon culturally different from and chronologically earlier than the urban Harappan is not yet available" (p. 45)

555. Nissen, Hans J. "An Archaeological Surface Survey in Northwestern Sindh, Pakistan," in *From Sumer to Meluhha; Contributions to the Archaeology of South and West Asia in Memory of George F. Dales* edited by Jonathan Mark Kenoyer. Madison, Wisconsin: University of Wisconsin Department of Anthropology, 1994: 51-58.

A report on the unexpected finding in the Larkana district of Sindh of fifteen sites exhibiting a type of pottery previously unknown. The majority of this report consists of section and profile drawings of the best-preserved forms found at Khairpur Juso. Potential applications of this information to a re-evaluation of the prehistoric occupation of Sindh are discussed.

556. Xu Chaolong. "Cultural Changes in Sindh Prior to the Mature Harappan Period? A Clue Drawn from A Comparative Study of the Pottery," in *From Sumer to Meluhha: Contributions to the Archaeology of South and West Asia in Memory of George F. Dales* edited by Jonathan Mark Kenoyer. Madison, Wisconsin: University of Wisconsin Department of Anthropology, 1994: 59-70.

Based upon a chapter from the author's dissertation, this paper sets forth a comparison of the pottery forms known from the contemporary sites of Kot Diji and Amri (which have been excavated down to undisturbed natural soils), and their relationship to ceramics retrieved from the lowest levels at Mohenjo-Daro. All major forms are compared, resulting in the conclusion that "each site had its cultural sequence distinct from the others," (p. 68) with the earlier levels at Mohenjo-Daro already representing forms seen in the later mature Indus Valley culture.

557. Belcher, William R. "Multiple Approaches Towards Reconstruction of Fishing Technology: Net Making and the Indus Valley Tradition," in *From Sumer to Meluhha: Contributions to the Archaeology* of South and West Asia *in Memory of George F. Dales* edited by Jonathan Mark Kenoyer. Madison, Wisconsin: University of Wisconsin Department of Anthropology, 1994: 129-141.

Noting that "Ethnoarchaeology of fisher-folk is virtually non-existent in a formal, quantified sense," (p. 129) the author of this essay uses the literature of ethnography available on the Punjab as a source of information on net manufacture and use. This model is then compared with relevant materials found during the excavation of various Indus sites, such as actual fish remains (along with a discussion of habitats and behaviors) net weights, motifs depicting both fish and the use of throw nets on Indus pottery.

558. Fairservis, Walter A. "The Harappan Script: Is It Deciphered Or Can It Be Deciphered?" in *From Sumer To Meluhha: Contributions to the Archaeology of South and West Asia in Memory of George F. Dales* edited by Jonathan Mark Kenoyer. Madison, Wisconsin: University of Wisconsin Department of Anthropology, 1994: 173-178.

This paper is a summary of the approach taken by Fairservis to the decipherment of the Indus script, using the Dravidian language family of India as a model. Its opening section sets forth past successful decipherments where no bilingual text was available, such as Linear B, then lists the facts known about this writing system at the time of publication, ranging from its occurrence on seals and tokens to the regular appearance together of certain signs. Two examples of deciphered texts whose Dravidian-based reading makes sense in their excavated context are then presented. Researchers interested in a more in-depth treatment of this approach to the Indus script should also consult his more lengthy monograph *The Harappan Civilization and Its Writing* (Brill, 1992).

559. Khan, Farid. "The Potential of Ethnoarchaeology, with Special Reference to

Recent Archaeological Work in Bannu District, Pakistan," in *Living Traditions: Studies in the Ethnoarchaeolgy of South Asia* edited by Bridget Allchin.Columbia, Missouri: South Asia Publications, 1994: 83-99.

Using data from the Neolithic site of Sheri Khan Tarakai, the author addresses the processes of site formation, interpretation of specific site features (in this case, grain bins ,roasting areas and cobblestone wall cores) via ethnographic analogy, retrieval of features of ancient economic systems (the hunting of mountain goats) and the continuity of regional cultural phenomena. This last is illustrated through modern crane-keeping and training, (the bird a frequent symbol on Tarakai pottery) and a terracotta figurine of a woman showing a hairstyle still worn in the district.

560. Mughal, M.Rafique. "The Harappan Nomads of Cholistan," in *Living Traditions: Studies In the Ethnoarchaeology of South Asia*. Columbia, Missouri; South Asia Publications, 1994: 53-68

Between 1980 and 1991, the author conducted a site survey of the dried-up Hakra River depression in east-central Pakistan and its associated areas, establishing that this region had been intensively settled in prehistoric times. A number of these sites (dated to the Harappan period by surface potsherds) are interpreted through analogy with modern nomads of the area as either temporary settlements of grazers or permanent settlements made of perishable materials. The use of open-air firing technology involving circular pottery disks as filler is also noted as clarifying anomalous features at some sites.

561. Allchin, Bridget. "Environmental Conditions In The Lower Indus Valley In Harappan Times: A Plea For Research," in *South Asian Archaeology 1993* edited by Asko Parpola and Petteri Koskikallio. Helsinki: Suomalainen Tiedeakatemia, 1994: 43-46.

Admitting "we do not have any sort of comprehensive view of how far the climate and environment of the lower Indus Valley differed from that of the present day or what changes it passed through during the growth and maturity of the Indus Culture," (p. 44) the author outlines four areas of required data. These are tectonic events, the historic instability of the course of the river Indus, climatic changes in the target region, and the effect of increasing human populations on the vicinities of the cities and outlying settlements. While smaller scale studies integrating environmental factors have begun in several areas of the former Indus occupation area, the valley itself has been neglected. Completed surveys which may serve as sources of data are outlined.

562. Belcher, William R. "Riverine Fisheries and Habitat Exploitation of the Indus Valley Tradition: An Example From Harappa, Pakistan," in *South Asian Archaeology 1993* edited by Asko Parpola and Petteri Koskikallio. Helsinki: Suomalainen Tiedeakatemia, 1994: 71-80.

A study done as part of the Harappan Archaeological Research Project, focusing on the reconstruction of fishing as part of the Indus civilization subsistence pattern. Archaeofaunal remains found at the site (principally several species of catfish and cyprinids) along with fish hooks and net weights, are interpreted through ethnographic information on fishing in the Punjab during historical times. Seasonal variation in availability of riverine habitats is also noted.

563. Jansen, Michael. "Mohenjo-Daro, Type Site of the Earliest Urbanization Process in South Asia: Ten Years of Research At Mohenjo-Daro,Pakistan, and an Attempt At A Synopsis," in *South Asian Archaeology 1993* edited by Asko Parpola and Petteri Koskikallio. Helsinki: Suomalainen Tiedeakatemia, 1994: 263-280.

In 1979, the Aachen University Research Project Mohenjo-Daro was initiated to document "all the excavated remains prior to studying the *forma urbis* under formal and functional aspects," (p. 266) as many of the older interpretations from the 1930s were considered to be outdated. The Project encompassed approximately three hundred structural units found during eight separate excavations. This article attempts to present the preliminary results of analysis of the birth of this settlement using such parameters as stratigraphy, construction techniques, house types, and orientation.

564. Jarrige, Catherine. "The Mature Indus Phase At Nausharo As Seen From A Block of Period III," in *South Asian Archaeology 1993* edited by Asko Parpola and Petteri Koskikallio. Helsinki: Suomalainen Tiedeakatemia, 1994: 281-294.

An intriguing approach to the analysis of town planning during the Indus occupation of the site of Nausharo is taken in this research, the examination of blocks of living units through "the vertical growth of the whole structure, as shown by the relative stratigraphy of each cluster." (p. 283) Repeated reconstruction of the walls of residential blocks indicated an overall house plan defined by a series of features and coordinated with other units to maximize water drainage. This study was undertaken as part of an effort to determine "the presence or absence of specialized areas at Nausharo during the Mature Indus period." (p. 291)

565. Meadow, Richard H. and Jonathan Mark Kenoyer. "Harappa Excavations 1993: The City Wall and Inscribed Materials," in *South Asian Archaeology 1993* edited by Asko Parpola and Petteri Koskikallio. Helsinki: Suomalainen Tiedeakatemia, 1994: 451-470.

The objectives of the 1993 field season at Harappa built upon the 1990 discovery of a perimeter wall and gateway. As part of the focus on urbanism and its development taken by the Harappan Archaeological Research Project (specifically, when and how individual sections of the city came to be established), attention was given to tracing the extent of the wall and the various phases of its construction between 2600 and 1900 B.C. Inscribed steatite seals and tablets and terracotta objects bearing Indus pictographs retrieved during the clearance of sixteen hundred square meters are also summarized.

566. Parpola, Asko. *Deciphering The Indus Script*. New York: Cambridge University Press, 1994.

The latest and most comprehensive treatment of continuing research on interpreting the writing system of the Indus civilization, this volume by the editor of the *Corpus of Indus Seals and Inscriptions* opens with a brief overview of the culture. Data on similar scripts such as Sumerian, Etruscan and the Mayan hieroglyphs are next presented as background to the history of efforts to identify the Indus language (at least by family) and to attempt precise assignment of meanings to its signs. The fourth chapter, "Approaches to the Indus Script," begins with the appearance of potter's marks on sherds from the Early Harappan era (ca.3600-2600 B.C.) and summarizes the various ideas applied to the evolution of Indus symbols since their first discovery by Sir Alexander Cunningham in 1875. The suggestion in 1924 by Sir John Marshall that this script represented an ancient member of the Dravidian language group is seen as having been attested through the Soviet structural analysis projects of the 1960's. Parpola's discussion then moves to the history of various branches of Dravidian and sets forth evidence indicating that the Indus script is logo-syllabic in nature. Perhaps most fascinating is the final section, which offers interpretations for specific pictograms suggesting astronomical, astrological and religious meanings. The massive bibliography should be used as a starting point by all Indus civilization researchers dealing with questions involving this writing system.

567. Kenoyer, Jonathan Mark. *Ancient Cities of the Indus Valley Civilization*. Oxford: Oxford University Press,1998.

Written as an introductory work and catalog to accompany the exhibition *Great Cities, Small Treasures: The Ancient World of the Indus Valley* held in New York, Madison and Pasadena in 1998, this lavishly illustrated volume opens with a discussion of the processes which create and maintain urban society and the physical and climatic setting of the Indus region. Succeeding chapters discuss the character of Indus urban and village settlements, the unique (and still undeciphered) writing system, social structure and trade connections, religion, crafts and technology. The legacy for later Indian cultures based on this culture is examined in the final section. The exhibition catalog covers some two hundred and four artifacts, described in detail and illustrated in both black and white and color. Readers wishing to assess the progress of scholarship in this field as of 1998 will find the bibliography useful.

Sri Lanka

568. Davids, Thomas William Rhys. *On the Ancient Coins and Measures of Ceylon*. London: Trubner, 1877.

An early work on the ancient coinage and units of trade by a noted scholar of the Pali language, this volume begins by informing the reader that "Ceylon and Kashmir are the only parts of India which pretend to possess a continuous native history," (p. 1), then limits discussion to coins and measures mentioned in the Buddhist literature of Ceylon and such medieval coins as were known at the time of publication. An excellent example of the use made of numismatics in the late nineteenth century with regard to the retrieval of Sri Lanka's history and lineages. Illustration is limited to a panel of coin types and one engraving of a ruined Buddhist shrine. This work reappeared as a facsimile reprint from Obol International in Chicago in 1975 and is the sixth part of the 1878 series International Numismate Orientalia.

569. Muller, Edward. *Ancient Inscriptions in Ceylon*. London: Trubner and Company, 1883. 2 vols.

"The object of the present work is to give a collection of the inscriptions in Ceylon very much in the same way as the Corpus Inscriptionum Indicarum by General Cunningham." (p. 1) The author of this volume was appointed Archaeological Commissioner of Ceylon in the spring of 1878, succeeding Dr. Goldschmidt, whose death on May 7, 1877 ended his pioneering epigraphical investigations, which are referenced in full and summarized in the *Preface*. The textual portion of the set opens with a general account of the inscriptions, which Muller limited to a range from the oldest known to the sixteenth century and attempted to arrange in chronological order insofar as possible. He then discusses all inscriptions known by period and presents transliterations and translations of many lengthy texts. The majority of inscriptions noted by Muller come from caves used by Buddhist monks as retreats. He also comments that "with regard to the contents of the inscriptions, I am bound to state that I have been greatly disappointed. Most...are religious, they contain grants to different temples, but no historical information." (p. 17) An alphabetical list of words used in inscriptions recorded completes the first volume. The second volume reproduces selected inscriptions illustrating the growth of the Sinhalese script over time. The set was reprinted by Asian Educational Services in New Delhi in 1984 without an index.

570. Smither, J.G. *Architectural Remains, Anuradhapura, Sri Lanka*. Government of Ceylon, 1894.

The author of this massive highly detailed presentation of the chief building complexes at the ancient capital of Anuradhapura was the government architect of the island's colonial Public Works Department from 1866 to 1883, and compiled this tome after his retirement. Due to the limited availability of the first two editions, scholars will find the 1993 publishing run from the Academy of Sri Lankan Culture most accessible. The format of the work is a series of essays on eleven major structure groups (chiefly *dagabas* where holy relics were enshrined), followed by a bibliography of works related to the history of the city in print as of 1894 which combines colonial writings with the *Mahavamsa* and *Dipavamsa* chronicles. Over half the volume is occupied by sixty-seven plates, which offer exquisitely drawn plans, elevations and sections of the *dagabas*, and photographs documenting the appearance of each complex at the end of the nineteenth century along with details of architectural elements. Any researcher dealing with the archaeology of Anuradhapura should begin by examining the wealth of data included here. An index and listing of the rulers who governed from the city is included for reference.

571. Abbot, John A. "The Buried City of Ceylon," *National Geographic Magazine* 17 (November, 1906): 613-622.

A group of eight photographs accompanied by an historical essay covering the ruins of Anuradhapura, capital of the Sinhala kingdom destroyed by Tamil invaders. Mention is made of archaeological clearance work initiated by the colonial government beginning in 1876 and the fact that most sites located to date were buried beneath six to eight feet of debris. Erosion of the few prominent structures by monsoon rains and animal life is noted. In addition to the carved sills of one of the city's ancient public baths and a surviving shrine to the Buddha, the accompanying pictures also illustrate the Temple of the Tooth in Kandy and the Rock Temple at Polonnaruwa. Researchers investigating the prehistory of Sri Lanka will find the text useful in assessing the degree of priority accorded preservation by the Raj.

572. Scidmore, Eliza R. "Archaeology In The Air," *National Geographic Magazine* 18 (March, 1907): 151- 163.

An account of a visit to the fortress palace of Sigiriya, built as a refuge by King

Kasyapa. The work of clearance by the Archaeological Survey of Ceylon had by this time resulted in clear definition of the three-acre site, which contained several tanks and cisterns as well as a throne cut from the living rock. Sigiriya's subsequent history as a Buddhist monastery where the *Mahavamsa*, the island's unbroken historical chronicle, was compiled and its abandonment are noted.Photographs depict artists copying the famous painted gallery, the royal throne and the highly dangerous access paths. The name is seen as a corruption of *sinha-giri*, meaning Lion Rock, a reference to the former entrance to the system of concealed access stairs, which was constructed as a lion's head.

573. Sarasin, Drs. Paul and Fritz. *Die Steinzeit auf Ceylon*. Wiesbaden: Kreidel Verlag, 1908.

The fourth volume of a set issued by the Sarasin brothers reporting on their natural scientific researches in Ceylon, this tome's preface cites the 1903 discovery of evidence for a Stone Age in the Celebes at the Toala grotto near Lamontjong as an inspiration to their own work. Having worked extensively among the Vedda population of Sri Lanka in the 1880's and 1890's, the Sarasins returned to the island in January 1907 and carried out surface surveys for stone tools. Test trenches were opened at several caves and rockshelters, beginning with the Katragam grotto in southeastern Ceylon. The bulk of the text reports on the results of these investigations. Individual chapters, heavily illustrated with sections of full-page monochrome photographs of selected specimens, discuss artifacts of bone, mollusc shells and wood, animal and plant remains from the site of Bandarawela, the Nilgala cave and the region around the city of Kandy. Parallels are drawn with the culture of the tribal Veddas in an effort to offer an ethnographic model of possible Stone Age life. Bibliographies of available related scientific literature in German, English and French are appended to each chapter.

574. Scidmore, Eliza Ruhamah "Adam's Second Eden," *National Geographic Magazine* 22 (February, 1912): 105-173.

This lengthy travelogue and photo essay depicts the island civilization of Ceylon (later Sri Lanka) as it existed in the first decades of the twentieth century. While much of the text deals with cultural and religious subjects, note is taken by the author of recent archaeological investigations. The sites of Anuradhapura, the sacred mountain of Mihintale, the carven fortress of Sigiriya and the ancient capital of Polonnaruwa are included. She observes that "British rule has revived the region... along with this economic salvation British archaeologists have done an enormous work in uncovering,making accessible and making known these wonderful monuments of the early century." (p. 153)

575. Pole, John. *Ceylon Stone Implements*. Calcutta: Thacker, Spink and Company, 1913.

This publication is the first monograph written on the Palaeolithic and Neolithic stone tool industries of Sri Lanka. The author, a British tea-planter who had taken an interest in the subject, had the work privately published in Calcutta. Its contents are divided into two sections on known stone implements of chert and quartz respectively. The first five illustrations are color reproductions of the best examples of chert and Palaeolithic tools found to date, many from private estates, while the remaining illustrations are high quality black and white drawings of flake tools and choppers. The text is useful for its review of prior prehistoric investigations carried out on the island, chiefly by the Sarasin brothers, and its detailed reporting of finds made at numerous minor locations across Sri Lanka.

576. Codrington, H.W. *Ceylon Coins and Currency*. Colombo: A.C. Richards, 1924.

Considered to be the standard work on Sri Lankan numismatics since its publication, this highly detailed volume classifies and discusses all known types of coinage used or created in the island since the Roman era. The opening chapters present ancient standards of metrology applied to the production and grade of various forms of money, and review the principal sources of data on coins used between the settlement of the Sinhalese and the rise of Polonnaruva (chiefly the *Mahavamsa* chronicle and its commentaries). Chapters four through thirteen analyse Roman and Byzantine coins, medieval coinage of both Ceylon and India, and Portuguese, Dutch, and Muslim currencies.The money issued by the kingdom of Kandy in the seventeenth century is treated separately. An invaluable resource for the archaeologist are the seven appendixes, which provide the full texts of relevant sections of the *Mahavamsa* and other Pali and Sinhalese documents (with accompanying translations), inscriptions which mention currency, and Portuguese, Dutch and British colonial documents. The lengthy bibliography lists primary sources dating from 1615 to the early twentieth century. Seven photographic plates of sample coins are included.

577. Hocart, A.M., ed. *Memoirs of the Archaeological Survey of Ceylon, Volume 1*. Colombo: A.C. Richards, Acting Government Printer, 1924.

In the preface to this first volume of what would eventually become a seven-volume set, A.M. Hocart, then Archaeological Commissioner, introduces the reader to the work of his late predecessor, E.R. Ayrton. Studies and papers completed by Ayrton on his excavations at various building sites within the city of Anuradhapura (chiefly the Ratana Pasada or "Elephant Stables," the Western Monasteries, and the Citadel) comprise the majority of this publication, with two additional notes and later materials added by Hocart as noted. Seventy-seven photographic plates provide an invaluable record of the state of these sections of Anuradhapura in the first two decades of the twentieth century.

578. Hocart, A.M., ed. *Memoirs of the Archaeological Survey of Ceylon*, Volume 2. Colombo: H. Ross Cottle, Government Printer, 1926.

This second volume of what would eventually become a seven-volume set chronicling important work done during the first five decades of archaeological work in Sri Lanka presents architectural drawings and analysis of three major temples at Polonnaruva. Hocart, editor of the *Memoirs* and then Archaeological Commissioner of Ceylon, observes in the preface that "the three...temples discussed were excavated by H.C.P. Bell, and two of them were partially restored by him." (p. vii) The papers which comprise this work resulted from the resumption of conservation work on the Lankatilaka in 1921 by Hocart and the discovery that no plans or systematic account of the building existed. In 1922, further conservation was undertaken at the Northern Temple, which resembled the Lankatilaka closely in plan despite later additions, and the smaller Thuparama. Hocart is quite frank about the lack of records from the previous seasons. "The original excavator is always best qualified to describe his results, even if complete records of his excavations are available...there were no complete records, finds were not to be traced, and I had therefore to confine myself to what could be seen at the present day." (p. *vii*) High quality ground plans and sections make this an invaluable resource for these structures. Over half of this *Memoir* is taken up with eighty-five sepia-tone photographic plates illustrating the condition of these temples at the time of publication and the artifacts retrieved during excavations at the monastic community site of Veherabandigala, said activity reported in the final section of text. Researchers interested in Bell's original work at Polonnaruva should consult the 1993 biography *H.C.P. Bell: Archaeologist of Ceylon and the Maldives.*

579. Hocart, A.M. *The Temple of the Tooth in Kandy.* London: Luzac and Company, 1931.

In this, the fourth volume of the *Memoirs of the Archaeological Survey of Ceylon,* the director of the Survey focuses on the famed shrine of Kandy (considered the chief temple of the entire island due to its possession of the left eyetooth of the Buddha) as a close model of the vanished temples of Anuradhapura. The work begins with a history of the relic, then passes to a detailed review of the physical layout and structure of the entire complex, with detailed plans and cross sections of all major structures included. The rituals carried out within the Temple of the Tooth are also presented through the cooperation of local Buddhist clergy.

580. Paranavitana, S. *The Excavations in the Citadel of Anuradhapura.* Colombo: Ceylon Government Press, 1936.

Published as the third volume in the *Memoirs of the Archaeological Survey of Ceylon,* this account reports on the results of field excavations carried out within the Citadel of the ancient capital between 1928 and 1933. The city of Anuradhapura was first surveyed by H.C.P.Bell in 1893, and the introductory pages summarize the location and investigations of the Royal Enclosure up to 1928. The thirty-five pages of text focus on the 1928 and 1929 seasons, the buildings and well uncovered and mapped at this time northwest of the *Mahapali* (the royal almshouse), and clearance done around this structure as well. In 1930 and 1931, no work was done, with excavation resuming in 1932 and completed in 1933. Lists of associated artifacts and high-quality architectural drawings and sections are included. Thirty-five black and white photographic plates illustrate the overgrown condition of much of Anuradhapura at this time, all buildings examined in the four seasons of active research, pottery, beads, architectural elements and coinage.

581. *"An Ordinance to Provide for the Better Preservation of the Antiquities of Ceylon, June 15, 1940,"* in *The Legislative Enactments of Ceylon, In Force on the 30th Day of June, 1956. Volume 7.* Revised Edition. Colombo: Government Printer, 1958: 159-182.

More widely known by the short form of its title, the Antiquities Ordinance of 1940 is the basic piece of modern legislation which governs the ownership, management, excavation and disposition of archaeological remains in Sri Lanka. All antiquities are defined as being "the absolute property of the Crown," (p. 159) with excavation limited to those persons who have been licensed to do so by the Archaeological Commissioner. The six main sections of the Act regulate the concept of antiquities as property, the discovery of antiquities (useful for the list of offenses relating to unauthorized digging or discoveries which are kept unreported), ancient monuments (defined as "any specified monument which dates or is believed to date from a period prior to the 1st day of January, 1850," [p. 165]) the creation of archaeological reserves, the export of antiquities, and the powers and duties of the Archaeological Commissioner. Legal sanctions of a heavy fine and imprisonment of up to three months are reserved for persons violating these regulations where the Act does not spell out a different punishment. Perhaps the most interesting section of the Act is its lengthy definition of exactly what may be regarded as an "antiquity." Objects falling within this category are "statues, sculptured or dressed stone and marbles of all descriptions, engravings, carvings, inscriptions, paintings, writings, and the material whereon the same appear, all specimens of ceramic, glyptic, metallurgic and textile art, coins, gems, seals, jewels, jewellery, arms, tools, ornaments, and all other objects of art which are movable property." (p. 181)

582. Norton, Wilson K. "Sigiriya, A Fortress In The Sky," *National Geographic*, 90 (November, 1946): 665-680.

Written by a field photographer of the Office of Strategic Services, this is by far the most detailed of the three articles published by *National Geographic* on Sigiriya. The text lays out the full story of the construction and eighteen-year occupation of the fortress, while the author's photographs illustrate the remains of the great lion figure whose maw gave access to the staircase, the remaining murals of royal ladies and their attendants and several of the tanks. Initial archaeological work at the site in 1898 is mentioned. Researchers desiring color reproductions of Sigiriya's murals should consult the 1987 article by Lindley Vann in *Archaeology*.

583. Paranavitana, S. *The Stupa In Ceylon.* Colombo: Ceylon Government Press, 1946.

Published as the fifth *Memoir* of the Archaeological Survey of Ceylon, this study focuses on an architectural form unique to Buddhism and its evolution in Sinhalese culture. A stupa (or *dagaba* in Sinhala) is intended "to enshrine a particle, in most cases a minute one, of the corporeal remains of the Buddha or a saint" (p. 1) which is then venerated through regular ceremonies. The opening chapter places the stupa form in the context of South Asian architectural history in general and defines the terms used for its component parts. Difficulties facing the archaeologist in studying these sites include rebuilding by subsequent generations, deliberate theft of stone elements for reuse, and partial erosion by natural forces. Separate chapters address the significance and variety of the various sections of a typical stupa; the terraces, dome and the superstructure, the *vahalkadas* (ornamental projections facing the entrance gateways), the surrounding precincts and concentric galleries of encircling pillars.Twenty-two black and white photographic plates and numerous line drawings and figures illustrate major stupas of the island as they were in the late 1930's, sites represented including Mihintale, Anuradhapura, and Polonnaruva. The original research was completed by 1939, with publication delayed due to World War II.

584. Paranavitana, Senarat. *Sigiri Graffiti: Being Sinhalese Verse of the Eighth, Ninth and Tenth Centuries*. London: Oxford University Press for the Government of Ceylon, 1956.

Compiled by the Archaeological Commissioner of Ceylon, this two-volume set makes available to scholars six hundred and eighty-five examples of graffiti from the fortress mountain and palace of Sigiriya. The first volume serves as a detailed introduction to the history and significance of Sigiriya, then moves to the language in which the graffiti were written between the sixth and thirteenth centuries A.D. Paranavitana explores its grammar and syntax, alphabetic styles,the literary quality of the documents and their subject matter, finally presenting a listing of all identified authors and place names. Sixty-five plates illustrate selected writings from the corpus of inscriptions and completes the first volume. The second volume provides the transliterated texts of the graffiti and their translations, along with a glossary-index keyed by graffito number. Standards of transliteration are the same as those used in the series *Epigraphia Zeylanica*. Readers dealing with the archaeology of Sigiriya will find this set a valuable supplement to the excavation reports.

585. Allchin, Bridget. "The Late Stone Age of Ceylon," *Journal of the Royal Anthropological Institute* 88 (1959): 179-201.

Noting that "it is fifty years since the first account of the stone age of Ceylon appeared, based upon explorations in the field and excavations," (p. 179) the author then offers a considered synthesis of archaeology and ethnography to reconstruct this era of Sri Lankan prehistory. Beginning with an overview of Stone Age archaeology in the island up to the time of publication, a summary of the life patterns of the Vedda aborigines and their technology is set forth. Cave and living sites were the principal types of archaeological deposits dating to this period, and lengthy reports on finds at seven caves (Kataragama Galge, Nilgala Cave, Udupiyan Galge, Bambara Gala, Lunu Galge, Beigalge and Batadomba Lena) and the open-air tool manufacturing site of Bandarawela are included. Three pages of line drawings illustrate the full range of stone implements known using samples from Bandarawela. While the Vedda model is used with due caution, Allchin calls for further work at selected cave sites to determine the date of appearance of the distinctive island Stone Age cultures and the length of their survival.

586. Devendra, D.T. "Seventy Years of Ceylon Archaeology," *Artibus Asiae* 22 (1959): 23-40.

This detailed and highly readable account begins with a review of the unique conditions under which archaeology took root in Sri Lanka in the nineteenth century. Chief among these are the close relationship of most major monuments to the island's active Buddhist community and clergy and the absence of delegation of authority for conservation and preservation to local government. The seventy years of the title refers to the first instruction given to H.C.P. Bell on November 20, 1889 for the initiation of work at Anuradhapura, although prior researches on architecture, inscriptions, and translations of the *Mahavamsa* and *Dipavamsa* chronicles done before that time are also noted in detail. A central feature of archaeology in Sri Lanka up to 1959 had been the conservation of major Buddhist shrines and monuments, many in the ancient capitals of Anuradhapura and Polonnaruva. The author follows the successive administrations of the Archaeological Survey from 1889 to current times, noting the most important field work done during each period as well as the significant publications and scholarly efforts which appeared in each decade, an invaluable service for retrospective research. Conservation is less complex than in India, as some factors such as earthquakes, erosion through river course changes, and the action of mineral salts are absent, the most common problem being the necessity of keeping encroaching vegetation at bay. The corpus of collected inscriptions (at this time exceeding two thousand) is discussed, with known types ranging from dedications of meditation caves for Buddhist monks to copper plates. Of particular note for the unusual history of Sri Lankan archaeology is the effective means of education on the need for reporting and preserving antiquities carried out within Sinhalese culture in partnership with the Survey. While no bibliography is provided, readers will find the numerous references scattered through the text to be a useful guide.

587. Sestieri, Pellegrino Claudio. "Important Monuments of Ceylon," *Archaeology* 12(4) (December, 1959): 223-233.

In 1958, the author was invited by the government of Ceylon to take the position of technical advisor for archaeology, and served as the nation's archaeological commissioner through 1959. This article is based upon his first-hand knowledge of the major sites and monuments. Beginning with mention of the palaeolithic materials from Balangoda in the central region and the burial urns of Pomparippu on the west coast, this essay emphasizes the uniformly Buddhist character of much of the island's ancient remains. Sites examined are the sacred buildings on the mountain of Mihintale (reached by two thousand steps), the capitals of Anuradhapura and Polonnaruwa, and the fortress of Sigiriya. Readers will find Sestieri's discussion of the various types of Buddhist structures useful as background for other site reports. He observes that only during his stay were excavations undertaken for the first time at Anuradhapura, with pottery samples taken and an attempt at constructing a stratigraphic sequence, as "since its beginning, sixty years ago, the Archaeological Department's main work has been the clearing of the jungles …to reveal the most important groups of monuments, which then had to be restored and preserved." (p. 225)

588. Deraniyagala, P.E.P. "Prehistoric Archaeology in Ceylon," *Asian Perspectives* v.7, nos. 1-2 (Summer-Winter 1963): 189-192.

A concise overview of the history of prehistoric archaeological investigation Sri Lanka's Stone Age. The author emphasizes the then-recent findings of hominid remains, the first stone tools on the island (termed the Ratnapura industry from their geologic context) and the extinct humans known from Balangoda.

589. Begley, Vimala. "Archaeological Exploration In Northern Ceylon," *Expedition* 9 (4) (1966): 21-29.

In February and March of 1967, the author directed a preliminary archaeological survey of the Jaffna, Mannar and Anuradhapura districts of northern Ceylon, with the aim of identifying a proto-historic site whose subsequent excavation might assist in constructing a cultural sequence for the region. General problems of Sinhalese archaeology noted are the historic emphasis of the Archaeological Survey on preservation and epigraphy, the total absence of absolute dates and stratigraphic control for any period, and the difficulty of locating surface remains due to dense vegetation. In addition to the previously known site of Mannai (Tirukesvaram), the most extensive testing done was carried out at Kantarodai, near the tip of the Jaffna Peninsula. Cist and urn burial sites were also identified. This article presupposes a degree of knowledge of the history of southern India and is valuable for the extensive bibliographic citations included in the text.

590. Deraniyagala, P.E.P. "Archaeological Seminar on the Prehistory and Protohistory of Ceylon, 21 August 1970," *Asian Perspectives* 15 (1972): 156-157.

An overview of the three joint projects conducted in Ceylon in 1970 by the Archaeological Department and the Smithsonian Institution. They included a survey of the eastern coast for sites indicating prehistoric contacts with Southeast Asia, re-excavation of the mesolithic burial site of Bellan-bandi, and field work at Kantarodai, this last confirming that the Sri Lankan Iron Age was not preceded by a Neolithic stage. Results of the season were summarized at the title seminar, where the importance of applying current methodologies to local data was stressed.

591. Lukacs, John R. "Dental Anthropology and the Biological Affinities of an Iron

Age Population from Pomparippu, Sri Lanka," in *Ecological Backgrounds of South Asian Prehistory* edited by Kenneth Kennedy and Gregory Possehl. Cornell: South Asia Program, 1974: 197-215.

The Iron Age assemblage of human remains of the title comes from urn burials at Pomparippu, Sri Lanka unearthed in the 1956-57 and 1970 field seasons. Following a detailed presentation of cusp morphologies and tooth shapes, parallels are drawn with the Late Stone Age skeletal remains from another Sri Lankan site, Bellan Bandi Palassa. Overall, "the complex of dental traits which characterize the...population of Pomparippu are unique. They represent a mixture of genetic and ontogenetic features not found in association with other human populations in Sri Lanka, living or fossil." (p. 207)

592. Bandaranayake, S. "Buddhist Tree-Temples In Sri Lanka," in *South Asian Archaeology 1973* edited by J.E. Van Lohuizen-De Leeuw and J.M.M. Ubaghs. Leiden, Brill, 1974: 136-160.

This essay sets forth in detail the ritual significance of a particular type of public shrine, one dedicated around a specific living tree, in both the pre-Buddhist and Buddhist eras of Sri Lankan history. Identification of such structures within the island's archaeological record was first made in the 1940's, although one such building had been cleared in 1895. Bandaranayake reviews the discussions within Ceylonese archaeology and presents the ground plans of several such temples as illustration, relating them to the appropriate sections of Buddhist scriptures.

593. Deraniyagala, S.U. "Prehistoric Research In Sri Lanka, 1885-1980," in *P.E.P. Deraniyagala Comemmoration Volume* edited by Thelma Gunawardana et.al. Colombo: Lake House Publishers, 1980: 152-207.

This detailed essay offers the reader a valuable summary of the state of knowledge and theoretical discussions of the prehistory of Sri Lanka as they evolved during the first century of active scientific investigation. Beginning with the surface collections of chert and quartz artifacts made by Green and Pole in 1885, all major and minor fieldwork is presented in chronological order. Detailed illustrations and maps show the stone tools from the Ratnapura Beds, sites known from various physiographic regions of the island, and sample artifacts. Much of the material contained in this essay was reworked into the first chapter of the author's 1988 thesis *The Prehistory of Sri Lanka*. Researchers will find the bibliography invaluable but should also consult the later work for relevant articles published after 1980.

594. Kennedy, Kenneth A.R. "The Antiquity of Human Settlement In Sri Lanka," in *P.E.P.Deraniyagala Comemmoration Volume* edited by Thelma Gunawardana et.al. Colombo, Sri Lanka: Lake House Publishers, 1980: 237-245.

This overview paper examines the problematic nature of determining the age of human presence on Sri Lanka, contrasted with the clearly established sequence of development available for southern India. Beginning with an assessment of the Pleistocene era Ratnapura fauna, "the earliest…with which archaeological remains might be associated," (p. 238) the author notes problems of dating and species survival as complicating factors. The more solidly documented Mesolithic era (marked by a variety of stone tool technologies ,some of which were being manufactured by tribal people such as the Veddas up to the beginning of the twentieth century) and the known physical anthropology of its populations is then analysed. Kennedy suggests that the distribution of sites thus far known suggests a pattern of sedentary hunting and gathering cultures.

595. Silva, Roland and Jan Bouzek. "Mantai- A Second Arikamedu?" *Antiquity* 59 (March, 1985): 46-47.

A report on surface collections made in March, 1983 at the site of Mantai on the northwest coast of Sri Lanka, the major harbor of the island until the eleventh century. Comparisons are drawn with the well-known trading site of Arikamedu in southeastern India on the basis of fragments of imported Roman pottery and glass unguent jars.

596. Kennedy, Kenneth A.R. et.al. "Upper Pleistocene Fossil Hominids from Sri Lanka," *American Journal of Physical Anthropology* 72 (1987): 441-461.

Between 1978 and 1983, "the most ancient specimens of anatomically modern *Homo sapiens* found thus far in South Asia" (p. 441) and dating to 16,000 B.P. and 12,260 B.P. respectively were collected from the caves of Batadomba lena and Beli lena Kitulgala in far southern Sri Lanka. This article is a detailed presentation of the results of the morphometric analyses performed on the remains of the thirty-eight individuals found at these sites. Continuity of traits with the physical measurements of the aboriginal Vedda population of the island indicates unbroken human occupation of Sri Lanka since the Upper Pleistocene. Charts of dental cranial and postcranial measurements, and photographs of sample mandibles, teeth and crania are included for reference. The lengthy bibliography will be useful for readers unfamiliar with extant literature on the physical anthropology of this region.

597. Deraniyagala, S.U. *The Prehistory of Sri Lanka, An Ecological Perspective.* Ph.d. thesis, Harvard University 1988. 2 volumes.

Subsequently published in 1992 by the Department of Archaeological Survey of the Government of Sri Lanka, this massive research project combines an analysis and synthesis of the available data on the geological and climatic histories of the island over a period of 28,000 years with the results of archaeological excavation. Noting that "for its size, Lanka has probably a more extensive literature relating to the Stone Age, particularly in its latter phase, than any other part of southern Asia," (p. 1) the text begins by presenting the history of archaeological research, starting with early surface collections in 1885. Deraniyagala outlines four basic stages in the growth of archaeological knowledge (establishing a chronology, description of individual cultures in space and time, comparison between cultural assemblages and formulation of generalizations) and views the archaeology of Sri Lanka as not having advanced beyond the first two, a situation the present research is intended to begin exploring. The chapters of this work offer strategies and tactics for addressing the levels of synthesis needed in the third and fourth stages, present the Quaternary chronology and environment of the island, core traits of prehistoric subsistence, settlement and technology, and ethnographic data on such hunting and gathering societies as the Veddas. Four appendixes provide radiometric dating evidence from the prehistoric, protohistoric and Early Historic eras and recent relevant Indian data. The picture that emerges is one of relative stability in both the island's ecosystemic division into wet and dry zones and in human adaptation to them. The huge bibliography will assist research on any aspect of Sri Lanka's past, while the "History of Research" section in the first chapter provides a compact summary of local archaeological investigations at Stone Age sites.

598. Bandaranayake, Senake. "The Settlement Patterns of the Protohistoric-Early Historic Interface in Sri Lanka," in *South Asian Archaeology 1989* edited by Catherine Jarrige. Madison, Wisconsin: Prehistory Press, 1992: 15-23.

The "relatively late and extremely rapid transition from stone-age hunting and gathering to advanced, and literate, agrarian civilization" (p. 15) which marks the first millennium B.C. in Sri Lanka is the focus of this essay. Only recently taken as a distinct focus of Sri Lankan archaeology, a decade in field investigation has centered on the period after 500 B.C. Field surveys and excavations previously carried out at the Early Buddhist rock shelter monasteries and megalithic grave complexes have been augmented by study of actual village sites and associated irrigation works, particularly in the region around Sigiriya and Dambulla, in an attempt to map the environmental and spatial limits of these transition settlements.

599. Banadaranayake, Senake. "The Periodization of Sri Lankan History and Some Related Historical and Archaeological Problems," in *Asian Panorama: Essays in Asian History, Past and Present* edited by K.M. de Silva et.al. New Delhi: Vikas, 1990: 3-24.

Approaching the archaeological record of Sri Lanka from the viewpoint of historical analysis, this essay attempts "to place on the agenda of contemporary Sri Lankan historiography the central problem of periodization." (p. 22) Beginning with an overview of the different eras into which the island's history has been divided by various writers, Bandaranayake synthesizes a general chronological framework reaching from prehistoric times to the nineteenth century. Each category's validity is then assessed in terms of available epigraphic and archaeological evidence. Archaeologists unfamiliar with the frames of reference used by many historians of Ceylon will find this discussion useful.

600. Prickett, Martha. "Sri Lanka's Foreign Trade Before A.D. 600: The Archaeological Evidence," in *Asian Panorama: Essays in Asian History, Past and*

Present edited by K.M. de Silva et.al. New Delhi: Vikas, 1990: 151-180.

Due to its geographic location and range of natural resources, Sri Lanka has long served as an important link in the trans-Indian Ocean trading networks. Literary references indicate that many items of both the export and import trade were materials not conducive to preservation, such as silks, textiles and spices. The predominant types of foreign imports known from the archaeological record are principally ceramics and coinage, carvings in stone and ivory, metals, glass and animal bones "of imported horses and of exported elephants." (p. 151) This article begins by examining available historical writings that mention the island, the oldest dating to the fourth century B.C. Following a general review of the prehistoric and protohistoric eras, six excavated occupation sites dating before 600 A.D. are summarized, including Anuradhapura, Sigiriya, and the ports of Kuchchaveli and Mantai. A lengthy table detailing the distribution of trade objects is included. Conclusions based upon the patterns of artifact distribution complete the work. Researchers will find the map of Roman coin finds and ports known to have been active before 600 A.D. useful for reference. A version of this paper including color plates of sample pottery types was published in the collection *Sri Lanka and the Silk Road of the Sea* under the title "Durable Goods: The Archaeological Evidence of Sri Lanka's Role in Indian Ocean Trade," in 1990.

601. Pathmanathan, S. "The Bronze Seal of the Nanadesis from Hambantota (Sri Lanka)," in *Asian Panorama: Essays in Asian History, Past and Present* edited by K.M. de Silva et.al. New Delhi: Vikas, 1990: 139-150.

In 1985, a solid cast bronze seal belonging to the corporation of travelling merchants known as the Nanadesis was discovered near Hambantota in southern Sri Lanka, "the only one of its kind to have been brought to light so far." (p. 139) This article discusses aspects of the seal's design and iconography and the fifteen inscriptions from the island recording the presence and activities of this commercial group. Sites bearing such inscriptions include Anuradhapura and Polonnaruwa. Dates for these inscriptions are estimated at the eleventh to twelfth centuries A.D. on palaeographic grounds.

602. *Sri Lanka and the Silk Road of the Sea* edited by Senake Bandaranayake et al. Colombo: Sri Lanka Commission for UNESCO and the Central Cultural Fund,1990.

A collection of thirty papers which takes as its theme the legacies of maritime trade and cultural exchange upon the historical development of Sinhalese civilization over more than two millennia. Several entries discuss the results of archaeological survey and analysis at sites ranging from the ancient capital of Anuradhapura to the port of Mantai. The collection was created as part of the Maritime Silk Route Seminar, held in Colombo in association with the UNESCO Maritime Silk Route Expedition, part of the "Silk Roads, Roads of Dialogue" project.

603. Ratnayake, Hema. "The Jetavana Treasure," in *Sri Lanka and the Silk Road*

of the Sea edited by Senake Banadaranayake et al. Colombo: Sri Lanka Commission for UNESCO and the Central Cultural Fund, 1990: 45-60.

The treasure of the title is a massive collection of artifacts of both domestic manufacture and foreign origin dating to the second and third centuries A.D. uncovered during structural technology investigations beneath the Jetavana stupa at Anuradhapura. This text is a preliminary report on the assemblage, undergoing analysis at the time of writing. A ground plan and cross-section of the stupa and color plates illustrating a selection of the pottery, intaglios, beads, glassware, marbles and ivory objects are included. Readers should consult the bibliography for further data on this phase of work at Anuradhapura.

604. Tampoe, Moira. "Tracing the Silk Road of the Sea: Ceramic and Other Evidence from the Partner Ports of the Western Indian Ocean (8th-10th c. A.D.)," in *Sri Lanka and the Silk Road of the Sea* edited by Senake Banadaranayake. Colombo: Sri Lanka Commission for UNESCO and the Central Cultural Fund, 1990: 85-103.

In contrast to other discussions of the ancient trading network of the Indian Ocean, this paper focuses on combining literary and archaeological evidence from five specific sites of the Early Islamic period to illustrate both local diversity and foreign influences. A useful history of the various sailing routes utilized between China and the Persian Gulf ports is provided as background. Sites reviewed within the South Asian region are Banbhore at the mouth of the Indus (excavated in the 1960's) and Mantai at the northwestern tip of Sri Lanka. Emphasis is placed upon the use of Islamic and Chinese trade ceramics as indicators of participation in the trade net. A page of known illustrations of ancient trading vessels from this time ranging from coinage to reliefs at Sanchi and Bharhut augments the text. Maps of the land and sea Silk Routes, the major medieval Indian Ocean ports, and a lengthy bibliography are included.

605. Prickett-Fernando, Martha. "Mantai-Mahatittha: The Great Port and Entrepot in the Indian Ocean Trade," in *Sri Lanka and the Silk Road of the Sea* edited by Senake Bandaranayake. Colombo: Sri Lanka Commission for UNESCO and the Central Cultural Fund, 1990: 115-121.

Beginning in 1886, several excavations have been carried out at the great horsehoe mound of the ancient port of Mantai on Sri Lanka's northwestern coast. This article reviews data retrieved from the most recent seasons between 1980 and 1984, with all periods of occupation from the late Mesolithic to historic times summarized. The author emphasizes that, while artifactual data accords well in some respects with Mantai's documented role as the chief port for Anuradhapura, the total excavated area "involves only 2% of the mound's surface." (p. 115) A schematic plan, a north to south cross-section of the mound, and an aerial photograph of the entire site are included. Researchers will find the detailed references useful for tracking the state of publication of this site.

606. "The Galle Tri-Lingual Inscription," in *Sri Lanka and the Silk Road of the Sea* edited by Senake Bandaranayake. Colombo: Sri Lanka Commission for UNESCO and the Central Cultural Fund, 1990: 217-219.

A presentation of translations of the Persian, Chinese and Tamil texts of an inscribed slab discovered in 1911 at the ancient port of Galle in southwestern Sri Lanka. They record the donation of dedicatory offerings to local shrines for the purpose of making merit given in the year 1411.

607. Prematilleke, P.L. "Chinese Ceramics Discovered in Sri Lanka- An Overview," in *Sri Lanka and the Silk Road of the Sea* edited by Senake Bandaranayake et.al. Colombo; Sri Lanka Commision for UNESCO and the Central Cultural Commission, 1990: 233-244.

A general discussion of the highly varied types of common and specialized trade pottery wares from China dating to between the seventh and fifteenth centuries found at interior and coastal Sri Lankan locations. Specific sites noted are the port of Mantai, Vankala and Allaipiddy, and the monastery complexes of Abhayagiri and Jetavanarama at Anuradhapura and Polonnaruva. Note is made of the major ports of the island during this period. Two pages of color photographs present examples of the major wares found.

608. Carswell, John. "The Port of Mantai, Sri Lanka," in *Rome and India: The Ancient Sea Trade* edited by Vimala Begley and Richard Daniel De Puma. Madison, University of Wisconsin Press, 1991: 197-203.

A report on excavations begun in 1980 at Mantai, site of a heavily referenced ancient port at the extreme northwestern tip of Sri Lanka. A sequence of occupation at the site from the Mesolithic period at the beginning of the second millennium B.C. to the eleventh century A.D. has been established. An aerial photograph illustrates the final form of the city and its underlying town plan, a chief objective of the project. Evidence of Mantai's importance as a center for bead manufacture is also reviewed. Field work at the site was halted after 1984 due to political unrest in the region.

609. Bell, Bethia N. and Heather M. *H.C.P.Bell: Archaeologist of Ceylon and the Maldives*. Denbigh, Wales: Archetype Publications, 1993.

The only book-length biography of the first head of the Archaeological Department of Ceylon (1890-1912), this work includes both a personal history and the story of the development of archaeology as a distinctive science in Sri Lanka. Of particular value for this latter is the fourth chapter, "Archaeology Before 1890: The Collecting of Records," (covering the establishment of the Archaeological Commission in 1868 and the Government Oriental Library in 1870 "to contain the rare manuscripts obtained or copied" (p. 27) as well as the formal campaign to counter the vandalising of ancient inscriptions. Bell's own field work at Anuradahapura (1890-1900), his exploration of the fortress of Sigiriya and its frescoes, the widespread restoration work carried out at many major Buddhist *dagabas* on the island including Mihintale, and his seasons of work on the Hindu and Buddhist shrines at Polonnaruwa are discussed in individual chapters, as is his later work in the Maldive Islands. The numerous black and white photographs depict both the state of several major sites in the late nineteenth and early twentieth centuries and the types of excavation and recording techniques used at this time. Detailed notes and references for each chapter are appended.

610. Abeyratne, Mohan. "TL Dating of Sri Lankan Archaeological Sites," *Quaternary Science Reviews* 13 (5/7) (1994): 585-588.

In 1985, thermoluminescent dating was established in Sri Lanka at the Research Laboratory of the UNESCO-Sri Lanka Cultural Triangle Project. This article reports on a test run to ascertain the degree of agreement between dates obtained through this process and historical information from other sources such as the *Mahavamsa*. Samples used included bricks from two stupas at Anuradhapura, pottery from test pits at Sigiriya, and sediment from Beli-Cave in southwest Sri Lanka, where microliths had been found. Results indicated close correlation of the two sources. Full details of the process of calculation involved are provided.

611. Seneviratne, Sudharshan. "The Ecology and Archaeology of the Seruwila Copper-Magnetite Prospect, North East Sri Lanka," in *From Sumer To Meluhha: Contributions to the Archaeology of South and West Asia in Memory of George F. Dales, Jr.* Madison, Wisconsin: University of Wisconsin Department of Anthropology 1994: 261-280.

Noting that "the ecological significance of resource zones sustaining pre-Industrial metallurgical operations as a critical factor… is seldom taken up for discussion in archaeo-metallurgical studies in South Asia," (p. 261) this report begins by presenting the basic geology of the Seruwila area, "the largest copper-magnetite deposit of the Bihar-Orissa region." (p. 278) Associated inscriptions and archaeological finds indicate mining activity beginning in the Early Iron Age. Historical models of metalcraft are used to reconstruct a possible model for the industry. Speculation on the place of the Seruwila ores in a regional economic net including southern India is also advanced.

612. Coningham, Robin. "Notes On the Construction and Destruction of Ancient Sri Lankan Buildings," in *Living Traditions: Studies in the Ethnoarchaeology of South Asia*. Columbia, Missouri: South Asia Publications, 1994: 69-82.

The data reported in this piece were obtained while the author worked at the Citadel of Anuradhapura in 1990 and 1991, during which the problem of interpretation of the remains in the context of local architectural methods and techniques was raised. After a brief overview of the occupational history of the city, attention is focused on a pillared hall which had been massively disturbed by a series of pits dug to facilitate the removal of columns for re-use. The pattern of these suggested a conscious approach to the task rather than simple salvage.

Techniques used by the work crew during the dismantling of the hall to allow access to layers below offered explanations of the movement of stone in ancient construction. The problem raised of the delineation and recovery of wattle and daub structures as part of site occupation data is also discussed, with the example of the Citadel site of Salgaha Watta used as the basis of an exploration of this method of construction. Photographs of modern houses built by this method are included as illustration.

613. Coningham, Robin A.E. "Monks, Caves and Kings: A Reassessment of the Nature of Early Buddhism In Sri Lanka," *World Archaeology* 27 (2) (October, 1995); 222-242.

A comparison of the physical evidence known from the archaeological record for the establishment of Buddhism in Sri Lanka in the third century B.C. with the written records of the Pali chronicles. Inscriptions on over one thousand cave dwellings occupied by the monks make it clear that a varied pattern of donation, including private citizens as well as royal patrons, was in effect. Using modern forest-dwelling monks (and their social and religious significance) as a model, a history of Buddhism's integration into an extant pattern of royal donation in Sri Lanka is constructed.

614. Weisshaar, H.J. and W. Wijeyapala. "The Tissamaharama Project 1992-1993 (Sri Lanka): Metallurgical Remains of the Akurugoda Hill," in *South Asian Archaeology 1993* edited by Asko Parpola and Petteri Koskikallio. Helsinki: Suomalainen Tiedeakatemia, 1994: 803-814.

A report on the results of the first two seasons of field work at the site of Mahagama, capital of the ancient kingdom of Ruhuna in southern Sri Lanka. Massive amounts of debris associated with the smelting of bronze and copper were located, as were several furnaces in the five periods of occupation revealed by stratigraphic analysis. Of unique value for the history of metallurgy was the discovery of a long furnace on a plan previously unknown in Sri Lanka or elsewhere in South Asia.

615. Bopearachchi, Osmund. "Seafaring in the Indian Ocean: Archaeological Evidence from Sri Lanka," in *Tradition and Archaeology: Early Maritime Contacts in the Indian Ocean* edited by Himanshu Prabha Ray and Jean-Francois Salles. New Delhi: Manohar, 1996: 59-77.

A preliminary survey of the available data on the ancient trade relations of Sri Lanka obtained from various excavations within the island as well as epigraphic sources and historical texts. Types of artifacts used as indicators of foreign contact include coins, ceramics, beads, seals, glass and ivory. Sites mentioned include the ports of Mantai and Gokunna, the Buddhist monasteries of the Jetavanarama and Abhayagiriya at Anuradhapura, the Alahana Parivena religious complex at Polonnaruwa, and Sigiriya. A map of ancient ports and the find spots of Indian punch-marked, Roman and Chinese coins is provided, as is a lengthy bibliography.

616. Weerakoddy, D.P.M. *Taprobane: Ancient Sri Lanka As Known to Greeks and Romans*. Turnhout: Brepols, 1997.

This unusual volume by a renowned Sri Lankan historian and classicist examines over forty foreign accounts of the island, known from Greek and Roman sources under the name Taprobane, written between the fourth century B.C. and the sixth century A.D, including later accounts based on them. Among the authors reviewed are Strabo, Pliny, Claudius Ptolemy and Cosmas Indicopleustes. The diplomatic mission sent from Sri Lanka to Rome in the first century A.D. is also profiled. Original texts cited and their translations are provided in the final chapters. The foreword discusses the extent of archaeological investigation of the ancient trading ports up to the late 1990s. The role of this type of information and the possibilities of checking specific points against both Sinhala literature and the archaeological record are evaluated.

Periodicals and Series

617. *Asiatic Researches* Calcutta: Asiatic Society of Bengal, 1788-1839.

The subtitle of this, the first scientific periodical to be published in modern India, defines the scope of its researches as "comprising history and antiquities, the arts, sciences, and literature of Asia." Published by the Asiatic Society, founded in 1784 by Sir William Jones, it had by the time of its demise in 1839 printed no fewer than three hundred and sixty-seven essays on topics ranging from geology and botany to ancient inscriptions. The full set of this title (including an index to the full run) was reprinted in 1979 by Cosmo Publications of New Delhi in twenty-four volumes. Its irregular publication was succeeded, and partly paralleled by, a periodical originally named "Gleanings In Science", renamed by its second editor, James Prinsep, the *Journal of the Asiatic Society of Bengal* in 1832.

618. *Journal of the Asiatic Society of Bengal.* Calcutta: Baptist Mission Press. 1832-1956/7.

On March 7, 1832, the Asiatic Society passed a resolution "that the monthly journal... *'Gleanings In Science'*...be permitted to assume that of the 'Journal of the Asiatic Society ...' and that the first object of the work should be to give publicity to such oriental matter as the antiquarian, the linguist, the traveller and the naturalist may glean, in the ample field open to their industry in this part of the world." (p. vii) The first article published which is directly connected with the presentation and analysis of relics of the Indian past was authored by the editor, James Prinsep, and appeared in the September 1832 issue under the title "On the Ancient Roman Coins in the Cabinet of the Asiatic Society." This and other selected articles have been entered in the present bibliography.

619. *Journal of the Asiatic Society of Bombay* Bombay: The Society, July, 1841-December, 1954

In the preface to its initial issue (which covered materials submitted between July 1841 and July 1844), the editor noted that the subjects of interest to the publication were to be "the Antiquities, Philology, Geography and History of Western India." (p. iii) Beginning with the work of the Society's founder, Sir James Mackintosh, the history of its scholarly activity is reviewed, commencing with three quarto volumes published between 1804 and 1821. The affiliation of the then-Literary Society of Bombay with the Royal Society in England in 1827 resulted in all research reports from India being sent to England and published in the *Transactions* of the parent society. By 1841 it was clear that the Bombay group had lost the research initiative which similar societies in Madras and Bengal had retained by publishing the results of their own work locally. The *Journal* was created to close this gap.

620. *Indian Antiquary* Bombay: James Burgess, January, 1872-December, 1933 and Series 3, January 1964- October, 1971.

On January 5, 1872, the first issue of the monthly *Indian Antiquary* appeared, being a privately funded project of Dr. James Burgess. The preface to the first volume noted that the periodical had been created due to "the great interest displayed by both Indian and European scholars, on all subjects relating to Indian Antiquities." (p. 1) The term *antiquity* was interpreted very broadly, with topics deemed suitable for inclusion ranging from numismatics, history and genealogy, art and architecture to anthropology, ethnographic data and archaeology. Translations of related materials appearing outside India were to be reprinted as available. Access to the contents of the sixty-two volumes issued between 1872 and 1933 may be had via the *Descriptive Index to the Indian Antiquary* compiled by Sibadas Chaudhuri and issued by the Centre for Asian Documentation in Calcutta in 1978.

621. *Archaeological Survey of India Reports: New Imperial Series*. 1874-1931.

Many numbers of this set of fifty-one volumes were also issued as individually named works or series of publications by a variety of publishers and agencies in both Great Britain and India. Examples of this complexity are volumes 13 and 14, which were the first two volumes of *Epigraphia Indica*, and several of James Burgess' reports issued as the *Archaeological Survey of Western India*. The final volume in 1931 was a listing of those monuments in Bihar and Orissa which qualified for protection under Act VII of 1904. Subject areas emphasized by the volumes in this series are the architectural schools of specific sites and historic periods (including types of color and tile decoration), the astronomical observatories of Jai Singh, inscriptions from several regions of the subcontinent (issued as *South Indian Inscriptions, Epigraphia Carnatica* and *Epigraphia Indica*), the cave temples of Ellora, medieval shrines of the Deccan, and inventories of all major antiquarian remains in various Indian states. The *New Imperial Series* was reissued in the 1980's and 1990s and is included in the South Asian Microfilm Project (SAMP).

622. *Archaeological Survey of Western India. Reports.* Bombay: Government Central Press, 1874-1891.

This set of twelve reports (most written by James Burgess and associates) constitutes the earliest formal scientific observation and analysis of this region of India done by the colonial British scientific establishment and reflect the varied approaches current in the investigation of India's past during its first years. The series began in 1874 with a memorandum on the Buddhist caves at Junnar, moving the following year to present three regional accounts of sites in Gujarat, the Bombay Presidency, Sind, Hyderabad, the Central Provinces and Berar. A more lengthy report on the state of the cave temple complex at Ellora and the Hindu and Jain cave shrines of western India (intended as a supplement to the work *The Cave Temples of India*) appeared as the fifth volume in 1883. Muslim era architecture of five Gujarati cities was covered in the sixth volume in 1896, with the two-volumes of the seventh focused solely on the architecture of Ahmedabad between 1412 and 1520. Archaeology reasserted itself in the eighth number in 1879, which contained accounts of archaeological remains from three local districts in Sind along with plans of tombs. The final four publications examine the ancient architecture of the state of Baroda in northern Gujarat, inscriptions from several of the cave temples, and antiquities in the Bombay Presidency. Researchers will find the accounts essential background to later field work in Gujarat and Maharashtra but should have a map of India handy for reference when reading them.

623. *Corpus Inscriptionum Indicarum.* Calcutta: Superintendent of Government Printing, 1877-

This set of seven lengthy volumes was initiated in 1877 with the publication of Sir Alexander Cunningham's *Inscriptions of Asoka (*which was reprinted in no fewer than seven editions in the ninteenth and twentieth centuries). The second volume appeared in two sections, presenting inscriptions in Kharoshthi script other than those of Asoka, and inscribed materials from the stupa at Bharhut. In 1888, volume three by John Fleet analysed the inscriptions of the first kings of the Gupta dynasty and their successors. Numbers four through seven examine the remaining evidence from the Kalachuri-Chedi era, the Vikataka dynasty of the Deccan, the Silahara rulers of Maharashtra, and several lesser known ruling houses prominent before 1000 A.D.

624. *Archaeological Survey of Southern India* (Madras, 1882-1903).

A series of seven volumes reporting on the investigations, excavations, planning, mapping and epigraphical work done by the Survey at various sites in the region during the late nineteenth and early twentieth centuries.Researchers will find the contemporary account by James Burgess of the salvage work done at the remains of the Amaravati stupa in Andhra Pradesh following the destructive clearance project ordered by the Madras Government in 1880 useful for the history of regional archaeology. Other subjects explored include lists of Tamil and Sanskrit inscriptions collected in the Madras presidency, a review of architectural and archaeological remains in Coorg, a study on Pallava architecture and accounts of the dynasties of southern India. The old series of reports appeared between 1882 and 1886, with the new series initiated in 1887 as part of the expanded publication program of the Archaeological Survey of India.

625. *The Taprobanian.* Bombay, Education Society's Press, 1885-1888.

One of the earliest of the scientific journals devoted exclusively to researches on the island of Sri Lanka, this periodical appeared for only three years between October 1885 and June 1888. It was edited by Hugh Nevill of the Ceylon Civil Service, who notes in the preface to volume one that "this Journal is founded chiefly in the hope that the columns for Notes and Queries may become a source for details, available hereafter for the elaboration of any special subject...the result of co-operative research in Ceylon and Dravida, will elucidate much valuable material." Its subtitle reflects the encyclopedic approach to science taken by many members of the colonial bureaucracy, a tradition reaching back to Sir William Jones and the founding of *Asiatic Researches* in 1788.*The Taprobanian* is described as "A Dravidian Journal of Oriental Studies in and around Ceylon in Natural History, Archaeology, Philology, History, etc." A series of five articles entitled "Archaeological Reports" provides the reader with valuable descriptions of a wide variety of major and minor sites as they existed in the late nineteenth century. Illustrations are limited to full-page line drawings and plans. While an index is available for the first volume, later issues must be scanned by page headings for specific subjects.

626. *South Indian Inscriptions.* Delhi: Manager of Publications, 1890-1962.

This series of publications was initiated in 1890 with the aim of making available to the scholarly community texts of inscribed materials scattered across a wide area of southern India, continuing the tradition begun by Sir Alexander Cunningham with the first volume of *Corpus inscriptionum indicarum* in 1877. The first thirteen volumes have Madras as the imprint. Emphasis is on Tamil inscriptions, their relationship to Sanskrit, and the records of the Chola, Pandya, Pallava and Vijayanagara dynasties. Most useful to the archaeologist as a source for inscribed materials now lost or eroded to illegibility. By 1962, fourteen volumes of the set had been published.

627. *Epigraphia Indica and Record of the Archaeological Survey of India* (1892-1963) Calcutta: Superintendent of Government Printing, India.

The purpose of this periodical (originally conceived in a proposal of 1887) was to provide "for the printing of a Record to include not only translations of inscriptions- Sanskrit, Persian, Arabic and other- but lists of them and other miscellaneous antiquarian information." Beginning as an annual publication, it became biennial in 1894. Its general format for the presentation and analysis of data provides background on the history of each particular inscription if known, a copy of the rubbing taken from the original, a transcription of the text using the original script, and an English translation with accompanying notes. The link of this field of historical study to the archaeology of the subcontinent was recognized in the preface to the first issue in 1892, which notes that "Indian inscriptions- more so even than those of any other country- are the real archives of the annals of its ancient history." (p. 1) Researchers dealing with any of the major investigations of India's prehistory made before World War II will find frequent bibliographic references to this periodical.

628. *Annual Report, Archaeological Survey of India*. Calcutta: Superintendent of Government Publication, 1902-1938.

Initiated as part of the revitalization of the Survey under the viceregal administration of Lord Curzon, this series of reports was written by the Directors General. Between 1902 and 1931, the majority of the reports in this series appeared under the aegis of John Marshall.

629. *Epigraphia Indo-Moslemica* (1907-1950) Calcutta, Office of the Superintendent of Government Printing.

While the recording and translation of inscriptions from the Muslim era of Indian history had always been a part of fieldwork from the first days of epigraphic research in the subcontinent, the sheer volume of such materials available eventually forced the recognition that this subject required a separate scientific publication. The standard format of articles is the presentation of the original inscription (in both print and photographic form) accompanied by textual analysis discussing the identification of places, persons, beings and concepts referred to. Each volume has its own index. Editorship was part of the duties of the Government Epigraphist for Moslem Inscriptions. Researchers should be aware that this publication was suspended during World War II, creating a gap between the 1939-1940 and 1949/1950 issues. Most useful archaeologically as a source of fuller treatment of inscribed materials from specific sites as a supplement to formal site reports. After 1950, this publication was known as *Epigraphia Indica: Arabic and Persian Supplement.*

630. *Memoirs of the Archaeological Survey of India* (1919-)

This continuing basic series of over ninety monographs constitutes the formal scientific reportage issued by the Survey for public dissemination following its revitalization by Lord Curzon in 1902. Begun in 1919 with Ramaprasad Chanda's *Dates of the Votive Inscriptions on the Stupas at Sanchi*, an examination of the subjects covered in this set reveals several distinct patterns. Prior to the discovery of the Indus Valley culture at Mohenjo-daro and Harappa in the period 1923-1925, the *Memoirs* continued the traditional subject approaches to the Indian past established during the first period of active Survey work under the direction of Sir Alexander Cunningham in the later nineteenth century. Topics frequently published on include possible links between specific literary documents and archaeological evidence, studies of sculptural groups and individual pieces from selected sites, the number and condition of architectural monuments and structural remains at individual localities, religious cults and their practices, and evidences of ancient science (notably astronomy) in the subcontinent. Examples of this school are *The Origin and Cult of Tara* (1925), *The Temples of Palampet* (1922), *Pallava Architecture* (1924) and *Antiquities of Bhimbar and Rajauri* (1923). Field excavation was also being done, albeit on a limited scale, as evidenced by reports such as John Marshall's 1921 work *Excavations at Taxila*. The period between 1925 and 1939 shows an increase in the publication of analyses generated by the restructuring of the accepted cultural sequence of the region's past caused by the Indus discoveries, technical laboratory reports dealing with major sites, and increased efforts at regional site survey. Typical of this period are *Exploration in Orissa* (1930), *Animal Remains from Harappa* (1936), Aurel Stein's accounts of his travels across the northwestern Indus Valley and southeastern Afghanistan, and *Sravasti in Indian Literature* (1938). The mobilization occasioned by World War II severely disrupted archaeology within the Indian subcontinent, a situation reflected in the *Memoirs* issued during wartime, all of which focused on analyzing artifacts gathered in previous season, such as *The Beads from Taxila* (1940). The immediate postwar era was overshadowed by the coming of independence and the upheaval of Partition, resulting in many of the famous and long-worked sites of the Indus culture winding up beyond the Survey's reach across the new border with Pakistan. During the fifty years since, new geopolitical realities forced a re-focusing of Survey fieldwork within India's new borders (notably in the investigation of regional variants of the Indus civilization (most especially in the western state of Gujarat) with greater attention paid to known historical sites and interdisciplinary joint projects with foreign universities becoming more common.Indian archaeologists also took their place in the field of international archaeological conservation. The diversity of this new phase of the Survey's work is mirrored in such *Memoirs* as *Excavations at Kausambi 1949-50* (1969), *Nagarjunakonda, 1954-60 (1975), Excavations at Satanikota, 1977-80 (1986)*, and *Angkor Vat, India's Contribution to Conservation, 1986-1993 (1994)*. The *Memoirs* also have a varied publication history. Until approximately 1935, they were printed in Calcutta by the Superintendent of Government Printing, subsequently renamed the Central Publication Branch of the Government of India. Between 1935 and the mid-1970's, their center of production shifted to Delhi, under the Manager of Publications, followed by formal publication by the Archaeological Survey of India after 1975 in New Delhi.

631. *Man In India.* Calcutta: A.K. Bose. (March, 1921-)

The first issue of this periodical is subtitled "a Quarterly Record of Anthropological Science with special Reference to India." In this context, anthropology refers more to social and cultural anthropology, ethnographic fieldwork, and linguistics than to archaeology, although coverage of the last is not totally absent. The earliest article on prehistory which *Man In India* printed appeared in the September 1921 number, and was a lengthy note on "Indian Paleoliths."

632. *Journal of Indian History*. Trivandrum, Kerala: University of Kerala, November, 1921-

The official journal (issued three times a year) of the Department of History at the University of Kerala, this is an excellent example of the type of local professional publication in which much of the initial periodical coverage of South Asian archaeological excavations and discoveries first appeared. While most useful as a source of additional data on specific eras of southern India's history, reports of excavations, field surveys and interpretations of inscriptions are also included. Representative entries have been entered in the present bibliography under the appropriate political unit.

633. *Memoirs of the Archaeological Survey of Ceylon* (1924-1969): irregular. Colombo: Acting Government Printer.

The contents of this series of seven volumes spans the entire modern history of archaeology in Sri Lanka, from colonial times to the postwar era. While some volumes are devoted to one single subject, others represent the collections of unpublished work by active field workers. The initial volume of 1924 is prefaced by A.M. Hocart, then Archaeological Commissioner, with a summary of the work of his late predecessor, E.R. Ayrton, whose work at Anuradhapura appears in his own words in its contents. The second volume, which appeared in 1926, contains an update and synthesis by Hocart of his own recent work with data obtained by H.C.P. Bell on three of the temples at Polonnaruva.Two years later, more of Ayrton's early work at Anuradhapura (this time in the Citadel) was built upon by S.Paranavitana, who excavated the area in 1928 and 1929, although the third volume of the *Memoirs* reporting on these seasons did not appear until 1936. Kandy's famed Temple of the Tooth was the focus of a study by Hocart issued as the fourth *Memoir* in 1931. Paranavitana also conducted an intensive study of the evolution of the stupa form as a feature of sacred architecture and the varous functions of its component parts, which appeared as the fifth *Memoir* in 1947 under the title *The Stupa in Ceylon*. The final two *Memoirs* continued this pattern of analysis of individual structures, treating the shrine at Devundara (the southernmost point of the island) and excavations at the Kotavehera complex at Dedigama in the southwest. Selections from the *Memoirs* have been entered separately in the present bibliography.

634. *Annual Bibliography of Indian Archaeology*. Leiden, Kern Institute, 1926-

This publication was the first attempt at gathering bibliographical information on the rapidly expanding literature of Indian and South Asian archaeology and related disciplines and making it available to researchers on a regular basis. The preface to the second volume, covering 1927 and issued in 1929 "with the aid of the government of Netherlands India," notes the warm reception given to the first, which contained five hundred and forty entries. The general format of all volumes in this series was to begin with a group of articles reporting on the more notable discoveries and researches of the year (or, in the case of some later volumes, years), followed by the body of the bibliography itself. These essays include a review of the first seasons at Mohenjo-daro written by Sir John Marshall. Content annotations are provided in English for the first volume only, later numbers leaving extracts from publications in French and German in their original form, as "students of Indian archaeology may...be supposed to be familiar with those two languages." (volume 2, p. vi) Topics included as subject headings in addition to archaeology are architecture, painting, iconography, palaeography, epigraphy, chronology, ancient history and geography, and numismatics. Each section begins with a review of relevant periodicals and journal articles, followed by books and research monographs. Separate sections cover Ceylon, "Further India" (an older term for South East Asia and most frequently applied to Thailand, Burma, Cambodia and Viet Nam), and Indonesia. A section of black and white plates is included as illustration for the opening essays. The *Annual Bibliography* appeared regularly up to 1939. When publication resumed after World War II, volume fifteen covered 1940-1947. By the time volume sixteen for 1948-1953 appeared in 1955, the editors were obliged to note the disappearance of several longstanding sources of income for the project and the lack of cooperation of authors and publishers in keeping the Institute staff informed of new materials. The blurring of lines between Indian archaeology and its interrelated fields, together with the increasing number of potential publications for the *Bibliography*, was coped with by limiting the concept of "Indian archaeology" more narrowly than in earlier issues, with items on Mesopotamia and Muslim architecture omitted. The *Introduction* was discontinued with volume seventeen for 1954-57, the plan being to issue summaries of new discoveries every five years through the monograph series of the Kern Institute. By volume eighteen (1958-1960) the backlog of unpublished data had been eliminated. Successive volumes appeared every two years up to 1972.

635. *Ancient India*. New Delhi, Director General of Archaeology in India, v.1-22, 1946-1973.

Subtitled the "Bulletin of the Archaeological Survey of India," this irregular publication was for twenty-seven years the official periodical of record for postwar government activity and policy in excavation and preservation. The preface to the first issue of January, 1946, written by Sir Mortimer Wheeler, described the new journal as "the outcome of war-conditions, which stopped the printing of annual reports on the old lavish scale...but...also an experiment in a new and timely form of publicity of a kind which has not been previously tried in India." (p. 1) *Ancient India* was intended to take the topic of archaeology regularly to the educated public of the nation, raise awareness of archaeological matters, and publish technical materials of interest chiefly to the practicing archaeologist. Volumes 20 and 21 of *Ancient India*, covering 1964 and 1965, appeared in 1967, and the final volume for

1966 was not published until 1973. Selected articles have been entered in the present bibliography. Researchers should consult the journal issued by the Indian Archaeological Society since 1967, *Puratattva*, for ongoing coverage of fieldwork being done in the subcontinent.

636. *Indian Archaeology*. New Delhi: Ministry of Scientific Research and Cultural Affairs, Department of Archaeology, 1958-

An annual publication intended as an ongoing summary of archaeological projects in India. Readers seeking a full picture of scientific journal coverage of current field investigations should also consult the Indian Archaeological Society's later periodical *Puratattva*, whose first issue appeared in 1967.

637. *Pakistan Archaeology*. Karachi: Government of Pakistan,, Ministry of Education, Department of Archaeology. 1964-

The equivalent in Pakistan to *Ancient India* and the annual review *Indian Archaeology*, this publication is the official journal of nation's Department of Archaeology. While the first issues appeared yearly, the ninth volume covering 1973 was not published until 1979. Contents are typically detailed reports on recently completed and continuing excavations, although epigraphy and laboratory analysis are also included. Selected papers from *Pakistan Archaeology* have been entered in the present bibliography.

638. *Puratattva: Bulletin of the Indian Archaeological Society*. Varanasi: The Society, v.1, 1967-The preface to the first number of *Puratattva* both announces the formation of the Indian Archaeological Society (based at Banaras Hindu University) and defines the purpose of the bi-annual journal to be "primarily first-hand reports of archaeological field work…and their interpretation…a worthwhile collaboration between the archaeologists working in the field and natural scientists working in the laboratory." (p. vii) Since that time, this periodical has filled the intellectual void left by the demise of *Ancient India* (formerly issued by the Archaeological Survey of India) in 1966.

639. *Pragdhara: Journal of the Uttar Pradesh State Archaeological Organisation*. Lakhanau: The Organziation, 1991-

Begun in the early 1990's, this is an annual publication exemplifying the growth of archaeology at the local level of government within India through the establishment of city and provincial archaeological societies and associations. Text is in both Hindi and English.

Appendix A: Circles

The system of regional archaeological survey "circles" was set up in 1895. Researchers wishing access to the data contained in these early researches should consult Ratan Hingorani's *Site Index to A.S.I. Circle Reports* (New Delhi, American Institute of Indian Studies, 1978) which incorporated a series of earlier works done in 1969 and 1970. These previous indexes have been listed under their respective Circles.

Central Circle- covering Bihar, Orissa and the Central Provinces, including Berar. *An Index to the Annual Reports of the Bengal, Eastern and Central Circles of the Archaeological Survey of India* was issued by the American Institute of Indian Studies in Varanasi in 1969.

Eastern Circle (Calcutta)- became the Eastern and Central Circle.

Frontier Circle (Peshawar)- covering the Punjab, the Northwest Frontier Provinces and Baluchistan. An *Index to the Annual Reports of the Frontier Circle of the Archaeological Survey of India* was published in 1969 by the American Academy of Benares, covering the years 1904 to 1921.

Northern Circle (Allahabad)- covering the United Provinces. *An Index to Annual Reports of Mohammadan and British Monuments*, Northern Circle of the *Archaeological Survey of India*, appeared from the American Academy of Benares in 1969 and covered the years 1910 to 1921.

Punjab and Uttar Pradesh Circle- becomes the Northern Circle. *An Index to Annual Reports of the Punjab and U.P. Circle and Northern Circle* was created in 1969 by Ratna Hingorani and published by the American Academy of Benares in 1969.

Southern Circle- covering the provinces of Madras and Coorg. *An Index to Annual Reports of the Southern Circle of the Archaeological Survey of India*,covering the years 1893-1920/21, was compiled by Ratan Hingorani and published by the American Institute of Indian Studies in Varanasi in 1970. The Southern Circle was the first of the regional divisions to begin issuing reports of its field research, which appeared sporadically between 1881 and 1892 before settling into an annual format.

Western Circle (Bombay)- covering the provinces of Bombay and Sind. An *Index to the Annual Progress Reports of the Western Circle of the Archaeological Survey of India* compiled by Ratan Hingorani was published by the American Institute of Indian Studies in Varanasi in 1970.

Appendix B: South Asian Archaeological Law and Legislation

India

Indian Treasure Trove Act (Act VI of 1878)

Ancient Monuments Preservation Act of 1904

Antiquities Export Control Act (1947)

Antiquities Export Control Rules (1947)

Ancient Monuments and Archaeological Sites and Remains Act (1958)

Antiquities and Art Treasures Act (1972). This act was amended on July 2, and December 1, 1976.

Antiquities and Art Treasures Rules (1973)

Pakistan

Antiquities Act of 1968

Antiquities Act of 1975

Rules on Archaeological Excavation and Exploration (1977)

Export of Antiquities Rules (1979)

Sri Lanka

Antiquities Ordinance of 1940

Index

Chilas (Pakistan), 517-18

Childe, V. Gordon, 380, 401

China, 40, 207, 214, 432, 605, 606-07, 615

Chinese language, 607

Chingus (Kashmir), 290

Chinji (Siwalik Hills, Himachal Pradesh), 142

Chirki-on-Pravara (Maharashtra), 347

Chitor, 33

Chodavaram (Andhra Pradesh), 27

Chola dynasty (Sri Lanka), 103, 444, 626

Cholistan Desert (Pakistan), 515, 560

Chota Udaipur Escarpment (Gujarat), 270

Chovvannur (Kerala), 318

Chowdhury, K.A., 399

Chronology, 58, 100, 120, 184, 432, 463-64, 492, 597, 599, 634

Church of St.Augustine (Goa), 266

Churches, 266

Cists. *See* Megaliths

City of Victory: Vijayanagara, the Medieval Hindu Capital of Southern India (1991), 314

City planning. *See* Urbanization

Civilizations of the Indus Valley and Beyond (1966), 102

Clark, J.Desmond, 182, 184

Clarke, David, 139

Clason, A.T., 117

Claudius Ptolemy, 616

Climate, 508. *See also* Palaeoecology

Coastal trade. *See* Trade

Cochin (Kerala), 66

Codrington, H.W., 576

Coggin Brown, J., 41

Coinage. *See* Numismatics

Cole, H.H., 77, 354

Colonization, 119, 133, 443

Colour and Monochrome Reproductions of the Ajanta Frescos based on Photography (1930-1955), 232

Comfort, Howard, 441

Computers, 512

Conference papers, 111-12, 115-18, 121-22, 136, 140-41, 144, 152-55, 163, 174, 179-80, 185-88, 191, 201, 212, 253, 264-65, 275, 277, 282, 285, 289, 296, 308, 311, 319, 343, 347, 367, 414, 426, 458, 465, 473, 499, 500, 503-11, 515, 517-18, 525-28, 531-32, 534-36, 538, 540-44, 546-548, 561-65, 592, 598, 614

Conferences, 111-12, 115-16, 121, 131, 140, 144, 148, 152, 174, 179, 185, 191, 201, 212, 515, 590

Coningham, Robin, 612-13

Conservation, 7, 34-36, 39, 48-49, 53-54, 59, 72-73, 77, 101, 145, 186, 198, 219, 292, 298, 323, 352, 354, 449, 465, 469, 549, 571, 574, 578, 580, 586-87, 589, 609

Constitution of India, 64

Cooper, Zarine, 221-22

Coorg, 625

Copper, 54, 59, 99, 153, 158, 173, 177, 188, 203, 261-62, 264, 421, 425, 454, 469, 494, 514, 611, 614

Copper culture, 41, 111, 121, 145-46, 153, 159, 188, 203, 261-62, 264, 319, 342, 428

Copper hoards, 145-46, 153, 188, 261-61, 264

Copper metallurgy, 121, 203, 261-62, 264, 319, 421, 425, 428, 459. *See also* Metallurgy

Copper mines. *See* Mining

About the Author

ROBERT B. MARKS RIDINGER is Chair of the Electronic Information Resources Management Department at the University Libraries at Northern Illinois University, and he is Subject Specialist in anthropology, sociology, and geography at the University Libraries. He is the author of several bibliographies, including *African Archaeology: A Selected Bibliography* (1993) and *The Homosexual and Society: An Annotated Bibliography* (Greenwood, 1990).